Treasure
Lost at Sea

DIVING TO THE WORLD'S GREAT SHIPWRECKS

Robert F. Marx with Jenifer G. Marx

FIREFLY BOOKS

A FIREFLY BOOK

Published by Firefly Books (U.S.) Inc. 2004

First Printing

Publisher Cataloging-in-Publication Data
(Library of Congress Standards)

Marx, Robert F.
   Treasure lost at sea : diving to the world's great shipwrecks / Robert F. Marx ; with Jenifer G. Marx.
[192] p. : col. ill. , maps ; cm.
Includes index and bibliographical references.
Summary: An exploration of underwater archeological sites and shipwrecks dating from the beginning of recorded history to the present day.
ISBN 1-55297-872-9 (pbk.)
1. Shipwrecks. 2. Underwater archaeology. I. Marx, Jenifer G.
II. Title.
930.102804 21 G525.M379 2004

Published in the United States in 2004 by
Firefly Books (U.S.) Inc.
P.O. Box 1338, Ellicott Station
Buffalo, New York, USA
14205

Published in Canada in 2003 by Key Porter Books Limited.

Electronic formatting: Jean Lightfoot Peters
Design: Peter Maher

Printed and bound in Spain

Contents

INTRODUCTION

ROM TIME IMMEMORIAL, mariners have sailed the perilous seas. Archaeological evidence discovered on mainland Greece reveals that man had vessels capable of making open sea voyages in the Aegean more than 9,000 years ago. In the South Pacific, using outrigger canoes, the Neolithic Polynesians made impressive voyages as far north as Hawaii and as far south as New Zealand.

The sailors of past times were an intrepid fraternity, setting forth on uncharted seas for distant lands. Journeys by sea were measured in months or years, and the risks were great. Ten percent of all ships that embarked on long voyages were lost.

Since men first traveled on the seas, ships have sunk, carrying with them varied cargoes, maritime objects, weapons, implements and personal items. All over the globe, relics of civilizations that have long since vanished beckon from watery tombs. Like the artifacts that archaeologists patiently unearth on land, those found on underwater sites provide clues, often beautiful and sometimes poignant, for vividly reconstructing the past. Unlike many land sites, where the vestiges of the earliest cultures are covered by or mixed with those of succeeding eras, an ancient shipwreck is a historical time capsule.

Most ships sank quickly, mortally wounded in storms or wrecked on hidden reefs or submerged rocks. Some wrecks were partially salvaged by contemporary or later salvors, especially ships laden with valuable cargo that had gone down in shallow water. Until recently, however, many of the most fascinating wrecks lay beyond our reach. Early salvors were limited to "fishing" a wreck with grappling devices, or by free diving or using rudimentary diving bells.

The identity of the first divers is shrouded in the mists of antiquity. As early as 4500 B.C., however, brave and skillful divers were reaching depths in excess of 100 feet (30 m), on a lungful of air, to retrieve such treasures as red coral and mother-of-pearl shells.

Tradition credits Alexander the Great with the first descent in a sealed waterproof container. This event reportedly took place in 332 B.C., off the island stronghold of Tyre, during his epic conquest of the world. A thirteenth-century French illustration shows the young Macedonian inside a candle-lit glass barrel. He is surrounded by numerous species of marine life and observed by a huge whale. Unfortunately, we have no idea what Alexander's contraption was really like.

The diving bell was actually invented before Alexander's time. Writing in 360 B.C., Aristotle noted its use by Greek sponge gatherers: "In order that these fishers of sponges may be supplied with a facility of respiration, a kettle is let down to them, not full of water, but air which constantly assists the submerged men. It is forcibly kept upright in its descent, in order that it may be sent down at an equal level all around to prevent the air from escaping and the water from entering."

The Renaissance provides the next account of a diving bell. In 1531 salvors employed a bell in Lake Nemi, near Rome, in an attempt to locate two of the Emperor Caligula's pleasure galleys, which were said to have sunk laden with gold. The barrel-shaped bell, invented by the Italian physicist Guglielmo de Lorena, covered the diver's head and torso. It was raised and lowered by ropes, and a diver could walk about on the lake bed for nearly an hour before his air supply was exhausted.

In 1538 two Greeks designed a diving bell and demonstrated it at the Spanish court in Toledo before Emperor Charles V and 10,000 spectators. Larger than de Lorena's, this bell was spacious enough to accommodate both inventors, who sat on a plank bench. To the astonishment of the king and the crowd, the candles the Greeks had taken down with them were still burning when they surfaced.

News of the Toledo bell spread rapidly throughout Europe, stimulating the construction of many more. The diving bell was significantly improved in 1689 by Dr. Denis Papin, a French physicist, who devised a way to supply fresh air from the surface by means of a large bellows or pump. At about the same time, Edmund Halley, the famed English astronomer, built a diving bell that incorporated air-filled, leaded barrels with valves and tubes attached for transferring air into the bell. This was a more primitive method than Papin's but far more effective, because the pumps of the period were subject to frequent breakdowns and were not strong enough to deliver much pressure. Diving bells had a long reign, until the advent of the diving helmet in the nineteenth century, and were the main tool used to explore the underwater world, albeit in a very limited way.

The earliest mention of divers in quest of sunken treasure (defined as precious metals, money, jewels and works of art) is by Herodotus, a Greek historian who wrote around the middle of the fifth century B.C. He records that, near the beginning of that century, Xerxes, the king of Persia, had employed a Greek diver named Scyllias and his daughter, Cyane, to recover an immense treasure from several Persian galleys sunk during a battle with a Greek fleet. They brought up the treasure, but Xerxes reneged on the promised reward and detained them aboard his galley, doubtless for other diving jobs he had in mind.

Scyllias and Cyane jumped overboard in the midst of a storm and cut the anchor cables of the Persian ships, causing many of them to collide. The Persians attempted

Tradition credits Alexander the Great with the first descent underwater in a sealed container in 332 B.C., off the island of Tyre.

pursuit, but the culprits managed to escape by swimming underwater to Artemisium, a distance of nine miles (15 km), using reeds as snorkels.

By the third century B.C., diving for treasure on shipwrecks was so common among the Greeks that they had laws regarding the division of the finds. A diver received a tenth of the value of treasure recovered in 2 cubits of water or less (a cubit was about 20 inches [0.5 m]); a third of the value of recoveries between 2 and 8 cubits; and half the value of treasure recovered in depths in excess of 8 cubits. The part of the treasure not given to the diver was the property of the original owner; in the event of his death or dishonor, it became the property of the ruler from whose waters it was recovered.

Early in the sixteenth century, the Spanish established pearl fisheries on the islands of Cubagua and Margarita, off the northern coast of Venezuela. The supply of indigenous Carib divers was soon exhausted. Many died from European diseases. Others died from overwork at the hands of their greedy employers, who forced them to dive as many as sixteen hours a day. The first recorded strike in history took place in 1606 at Margarita Island when the divers ran out of tobacco, which they ate in the belief that it allowed them to stay underwater longer. After several divers were hung by their Spanish masters, the rest quickly resumed diving.

The next to be used as divers were enslaved Lucayan Indians, from the Bahamas, the first natives Columbus had encountered in the New World. The Spanish historian Oviedo, writing in 1535, described a visit to the pearl fisheries of Margarita where he observed the Lucayan divers, who were considered the best divers in the New World. He marveled at their ability, noting that they were able to descend to depths of 100 feet (30 m) and remain submerged for as long as five minutes. They had more stamina than the Caribs and could dive from sunrise to sunset, seven days a week, without appearing to tire. As Old World divers had done for millennia, they descended by grasping stone weights in their arms. They dove naked except for net bags around their necks, in which they deposited oysters they found on the bottom. So great was the demand for the Lucayan divers in the pearl fisheries that in only a few decades the Bahamas were bereft of their former inhabitants.

The Spaniards also used divers in salvage work. Every year from 1503 until the end of the colonial period in the early nineteenth century, ships from Spain carried supplies across the Atlantic to the settlements in the New World. On the return voyages, these ships carried the treasures and products of the colonies back to the mother country. Because of frequent storms and careless navigation, a great many were lost at sea. In major colonial ports such as Havana, Veracruz, Cartagena and Panama, teams of native divers, and later African slaves, were kept aboard salvage vessels, which were ready to depart on short notice to attempt the recovery of sunken treasure. From the sixteenth century to the end of the eighteenth, these divers recovered more than 100 million ducats ($1.25 billion in modern currency) from Spanish wrecks. This was only the intrinsic value; the collectors' value today would be at least 50 times that amount. On more than one occasion, they saved the Spanish crown from bankruptcy.

It was an American from Boston, William Phips, who made the greatest recovery of Spanish treasure in history. In 1641, a treasure fleet of more than thirty ships was struck by a hurricane in the Florida Straits. Nine galleons were dashed to pieces on the coast of Florida. The vice admiral's galleon, the *Nuestra Señora de la Concepción,* lost all her masts and filled with water. For a week, the galleon was barely afloat, carried along at the mercy of wind and current. She finally wrecked on a reef, now known as Silver Shoals, about 90 miles (150 km) north of the coast of Hispaniola. Only a few of the 600 persons aboard reached land. The Spaniards searched for this richly laden ship for years.

Spanish breath-holding free divers at work on a wreck in 1626 off Jamaica.

Spanish galleons in the sixteenth and seventeenth centuries ruled the high seas, carrying untold riches. For hundreds of years, treasure hunters have searched to recover the cargo from those ships that were lost.

Phips had been bitten by the treasure bug while listening to sailors' tales as a child. In 1681 he launched his first treasure hunt in the Caribbean, financed by savings he had accumulated as a shipwright and later from his own shipping business. He didn't find the vast treasure of his dreams, but he did locate several wrecks in the Bahamas that more than covered his expenses—a promising beginning for any treasure hunter. He decided to search for a Spanish galleon, reputedly laden with gold, that had been lost near Nassau. Phips wanted the best ship, men and equipment possible for the venture. Failing to raise enough money in Boston, he went to London in the spring of 1682 to enlist the aid of King Charles II. He waited eighteen months before he was granted a royal audience. His patience was rewarded when the king agreed to back the expedition in return for a large share of the profits.

After working for a month on a wreck near Nassau and finding nothing, Phips was determined to search for another wreck. His crew, however, irate at the failure to find the expected treasure, mutinied, planning to take over the ship and seek their fortune as pirates. Phips, backed by a handful of loyal men, quelled the mutiny and sailed to Port Royal, Jamaica, where he was able to sign on a new crew. It was there that he first learned of the lost *Concepción* on Silver Shoals.

In 1685, after an unsuccessful search for the *Concepción* in waters north of Hispaniola, Phips reluctantly returned to England empty-handed, only to find that Charles II had died during his absence. At first, the new monarch, James II, was not interested in tales of sunken Spanish treasure, and Phips was briefly jailed for nonpayment of debt. But eager backers eventually persuaded the king to grant permission for an expedition to Silver Shoals. In 1686 Phips sailed for the Caribbean with two ships in search of the elusive galleon.

In Jamaica he picked up two dozen pearl divers, escapees from the Spanish pearl fisheries of Margarita. On Silver Shoals, Phips drove himself and his men almost to the breaking point, especially the divers, who searched endless miles of reef from dawn to dusk. Perseverance was at last rewarded. The wreck was found by a diver who went to the bottom to take another look at a delicate branching coral called a sea fan. Upon surfacing, he reported sighting traces of a sunken galleon. Phips burst into tears of joy at the news. Over a period of weeks the divers brought up more than 32 tons of silver, vast numbers of coins, gold, chests of pearls, and leather bags containing precious gems. There was a constant struggle to bring up the treasure while fighting off encircling pirates. In the end, bad weather and a shortage of provisions put an end to the salvage operations. The total value of Phips's recovery in today's currency was more than $50 million. He was knighted by the grateful monarch, who later made him governor of the Massachusetts colony, and his share of the treasure made him one of the richest men in America. One of the observers sent by the king was Sir Hans Sloan, a naturalist who made drawings of the objects salvaged. The bequest of his great collection, in which natural history was quite prominent, became the nucleus of the British Museum.

The first interest in underwater archaeology—as opposed to treasure salvage—dates to 1775, when a group of English antiquarians sponsored an expedition to recover historical artifacts from the Tiber River near Rome. Greek divers with a diving bell labored for three years with little success, for they had no means of removing the centuries' accumulation of river mud that covered the artifacts. After that attempt there was very little interest in recovering sunken historical objects until early in the twentieth century, when artifacts brought up from the Mediterranean by Greek and Turkish sponge divers aroused the interest of archaeologists and historians.

The majority of the beautiful bronze statues now on display in the National Museum in Athens were recovered by sponge divers and by fishermen who accidentally snagged them in their nets. The spread of scuba diving in the early 1950s sparked intense interest in ancient shipwrecks in the Mediterranean. In 1952, Jacques Cousteau and a team of French divers spent almost a full year excavating a Roman galley loaded with amphorae in 160 feet (50 m) of water at Grand Congloué, near Marseilles. (Amphorae—tall, unglazed ceramic jars, usually narrow at the top and bottom—were used for thousands of years throughout the Mediterranean area and are found on virtually every ancient ship that was wrecked there.) Although some scholars sharply criticized the project because the French made no attempt to map the site or plot the finds *in situ,* the team was successful in recovering thousands of valuable artifacts. As a result of the international publicity the excavation generated, scholars began to recognize the archaeological potential of ancient shipwrecks. The project also stimulated underwater exploration by sport divers and led to the plundering of many wrecks along the French Mediterranean coast before laws were enacted to prohibit such activities.

The most challenging problem confronting all archaeology is the accelerating pace at which sites are being destroyed. As bulldozers scar millions of acres each year and whole valleys are inundated to make reservoirs and recreational lakes, irreplaceable opportunities to unravel and illuminate the past are lost. Until recently most such depredations were confined to the land. Today, although many underwater sites of archaeological significance are looted and destroyed by scuba divers a much greater number are obliterated by dredging and landfill operations. In fact, hundreds of shipwrecks are demolished by such activities every year, with little outcry from either archaeologists or the general public.

It is governments who permit this deplorable destruction, and most underwater archaeologists are employed by governments. Years ago in Florida, legislation required a "cultural impact" study prior to any dredging or landfill projects. This is no longer required in Florida—or in any other state, for that matter. Due to the recent extensive beach erosion in Florida, an estimated 200 miles (320 km) of dredging and beach replenishment was carried out during the past eight years. Nothing is being done to protect the hundreds of shipwrecks that lie in these areas.

An eloquent example of site destruction is found at Cádiz on the south coast of Spain. Cádiz is an important seaport that has been in continuous use since 2000 B.C. On the bottom of Cádiz Bay lie several thousand shipwrecks of many types, nationalities and historical periods. The earliest known shipwrecks were Egyptian, followed by Phoenician, Greek and Roman merchantmen and warships. Countless craft of many European and north African nations were also lost there. Even the Vikings came to grief in Cádiz Bay. In A.D. 975, after months of sacking Mediterranean ports, a fleet of seventy Viking ships went to the bottom in a storm. In the sixteenth century alone, more than 600 ships were lost, most of them engaged in New World navigations.

The speed with which underwater objects deteriorate or decompose depends on a variety of factors. Because the bottom sediments of Cádiz Bay are unusually anaerobic (lacking in oxygen), shipwrecks may remain there in a remarkable state of preservation for a long time. This makes the bay one of the world's most important underwater archaeological sites. In most areas very few wooden remains have survived over the centuries, but such is not the case at Cádiz. Even intact Phoenician hulls are known to rest under this harbor's protective mud.

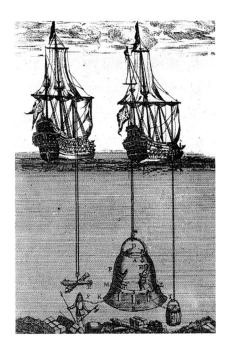

In this old print, a diving bell invented by Edmund Halley in 1720 is being used to salvage a shipwreck.

Many of the shipwrecks lie in less than 50 feet (15 m) of water, and some have been subjected to damage and destruction by such things as the huge seas caused during storms. Nothing can be done to prevent this from occurring in the future, other than actual salvaging of the shipwrecks.

Not only natural hazards threaten these sites, however. Human forces have caused greater destruction in the past three decades than natural forces over thousands of years. Under the auspices of the Archaeological Museum of Cádiz, a visual survey was conducted from 1960 to 1962. Within a 2-mile (3 km) radius of the modern port, fifty-four shipwrecks of the classical period and ninety-seven of later dates were located. During a 1988 survey of the same area it was discovered that more than two-thirds of these shipwrecks had been demolished by dredging operations, which are still going on today. Most of the dredged

material has been used as landfill and is now covered over by newly constructed buildings. Just a few years ago, a container-ship port was constructed at Cádiz in which the landfill completely covered over the remains of a Phoenician sunken city. Soon afterward, dismayed by this destruction, I organized The Save Cadíz Foundation, which sought protection of the remaining shipwrecks in Cadíz Bay from the United Nations Educational, Scientific, and Cultural Organization (UNESCO). Although UNESCO had been involved in saving ancient Egyptian monuments during the Aswan Dam construction, our pleas were ignored for political reasons. The Spanish government claimed that the economic benefits derived from making Cadíz into the most important port of the Iberian Peninsula far outweighed protecting the underwater cultural heritage. I tried to enlist the assistance of museums, universities and archaeological societies worldwide and, although almost everyone agreed that the destruction in Cadíz Bay was deplorable, very few showed interest in doing anything about it.

Co-author Jenifer Marx holding a gold scabbard tip with another diver, next to a cannon on a Spanish wreck in the Bahamas.

In neighboring Portugal the situation is equally grave. During the construction of a deep-water harbor at Sine in 1985, a port used first by the Carthaginians and later by the Romans, dredging operations obliterated at least four Punic shipwrecks and many others of later periods. Farther down the coast at Portimão, dredging operations also destroyed three shipwrecks of the classical period. No doubt many other shipwrecks were also lost forever in this port when more than one-third of it was covered over with fill to form the base for a large ship wharf.

In the area of Lisbon, where at least 500 ships have sunk since the late fifteenth century, the devastation is even worse. In a recent interview, the captain of a dredge boat reported that "rarely a day passes in which some vestiges of an old shipwreck are not seen spewing out of the discharge end of the dredge pipes." About 20 years ago construction crews working on the Cultural Center of Belém, a suburb of Lisbon, uncovered over a dozen old shipwrecks that had originally sunk in the Tagus River but had since been covered by landfill. Not one archaeologist in Portugal even examined these vestiges of the past, let alone did anything to recover the hulls or the artifacts they contained, nor obtained any pertinent archaeological data.

Angra Bay on Terceira Island in the Azores was the main port used during the colonial period by the Spanish ships returning from the New World and Portuguese East Indiamen returning from the Orient. In 1961 I conducted an underwater survey of the bay and located five Spanish galleons from the sixteenth and seventeenth centuries. I tried in vain for over a period of thirty-five years to obtain an excavation permit for these shipwrecks. In 1998 a team of local divers, led by a school teacher, with no archaeological training and very little scuba diving experience, began working for the local museum. From information I had given them they relocated the shipwrecks I had discovered in 1961 but did very little work on them. Despite awareness of these important shipwrecks, the government permitted them to be destroyed by dredging in the building of a new marina, which was completed in 2000.

The problem is also acute on the other side of the Atlantic. Dredging and landfill operations at Cartagena, Colombia, one of the most important seaports during the Spanish colonial period, have resulted in the destruction of more than 50 percent of the port's known shipwreck sites. At Veracruz, Mexico, another major colonial port, the devastation is deplorable. Probably less than 10 percent of the area's colonial shipwrecks remain. At Rio de Janeiro, Brazil, landfill used in constructing an airport completely covered the anchorage area used during the colonial period.

Shipwreck sites are being erased not only in protected harbors, but offshore as well. Such projects as laying offshore petroleum pipelines, building breakwaters, gathering land and beach replenishment materials and opening new entrances to ports and rivers require dredging operations. Some years ago, during the dredging of a new channel at Padre Island, Texas, one of the Spanish shipwrecks from the 1553 fleet that lay offshore was sucked up in the hungry jaws of the dredge pipe and spat out on a nearby beach.

Fishing boats also account for a great amount of destruction to shipwreck sites. Not only are archaeological objects caught in fishing nets, but the cables pulling the nets cut across the seafloor, and sometimes beneath it as well, destroying everything in their path. The practice of fishing with dynamite is equally destructive. On the other hand is the fact that fishing boats account for locating more shipwrecks worldwide than by salvors and archaeologists combined.

Beautiful gold and emerald jewelry found on the *Maravilla*.

For years I have been one of a small number of people struggling to educate governments about the unique historical and archaeological resources that they have in their waters and to encourage them to prevent further destruction of these sites. In every instance our pleas have met with indifference or hostile reactions from government bureaucrats. Their stock response is that national economic imperatives take precedence over the protection of shipwreck sites. In some instances we were told that they already have such an abundance of historical artifacts in their museums that those from the sea are of no importance or interest. We have also taken our battle to UNESCO, which was sympathetic but not constructively helpful in the past.

Finally in 1995 UNESCO formed a committee to study the protection of underwater cultural sites. It sponsored several meetings at which delegates from over 50 nations shared their views. In 1998 UNESCO officials presented the draft of a proposed law at a conference held in Lisbon. All 170 participants endorsed the draft. At a conference in Paris in November 2001 UNESCO adopted the "Convention of the Protection of Underwater Cultural Heritage." Delegates from 106 nations attended the conference; eighty-seven nations voted in favor of the convention, fifteen nations abstained and only four—the United States, Canada, China and the Philippines voted against. The convention will become a law when the parliaments of many nations have approved it, which may takes years to accomplish.

The convention defines "Cultural Heritage" as any man-made object one hundred years old or older. It would prevent sport divers and professional salvors from recovering anything from old shipwrecks. Several nations, such as Spain and Portugal, are also clamoring to have the convention include legislation mandating that all treasures and artifacts recovered from shipwrecks of their nations be returned to them. However, their request raises several questions. Does this mean that salvors must contact every person who ever bought a coin from them and return them to Spain and other countries? Would any nations wanting to conduct archaeological investigations on any shipwreck or sunken city first have to obtain permission—a lengthy process—from UNESCO? What happens when a dredge boat uncovers an old shipwreck? Must the owners wait months or years for permission so that archaeologists can excavate the site or just go ahead and destroy it?

The convention has many unanticipated negative outcomes; few nations even have the qualified underwater archaeologists, expertise and financial resources needed to undertake legitimate excavations. Passage of the convention would probably put an end to work on deep-water shipwreck sites, which are costly and complex to excavate. If and when the convention becomes law, its supporters will have won a Phyrric victory.

In the United States, nobody seems to want to step on Big Brother's toes by criticizing the shameful obliteration of our international heritage of underwater sites. Yet bureaucrats and scholars think nothing of trying to stop sport divers and treasure hunters from exploring shipwrecks, claiming that their plundering is destroying the sites at an alarming rate. The fact is that shipwreck plundering accounts for only a small fraction of the destruction of our underwater heritage.

Another major problem confronting underwater archaeology is the question of who owns shipwrecks and other underwater cultural sites. Throughout the world, all but twenty-one nations have specific laws concerning shipwrecks. In the United States up until 1999, thirty-seven states had laws (which differed widely from state to state) laying claim to sunken historical sites. In 1981 these laws were challenged in the Supreme Court by the late Mel Fisher, a Florida treasure hunter, and the states lost the rights to shipwrecks. Federal laws give the federal government control over natural resources within the 200-mile (320 km) limit except for state ownership of resources within the coastal 3-mile (4.8 km) area; however, these laws do not cover shipwrecks or other man-made objects. (By contrast, the right of states to manage archaeological

Co-author Jenifer Marx with a human skull and Mayan ceramic figurine found in a sinkhole in the Yucatan.

OPERATIONS UPON THE WRECK OF THE SAN PEDRO ALCANTARA MAN-OF-WAR.

This contemporary print shows salvors working in 1788 on the Spanish galleon *San Pedro Alcantara*, which sank off Peniche, Portugal.

sites buried on land is explicitly stated in U.S. law.) For a time, in the absence of a law recognizing the special nature of ancient shipwrecks, these sites were covered by the "finders-keepers" principle that applies to modern wrecked and abandoned commercial vessels. It meant that federal Admiralty law took precedence over state laws.

During a period of seven years, Congress labored over the passage of a new law granting states the right to jurisdiction over all shipwrecks one hundred years old or older within 3 miles (4.8 km) of the coast. Sport divers, treasure hunters and archaeologists contributed their points of view on the management of shipwrecks at congressional hearings held by the House Merchant Marine and Fisheries Subcommittee. In April 1987 the Reagan administration endorsed a bill entitled the *Abandoned Shipwreck Act of 1987*. The bill was approved by the Senate on December 19,

1987, by a vote of 64 to 34 and on April 14, 1988, by an overwhelming majority of the House of Representatives. On April 28, 1988, the president signed the bill, which is now known as *Public Law 100-298*.

The new law covers 5 to 10 percent of the estimated 50,000 shipwrecks inside the 3-mile (4.8 km) limit. Other shipwrecks both within and outside this limit continue to be covered by federal Admiralty law. The shipwrecks affected by the new law are (a) those defined as historic abandoned shipwrecks that are "substantially" buried in submerged state lands; (b) those held in coral formations; and (c) wrecks listed in the National Register of Historic Places (fewer than 150 are currently so designated). Each state has the right to determine how recovered artifacts and treasures are to be divided and to establish guidelines for the search and excavation of shipwrecks.

The proposed law enables states to guard against plundering of the sites within their jurisdictions, which few have done on their own. But the problem remains of protecting shipwrecks from the depredations of the innumerable dredging operations and construction projects undertaken in the name of "progress."

Raising a Spanish iron anchor off a wreck in the Bahamas.

In 1998 the question of ownership of foreign wrecks in U.S. waters hit the news. The debate revolved around Sea Hunt Inc., a salvage group led by Ben Benson, who had spent over $1 million locating two Spanish galleons off the coast of Virginia and was stopped as he prepared to salvage them. For some undisclosed reason the U.S. Justice Department, instead of protecting the rights of U.S. citizens, notified Spain and urged it to fight for ownership of both shipwrecks. A federal judge in Virginia ruled that the *Juno,* lost in 1802, still belonged to Spain and that the other galleon, *La Galga,* lost in 1750, could be salvaged by Benson, thanks to a 1763 treaty in which King Charles III of Spain renounced all his North American possessions. Again at the urging of the U.S. Justice Department, lawyers representing Spain took the matter to the Appellate Court and Spain ended up owning both shipwrecks.

Iron treasure chest full of Spanish gold doubloons and silver pieces of eight found on the flagship of the 1715 fleet, lost off the east coast of Florida.

Things became even more complicated when Spain then went to the International Court in the Hague demanding rights to all Spanish shipwrecks worldwide. While this matter was under review, Peru, Chile, Colombia, Ecuador and Mexico climbed on the band wagon. These nations declared that they, not Spain, own the treasures on Spanish wrecks since they were looted of natural resources—gold, silver, emeralds, pearls—by Spain, using slave labor. Spain then countered that all warships are protected and owned by the countries of origin under an international treaty and since all of her mighty galleons were armed with cannon and other weapons, they are covered by this treaty. Nevertheless, in many cases it is impossible to identify the nationality of a shipwreck. Finding Spanish coins on a shipwreck does not constitute proof that it is a Spanish wreck; Spanish coins were used worldwide by most nations and have been found on hundreds of non-Spanish shipwrecks. In fact, Spanish pieces of eight—1-ounce (30 g) coins of pure silver, struck by Spanish colonial mints in the New World between 1531 and 1815—were legal tender in the United States until 1857. Like the UNESCO convention, this matter will most likely take some time to resolve.

Outraged treasure hunters have formed an organization, the Institute of Marine Archaeological Conservation, whose worldwide associates lobby against both Spain's claims to the rights of all of her shipwrecks and the passage of the UNESCO convention into law. Peter Hess, a leader of this group, points out that some of the best archaeological work has been done by the private sector. Gone are the days when treasure hunters after riches heedlessly destroyed shipwrecks in their haste. Today most of them employ qualified archaeologists to oversee all operations.

For decades one of the easiest places in the world to work was in England where no search or salvage permits were required, even for foreign salvors. After a shipwreck was discovered the finder had only to notify the nearest receiver of wrecks and he or she would be officially named salvor in possession and could go on with the work. After the salvage effort was completed the receiver of wrecks would put an announcement in the local newspapers declaring that a find had been made and asking if any person claimed the site. On old wrecks there was no problem as the original owners would have died long before. In the case of more recent wrecks, claims of ownership are possible, and the original owner or his descendants might be given a small share of the objects recovered. In cases when a shipwreck was found to be of great historical importance it was sometimes declared a designated wreck, and the salvors had to employ archaeologists for its excavation. The government was not entitled to any share of the finds. If a museum wanted to buy some of the recovery an independent appraiser put a value on the objects, and they were sold at a fair market price. This law did not cover warships or planes, which are considered war graves and are protected from any disturbance.

In 1998 the Tampa-based Odyssey Marine International group located the warship HMS *Sussex* lost in 1694 off Gibraltar. They had to enter into an agreement with the British government that took four years to obtain and held up further exploratory and salvage work. It wasn't until October 2002 when the agreement between both parties was signed that they announced their discovery of this rich shipwreck. Odyssey will receive 80 percent of the first $45 million from the sale of treasure. Any proceeds between $45 million and $500 will be split 50–50 between Britain and the salvors. Above the figure of $500 million, which I doubt will ever be achieved, Britain gets 60 percent of the money. This agreement caused a great deal of furor among archaeologists as it is contrary to one of the provisions in the UNESCO convention, which states that governments should not make contracts with commercial salvors.

John Paul Jones is considered a great naval hero in the United States and one of the founders of the U.S. Navy. He is best known for the 1779 Battle of Flamborough Head off the east coast of England. While marauding in British waters with five privateering vessels during the American Revolution, he chanced upon a fleet of merchant ships under the protection of the British warship HMS *Serapis*. Aboard the *Bonhomme Richard,* engaged in combat and finding he was outgunned, Jones decided to board the *Serapis* and take her in hand-to-hand fighting. The *Bonhomme Richard* was soon ablaze, and when the British captain asked Jones if he wished to surrender he shouted back, "I have not yet began to fight." He was right as the Americans overpowered the British seamen and captured the *Serapis,* cutting the *Bonhomme Richard* adrift to sink a few hours later. This was the first major British defeat at sea in the war.

Numerous salvors have searched for the *Bonhomme Richard,* among them novelist Clive Cussler, but the wreck remained elusive as so many are. In 1998 a fishing boat snagged into a wreck and brought up various objects that were used to identify it as Jones's ship. When word of the discovery leaked out, dozens of sport divers descended on the site and began to plunder it. In April 2002 one of the local divers who had searched for the wreck for over 25 years publicly announced that he would lead a group to salvage the site. Fortunately, the receiver of wrecks immediately had the site declared a designated wreck to further protect it. Archaeologists from Scotland's St. Andrews University were then hired to positively identify the wreck. In the meantime a controversy has ensued as the British claim the ship was a pirate vessel and the United States regards it as a U.S. naval ship; a bit difficult to prove as the U.S. Navy had not been established at this time.

Around this same time another controversy developed in nearby Newport, Wales, when construction workers uncovered a well-preserved medieval trading ship dating from 1465. The local city government on whose property the find was made declared they owned the shipwreck and would have it excavated and placed on local display. Concerned history buffs in England and around the world, including actor Anthony Hopkins, raised an outcry, claiming that the Newport City Council had neither sufficient funding nor expertise to properly recover the ship. Finally the Welsh National Assembly stepped in and took over the responsibility of the ship's full recovery and conservation.

FOLLOWING PAGE: There are thousands of wrecks worldwide harbouring the promise of sunken treasure. The world's great shipwrecks are located off the shores of every continent.

VIKING WRE

ANNA CATHARINA

VLIEGENTHART

BRITISH AND IRISH
SHIPWRECKS

BISMARCK

EGYPT

SAN JUAN

LE CHAMEAU

TITANIC

SLOT TER HOOGE

SAN AUGUSTIN

MONITOR

WHYDAH

CENTRAL AMERICA

ANDREA DORIA

1715 SPANISH FLEET

BERMUDA
SHIPWRECKS

SANTA MARIA DE YCIAR

SANTIAGO

ATOCHA

MARAVILLA

MARGARITA

CONCEPCION

EL MATANCEROS

CAPITANA

LA NICOLASA

SANTIAGO DE PALOS

VIZCAINA

GALLEGA

OXFORD

HOLLANDIA

WITTE LEEUW

BOUNTY

ROMAN WRECK

BRITISH AND IRISH
SHIPWRECKS

WENDELA

LASTDRAGER

GRAN GRIFON

DUQUE DE FLORENCIA

GIRONA

TRINIDAD
VALENCIA

LAVIA

AMSTERDAM

JULIANA

SANTA MARIA
DE LA ROSA

MARY ROSE

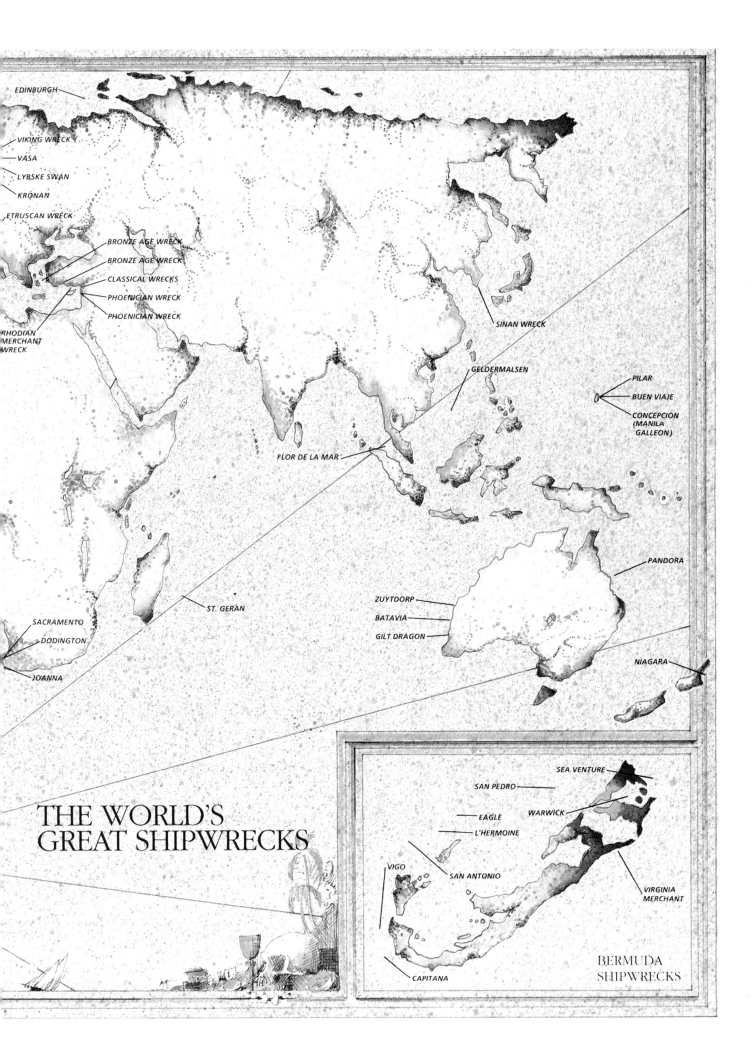

EDINBURGH

VIKING WRECK

VASA

LYBSKE SWAN

KRONAN

ETRUSCAN WRECK

BRONZE AGE WRECK

BRONZE AGE WRECK

CLASSICAL WRECKS

PHOENICIAN WRECK

PHOENICIAN WRECK

RHODIAN
MERCHANT
WRECK

SINAN WRECK

GELDERMALSEN

PILAR

BUEN VIAJE

CONCEPCIÓN
(MANILA
GALLEON)

FLOR DE LA MAR

PANDORA

ST. GERAN

ZUYTDORP

SACRAMENTO

BATAVIA

DODINGTON

GILT DRAGON

NIAGARA

JOANNA

THE WORLD'S
GREAT SHIPWRECKS

SEA VENTURE

SAN PEDRO

WARWICK

EAGLE

L'HERMOINE

VIGO

SAN ANTONIO

VIRGINIA
MERCHANT

CAPITANA

BERMUDA
SHIPWRECKS

1 THE CLASSICAL WORLD

S EARLY AS 3000 B.C. THE BABYLONIANS had established regular sea intercourse with India and may have ventured even farther on ocean voyages. The Egyptians began sea trading about 3000 B.C., and by 2500 B.C. were constructing wooden merchant ships well over 100 feet (30 m) long and propelled by big square sails. Incense, ivory and gold lured Egyptian trading ships into the Red Sea as far south as the Somali coast of Africa.

For much of the third millennium the Egyptians accounted for most of the sea traffic in the western Mediterranean. Then, around 2500 B.C., the Minoans on Crete rose to power in the Aegean. Minoan ships sailed far and wide in search of raw metals, which master smiths turned into exports of bronze weapons and tools and delicate gold and silver jewelry.

In the late Bronze Age maritime and commercial dominance of the Mediterranean passed to the bellicose Mycenaeans on the coast of the Greek mainland. The Mycenaeans were the middlemen in commerce between Europe and Asia; great seafarers and intrepid long-range traders who greatly advanced the science of navigation.

The greatest maritime people in ancient history, however, were the Phoenicians, who inhabited the area of present-day Syria and Lebanon. Ships in the ancient Mediterranean usually kept within sight of land, as an aid to navigation. But the Phoenicians, who had learned astronomy from the Babylonians, set their course by the stars and ventured beyond the Straits of Gibraltar into the vast, forbidding Atlantic.

In the eighth century B.C. the Etruscans and Greeks gained in importance and soon

Bronze first-century Roman bust found on a wreck off Sidon, Lebanon.

eclipsed the Phoenicians in maritime power. From the sixth century B.C. the Greeks were using merchant ships of up to 500 tons that were able to carry as many as 600 passengers on long voyages.

Rome started its rise to power in the early sixth century B.C., and by the time of Christ, Roman fleets dominated the Mediterranean. Following the decline of the Roman Empire in the third century A.D., the Byzantine Empire controlled the Mediterranean for three centuries, during which there is little evidence of long-range voyaging.

Until recently the only means of tracing the history and evolution of ancient shipping, from the earliest known Egyptian vessels of 2500 B.C. to the Phoenician, Babylonian, Carthaginian, Greek and Roman galleys, was through ancient literary references and by studying ships depicted on coins, sculpture, frescoes and mosaics. These methods yielded only meager information about the appearance, construction, means of propulsion and endurance of ancient vessels.

The greatest untapped source of information about the classical world lies at the bottom of the Mediterranean. Between 1500 B.C. and 1000 A.D. at least 20,000 ships are believed to have been lost. The sailing routes of ancient mariners tended to remain the same over the centuries, so there are certain areas where the seafloor is practically paved with ships.

Thanks to the development of scuba diving and other advances in underwater technology, much has been learned in the past four decades about the cargoes, weapons, tools, navigational

Mosaic of a Roman galley dating from the second century, B.C.

instruments, implements and other objects, including personal items, that these craft carried. Yet we still know virtually nothing about the ships themselves. Owing to the destructive forces of nature, little remains of ships wrecked in shallow water. Our information about the *trireme,* for example, is quite scanty, even though it was the most common warship in the Mediterranean for a period of more than 500 years, and thousands of these ships were lost at sea. (During the great Athenian expedition to Sicily in the summer of 413 B.C., more than 350 *triremes* were sunk off Syracuse in the course of a series of naval battles.)

Although shipwrecks have been salvaged in the Mediterranean for centuries, only in the past forty years or so has underwater archaeology entered the picture. The first serious project in the region was initiated by Peter Throckmorton, a professional U.S. diver who lived in Greece. In 1959 after sharing countless bottles of *raki* with garrulous Turkish sponge divers, he learned the locations of many places where divers had seen "old pots" or amphorae. Throckmorton spent a year checking about thirty-five of these locations off the Turkish coast and found that most were sites of ancient vessels wrecked over a span of more than 2,000 years.

One of these, in about 100 feet (30 m) of water off Cape Gelidonya, was the oldest shipwreck located to that date: a Bronze Age wreck from 1200 B.C. (The Bronze Age, which began in the early fourth millennium B.C., is the period in which humans first made bronze artifacts and learned to use the wheel and the ox-drawn plow.) Throckmorton immediately recognized the unique importance of the wreck on his first exploratory dive. Fortunately, he had found it just in time to save it from being dynamited by sponge divers, who had no interest in the ship's historical value and planned to salvage the cargo of copper and bronze to sell for scrap. He reported the shipwreck to Turkish authorities and the University of Pennsylvania's Department of Archaeology. Dr. Rodney Young, the director of the university's Institute of Classical Archaeology, offered to find the personnel and funds to mount a major expedition to the site. The following summer a team of twenty specialists, including Frederic Dumas, who had previous underwater archaeological experience off the French Riviera with Jacques Cousteau, and George Bass, a young graduate student in archaeology at the university, joined Throckmorton at Cape Gelidonya.

The depth of the wreck and the resulting dangers of decompression sickness limited each diver to sixty-eight minutes of underwater working time each day. However, the group was able to make the most of such short bottom time because each diver's daily assignment was specifically designated. After the men had thoroughly cleared the area of seaweed, they made drawings and plans of all visible traces of the wreck's cargo, then filmed a photographic mosaic. On the bottom the site looked like a conventional land excavation, with meter poles staked about and numbered plastic tags attached to all visible objects.

A thick lime deposit, as hard as concrete, blanketed most of the cargo, only an occasional piece of which protruded through the hard seafloor. Attempting to extract individual pieces underwater was too time-consuming and dangerous because of the fragility of many of the artifacts. Instead, using hammers and chisels, the divers broke away large chunks (called conglomerates) of material, some weighing as much as 450 pounds (over 200 kg), and sent them to the surface, where they were broken apart. Some of the larger masses were so difficult to separate from the bottom material that the divers had to use automobile jacks.

Until each day's recoveries could be treated, they were stored in a freshwater pond on the beach. When the conglomerates were broken apart, a thrilling array of Bronze Age artifacts from the ship's cargo came to light: bronze chisels, axes, picks, hoes, adzes, plowshares, knives, spades and a large number of copper ingots. An airlift, a type of underwater vacuum-cleaner used on the site's few sand pockets, uncovered further finds, including four Egyptian scarabs, oil lamps, polished stone mace-heads, apothecary weights, pieces of crystal, mirrors, awls, a cooking spit, whetstones, olive pits and the bones of animals, fish and fowl.

The expedition was a notable success and opened the door for future marine archaeological projects in the Mediterranean. George Bass, convinced of the importance of this fledgling field, has been engaged in marine archaeological projects in the Mediterranean ever since, particularly off the Turkish coast. Throckmorton dedicated himself to classical-era shipwrecks in the waters off Greece and Italy until 1985, when

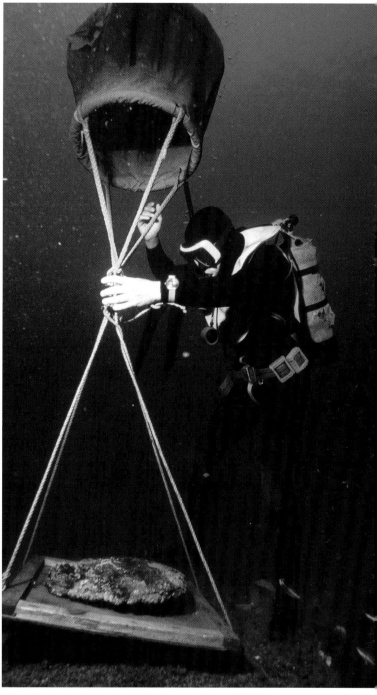

Diver raising a bronze ingot from the Etruscan wreck off Giglio, Italy.

he shifted his activities to the Caribbean, where he worked on shipwrecks of the Spanish colonial period until his death in 1990.

Before he went to Turkey to work on the Cape Gelidonya wreck, Bass consulted with land archaeologists and was surprised to hear the majority express the opinion that archaeology underwater was impossible and could never become an exact science. "Nothing much could be preserved underwater," they said and "It's not possible to execute proper archaeological plans underwater." The feeling was almost unanimous that excavating shipwrecks was too dangerous and far too expensive for the amount of information to be gained.

The Bronze Age shipwreck project proved otherwise. A remarkable portion of the cargo was in an excellent state of preservation, despite having been underwater for 3,200 years. The team was able to make accurate plans and drawings underwater that were more professional than many produced on current land excavations. Although most of the expedition's members had had little previous diving experience, no diving accidents of any kind occurred. To the amazement of the skeptics, the whole project, including the air fares of all personnel, cost less than $25,000—a modest sum and considerably less than that spent on many land excavations of the same duration. The only disappointment, one encountered by Bass and Throckmorton in most subsequent excavations as well, was the scarcity of wood from the original ship. The primary goal of an underwater archaeologist is to obtain as much data as possible about a ship's construction. The recovery of artifacts is of secondary importance.

Until the Bronze Age shipwreck project, it was commonly thought that it was easier to teach a professional diver archaeology than to teach diving to an archaeologist. George Bass took exception to this, since it takes years of study to become an archaeologist and no more than a few weeks to become a qualified diver. Thus far he has proved his point; his people have logged many thousands of hours on the bottom, working at various depths, and only one serious case of decompression sickness—"the bends"—has marred thirty diving seasons in the Mediterranean.

Bass differs with other archaeologists in believing that every underwater archaeological site can be surveyed and excavated stratigraphically (layer by layer) using methods the same as, or similar to, those employed on land sites. In the relatively deep water where he has worked, he has been proved right, because the deeper sites remain undisturbed by storms, wave action, currents and human activity. Most sites in the western hemisphere are in shallower water, however; they have been badly battered by nature and man and are scattered over large areas of the seafloor.

There is a marked contrast in bottom conditions on deep and shallow shipwrecks. Although the diver's time is limited on deep sites, such as those in the Mediterranean, once on the bottom a diver is able to work comfortably and generally enjoys good visibility. On most wrecks in shallower water, however, the diver works in rough seas and is hampered by poor visibility, which makes it impossible to utilize the same type of surveying, photographic and excavation methods and equipment used on the deeper wrecks.

In 1984 a Bass-led expedition from the Institute of Nautical Archaeology (INA) of Texas A&M University discovered another Bronze Age wreck: a 3,400-year-old shipwreck near the seaport of Kas off the southern coast of Turkey. This wreck of a trading ship from biblical Canaan was two centuries older than the previous Bronze Age ship. Dating from the time when Tutankhamen sat on the throne of Egypt and Troy was in its heyday, it has furnished us with an unparalleled look at seaborne trade in antiquity.

The ship, about 65 feet (20 m) in length, was laden with a cargo of raw materials that included 150 intact amphorae containing over a ton of resin, six tons of copper and tin ingots, cobalt-blue glass ingots, elephant tusks, dozens of logs of unworked ebony wood, jars of olives, tortoise shells and even pomegranates and hollow ostrich eggs. The wreck lies on a ledge in depths of between 150 and 170 feet (46 and 52 m), depths that restrict the time divers can work on the site each day. INA has spent six summers on the excavation, and it may be another five seasons before it is completed.

In 1990 while INA divers were working on the Canaanite site at Kas, a Greek sponge diver chanced upon what is believed to be the oldest known shipwreck in the world: a Bronze Age ship dating from 2250 B.C. The wreck, only 65 feet (20 m) deep, lies off the northern coast of the tiny Greek island of Dokos. A team of twenty divers, led by archaeologist George Papathanasopoulos, spent two summers on this early Helladic period site mapping and photographing the wreck. They recovered hundreds of ceramic objects and several stone anchors. Work on this extraordinary wreck was finally completed in 1995, but it will take many years of conservation and study of the artifacts before the final archaeological report can be written.

In 1995 INA archaeologists were conducting their annual survey along the Turkish coast and located the remains of a fifth century B.C. Greek wreck in 140 feet (44 m) of water just south of the resort town of Cesme on Turkey's Aegean coast. At that time, the INA team was busy excavating a Byzantine shipwreck and couldn't shift operations to this new site until the summer of 1999. Dr. Bass assembled an international team from the United States, Canada, Turkey, Spain, Bulgaria, Australia and the United Kingdom. The team consisted of archaeologists, historians, classicists, students, conservators, mechanics, a physician and a cook. Typically there were 30 people on the expedition, excluding visitors. All were volunteers, and living conditions ashore were Spartan to say the least. A base camp was built on a cliff overlooking the wreck site, and very few modern conveniences were provided.

In 1990 Bass left diving to the younger generation and supervised the operation from a two-man submersible named *Carolyn*. On the first dive on the site, he discovered dozens of two-handled Greek amphorae. After mapping the site, airlifts were used to remove the overburden, or sediment, covering the wreck site. In addition to over 200 intact amphora, most of the other finds consisted of ceramic objects such as small jars, plates, bowls and oil lamps, The most exciting find was a translucent alabaster flask. In some ways the excavation was a disappointment to Bass as no wooden remains of the small coastal trading vessel remained. Also, no personal items of the crew were found, which indicated that the survivors were able to take their possessions with them when the ship sank in a storm.

Multi-colored amulets and a necklace bead recovered from a sixth-century B.C. Phoenician shipwreck off Tyre, Lebanon.

THE PHOENICIANS

The greatest seafarers and traders of antiquity were the Phoenicians. For 2,000 years before the birth of Christ, the entrepreneurial Phoenicians set out from their centers at Byblos, Tyre and Sidon on Mediterranean coastal trading ventures and amazing long-range voyages that took them to Africa, Arabia, Spain and other parts of the ancient world, in search of gold, ivory, tin and copper (the last two essential for making bronze tools, weapons and other trade goods).

They exported timber and carved furniture crafted from the legendary cedars of Lebanon; Tyrian purple, the precious dye from the murex shell, which was highly prized by the ancients; as well as cloth, silk, glass (which they invented) and other trade items. It was from the Phoenician ports that many ideas, both in writing and in art, reached the western world via Greece. Tradition has it that the alphabet was developed

Small Phoenician amphorae found off Carthage, Tunisia.

by the Phoenicians to aid in their commercial enterprises and was introduced to Greece by Cadmus, the Phoenician prince who founded Thebes.

The Phoenicians were great middlemen and merchants. During their golden age under King Hiram of Tyre, Phoenician craftsmen, architects and materials were used to build Solomon's great golden temple at Jerusalem. They founded colonies at Carthage in the ninth century B.C. and in Sicily, Tunisia, Cyprus and Malta. Their descendants in Carthage went on to establish settlements in Algeria, on Spain's Balearic Islands and southern coast and along the Moroccan coast. It was from these sites that the intrepid Phoenician mariners embarked on the search for raw materials, reaching such distant places in that long-ago world as the Azores, West Africa, and the coast of England, at Cornwall. They also sailed to many lands in the Indian Ocean and were the first to circumnavigate Africa, a three-year voyage. It is not inconceivable that at least one Phoenician ship, sailing far into the Atlantic, was pushed westward by contrary winds or currents as far as the Americas.

In January 1973 I was invited by Emir Maurice Chehab, Lebanon's director general of Antiquities, to conduct an underwater archaeological survey in and around the ancient ports of Byblos, Sidon and Tyre. Our main objective was to locate one or more Phoenician shipwrecks. To that date, no Phoenician wrecks had been discovered. However, just a few days before I left for Lebanon to begin the expedition, the *New York Times* carried a story about a Phoenician wreck of around the fifth century B.C. that had been found by Israeli archaeologist Elisha Linder off the Israeli coast near Shave Ziyyon, quite close to the Lebanese border.

This find electrified the archaeological world. Not only was it the first Phoenician wreck ever found, but part of the cargo consisted of clay figurines of Tanit, the goddess of fertility and a major Phoenician deity. Archaeologists excavating at Carthage had previously found drawings and symbols of the goddess, as well as impressions on bronze coins, but these varying statuettes, from 6 to 15 inches (15 to 38 cm) high, were the first three-dimensional representations of Tanit to come to light. Unfortunately, no traces of the actual ship survived, since it had come to rest on a rocky bottom, where it lay unprotected by sediment. All wood had disappeared.

I headed for Lebanon with two diving friends, writer Milt Machlin and Tulsa businessman Jack Kelley. Our objective was to find a well-preserved Phoenician shipwreck hull, and our first stop was Byblos, according to tradition the world's oldest continuously inhabited city. Recent excavations there have revealed the existence of a Neolithic culture dating to 5000 B.C. Long before the Greeks and Romans arrived, Byblos was a powerful, independent city-state with its own king, culture and trade. It was here that the alphabet we use today was developed. During the third millennium B.C., it was the most important seaport in the Mediterranean, though it was eventually eclipsed by Tyre and Sidon.

The water at Byblos was a bone-chilling 45° Fahrenheit (7°C); but excitement kept us from minding the numbing cold. I'll never forget my first look at the seafloor off Byblos. I found myself in an underwater museum where the exhibits spanned thousands of years. Scattered over the bottom were numerous immense marble columns and hand-worked building stones, many carved with beautiful designs. Even more thrilling was our discovery of the cargo of an eighth-century B.C. Phoenician shipwreck. The amphorae and other ceramic objects had survived, but not the wood of the ship's hull. On surveying the site, we also found eight Phoenician stone anchors, the lower torso of a Roman terra-cotta man, and many ceramic artifacts and shards (fragments of pottery) from other wrecks, covering a span of 3,000 years.

We then went to Sidon, a city founded around 1400 B.C. and second only to Tyre in the heyday of the Phoenicians. It was destroyed many times by earthquakes and invaders, and very little of its ancient past is visible today. The most impressive building still standing, a fortress at the port entrance, was built by the Crusaders and dates back only to the twelfth century. After diving at Byblos, we found Sidon a bit of a letdown.

The seafloor was covered with tons of modern debris, many layers of which would have to be removed before any vestige of antiquity could be found. Even worse, thousands of projectiles and bombs, still armed, littered the bottom. During World War II a fleet of Vichy French warships at anchor off Sidon dumped their munitions overboard before surrendering to the British. Nevertheless, we were fortunate enough to find a cargo of amphorae from a second Phoenician ship; no traces of the ship itself remained.

We went on to Tyre, on Lebanon's southern border. I was eager to explore underwater there because the city, founded by the Phoenicians in 2750 B.C., was one of the most celebrated in the ancient world. Its flourishing maritime trade, colonies all over the Mediterranean and Atlantic coast, and famous purple dye and glass industries made it the most important commercial center in the eastern Mediterranean. Originally, Tyre consisted of a mainland settlement and a fortified island city a short distance offshore. In 333 to 332 B.C. Alexander the Great stopped with his army at mainland Tyre and was offered hospitality. The island dwellers, surrounded by a towering wall and with a fleet of galleys blockading the entrance to their two harbors, believed themselves invincible, however, and refused entrance to Alexander's army. Incensed by this breach of courtesy, Alexander laid siege to the island for seven months, during which many ships on both sides were lost in sea battles.

We were shocked, when we arrived at Tyre, to see a clamshell dredge being used to deepen the modern harbor on the north side of the town. As bucket after bucket of mud was brought up, we spotted many artifacts, including a couple of Roman amphorae, miraculously intact. We rented a boat from a fisherman, whose initial protestations of ignorance about traces of ancient shipwrecks disappeared after we ingested a staggering amount of the local brandy together. He took us to an area where he had snagged and raised several amphorae in his nets and put us right on top of the amphorae from a Roman wreck dating from the first century A.D.

Our first dive confirmed our suspicion that he had previously shown the site to others, who had plundered it. Where once there had been thousands of intact amphorae, there were only thousands of shards. Divers had used dynamite to dislodge amphorae from the coral growth in which they were embedded. We mapped the site for the government archaeologists and then dug into the mass of broken amphorae, finding two that were still whole. Nearby, we found a large number of Roman ceramic oil lamps, plates, small jars, ointment bottles and copper coins, all of which appear to have been lost when a small boat capsized.

We then searched visually closer to shore inside the southern harbor and made one exciting find after another. The bottom was almost completely paved with artifacts, samples of which we recovered for study by Emir Chehab, Lebanon's director general of Antiquities, and his staff. To cover larger areas, we hung on lines and were towed behind our boat. In two days we found four more shipwreck sites: a Phoenician wreck from the fourth century A.D., two Greek wrecks from the third and second centuries B.C. and a Byzantine wreck dating from about 600 A.D. The Phoenician and Greek sites were on rocky bottoms with no surviving traces of the ships that had carried cargoes of amphorae. Like the Roman wreck we found the first day at Tyre, all three of these had been dynamited and plundered, but we still brought up an interesting collection of artifacts. The Byzantine wreck was on a sandy bottom, and by digging in the sand we recovered part of its cargo of brightly colored plates and bowls, ceramic jugs and several mortars of basalt.

Our last day at Tyre began badly, but ended on a high note. We were using probes to determine the depth of sand and mud in the center of the southern part of the harbor. After about two hours on the numbingly cold bottom, I accidentally touched a venomous scorpion fish and immediately felt so severely nauseated that I had to return to the boat to recuperate. Soon, Jack Kelley surfaced to tell me that his probe had struck something solid not far beneath the sand. But he was almost out of air and too cold to go back down. I went back in, although I was still dizzy and on the verge of vomiting. I loosened Kelley's probe, which felt as if it had been stuck in wood. Digging by hand in loose, powdery sand is no easy task. In an hour, I was able to dig only a small hole about as deep as my arm.

Kelley rejoined me, and after digging a bit deeper we uncovered several Phoenician amphorae, which the Lebanese archaeologists on board dated to the fifth century B.C. While widening the hole and uncovering more amphorae, I suddenly spotted three clay figurines ranging from 5 to 13 inches (13 to 33 cm) long. Nearby, I found two more, and brought them to the surface. The two archaeologists were ecstatic, especially when Kelley came up with another two. Some, which were identical to those found at Shave Ziyyon—the two sites are only about 15 miles (24 km) apart—represented the goddess Tanit with her right hand raised in a gesture of blessing and her left hand either over her breast or holding a baby. Two of them portrayed her pregnant.

Our air was almost depleted and the sun was sinking fast, but I made one last brief dive. Forcing my hand as far down as possible in the deepest part of the hole we had dug, I felt hard wood. To me this was far more important than anything else we had found during our stay in Lebanon. It indicated that, buried in the protecting mud, there might be the structural remains of an ancient vessel. Only a complete excavation of the site would reveal whether we had found just a small section of the hull or a greater part of the wooden remains of a Phoenician ship.

On the day I returned to Lebanon in July 1974 to begin a three-month excavation of the site, Israeli commandos attacked and destroyed, at Tyre, more than forty fishing vessels that were suspected of carrying terrorists into Israel. The Lebanese government placed the area off limits and it remained off limits for three weeks while I waited in Beirut. In September and December of that year, I again attempted to get back to Tyre; but each time I was thwarted by the activities of the PLO terrorists, who were using Tyre as their main base in southern Lebanon. Unfortunately, continuing political unrest in Lebanon has prevented further exploration of this tantalizing wreck.

One of the strongholds of the Phoenicians, of which there were many along the Mediterranean shores, was Carthage in Tunisia. The most important collection of Punic inscriptions were found on land in 1874 on around 500 stone stelae from the second century B.C. They were shipped aboard the French warship *Magneta* back to France in 1875 for study by scholars in Paris. Unfortunately, just after the ship entered Toulon

Harbor it caught fire, exploded and sank. Soon after, helmet divers were employed and recovered a few of the stelae, as well as an incomplete marble statue of the Roman empress Sabine, wife of Hadrian. The rest of the archaeological treasures had sunk into the bottom sediment and couldn't be recovered at the time.

In 1994 the French Ministry of Culture enlisted the services of the Naval Archaeology Research Group led by Max Guerout. A magnetometer quickly located the wreck laying in 50 feet (15 m) of water with only 4 feet (1 m) of sediment covering it. Over the next four years Guerout and his team recovered 115 of the stelae as well as the face and midriff of the statue of the Empress Sabine, which were reunited with the rest of the statue on display at the Louvre Museum in Paris.

Apparently a Carthaginian ship made it across the Atlantic and reached the coast of Honduras, whether deliberately or acci- dentally is not known. In 1972 some tourists on a sailboat stopped at the fish- ing village of Yapadingding and while snorkeling stumbled upon a mound of third-century B.C. Carthaginian amphorae. Honduras museum staff identified the find as being a Spanish Colonial Period ship and only in 1990 when a vis- iting English archaeologist saw the amphorae was the importance of the find revealed.

Greek war galley depicted on a silver coin from the third century B.C.

THE GREEKS

In 1967, a diver spearfishing off the shore of Kyrenia, Cyprus, came across the remains of a mound of intact amphorae at a depth of 100 feet (30 m). The amphorae, dating to the fourth century B.C., were from the Greek island of Rhodes, and the chance find proved to be the most significant discovery of a Greek merchant ship to date. Dr. Michael L. Katzev, an American under- water archaeologist from the University of Pennsylvania, was invited by Cyprus's director of antiquities to survey the site. During his first dives, it appeared to Katzev that a very small ship might have sunk, because the mound measured only 10 feet by 6 (3 m by 2 m).

When Katzev laid out a grid around the site and used both a metal detector and a magnetometer to locate concentrations of metal, it became apparent that the site was much larger than his original estimate and lay concealed beneath the sand. A survey with metal probes suggested that a substantial amount of the ship's hull had survived, convincing him that the site warranted a full-scale excavation.

Katzev worked at Kyrenia for the next two summers with a team of underwater archaeology students from the University of Pennsylvania. They used airlifts to remove the sand covering and preserving the wreck and uncovered a time capsule of Greek seafaring. The whole bottom of a large merchant ship was exposed, and each fragment of wood was carefully photographed *in situ,* tagged and then taken to the surface for preservation.

The Rhodian merchant wreck produced a gold mine of interesting artifacts. Katzev was able not only to determine what Greek ships of this period were carrying for trade, but, even more fascinating, to reconstruct the daily life of its crew from the hundreds

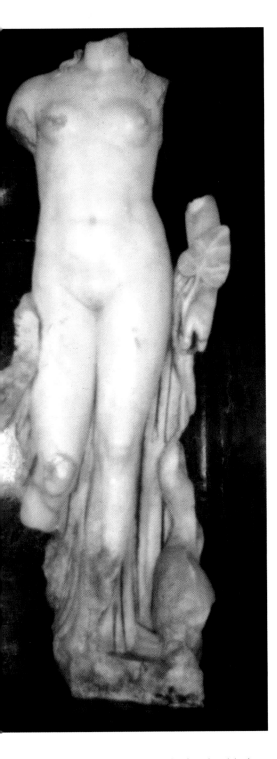

Greek marble statue of a female with the head missing, found off Ibiza, Spain, from the fourth century B.C.

of personal items found. More than 400 intact amphorae were raised, along with hundreds of other ceramic objects, including cups, bowls, plates, pitchers and jars. Wooden bowls and spoons were also found, as well as a large copper cauldron. There were even 10,000 almonds that had probably been stored in long-vanished sacks. The only treasure recovered consisted of five bronze coins. The ship's hull was reconstructed by Dr. Richard Steffy, and in 1989 a full-scale replica of the Kyrenia ship was built and successfully sailed. Today the reconstructed ship and its cargo are on display in an old Crusader castle in the port of Kyrenia.

A large number of other Greek shipwrecks have been found in recent years all over the Aegean, Mediterranean and Black Seas, but few have been surveyed and excavated by qualified archaeologists. An exception to this is one that was discovered accidentally in the shallow waters near Cala San Vicente off the north coast of Mallorca, Spain. Winter storms had removed a great amount of the sandy bottom during the previous winter, and in June 2002 some visiting German tourists found this fifth century B.C. Greek wreck while searching for lobsters. Local authorities got wind of the find when the Germans were seen carrying two of the amphorae at the airport. They were arrested, the amphorae were seized and the Centre d'Arqueologia Subaquatica de Catalunya brought in to survey the site. This organization began excavation soon afterward and will continue for several more years.

THE ETRUSCANS AND ROMANS

In 1961 an Englishman vacationing in Italy discovered the oldest known Etruscan shipwreck. Reg Vallintine, a sport diver, was spearfishing around Giglio Island off the Tuscan coast when he spotted several copper ingots and dozens of ceramic bowls and cups. Word of his find spread and, over a number of years, countless sport divers plundered the site. Once all artifacts visible on the surface were gone, the site was forgotten. Twenty years after Vallintine's discovery, Dr. Mensun Bound, an underwater archaeologist from Oxford University, spotted the ceramic handle of an old jar on a shelf in a friend's living room. It piqued his interest. Bound tracked down Vallintine, who had given his friend the artifact, and persuaded him to show him the Giglio site.

Bound was not discouraged by the barren seafloor he saw on his first dive. He had no doubt that beneath it lay a valuable archaeological site. Over the next five summers he excavated the wreck with an international team of volunteer divers, operating on the shoestring budget typical of most underwater archaeology projects. Airlifts were employed at a depth of 165 feet (50 m), and the team discovered that most of the ship's cargo and a section of the hull had escaped the plunderers.

The ship, which dated from the sixth century B.C., eventually yielded more than 7,000 priceless Etruscan artifacts. Among the most interesting was a magnificent bronze Greek warrior's helmet. A fair amount of the ship's lower hull remained in good condition, and Etruscan scholars rejoiced at the variety of well-preserved wooden artifacts recovered. These included an inlaid sofa leg, several flutes and a pair of olive-wood calipers with a Greek inscription, most likely used by the ship's carpenter. Etruscan wooden artifacts are extremely rare on land sites, because acid soil and dampness quickly rot wood.

Roman ships seldom ventured beyond the Straits of Gibraltar (known to the ancients as the Pillars of Hercules), except to sail time-proven routes to France, the Netherlands and the British Isles. The Romans were never superb sailors like the Phoenicians; they used their ships chiefly to transport their conquering legions and to carry grain, wine and other agricultural commodities. Roman merchant ships, though impressive in size, were clumsy and sailed badly. The number of Roman shipwrecks found along the ancient sea routes attests to a high rate of ship casualties.

Since the introduction of scuba equipment, more than a hundred Roman shipwrecks have been found in the Mediterranean and along the Atlantic seaboard, as far north as Holland and England. The majority were discovered by sport divers, and in almost every case they were plundered before archaeologists could investigate.

One of the most intriguing Roman shipwreck finds occurred in 1976 in Brazil. A young diver named José Robert Teixéira was spearfishing around a rock off Ilha do Gobernador, in the Bay of Guanabara, not far from the port of Rio de Janeiro. He saw many intact amphorae on the seafloor and brought up three of them. He assumed that they were Portuguese jars from the colonial period and sold them to an antique dealer for a small amount.

Some time later, one of the amphorae was mistakenly identified by the Brazilian Institute of Archaeology as of ancient Greek origin. News of the find soon spread and sport divers recovered dozens more amphorae. Local scholars, trying to solve the puzzle of how they had come to be in Brazilian waters, decided they most likely had been found in the Mediterranean and later thrown overboard by a vessel visiting Brazil.

Five years later, in 1981, while I was working in Brazil on several shipwrecks from the colonial period, the director of the Maritime Museum of Rio de Janeiro asked me to investigate the site. He didn't believe that the amphorae had been thrown overboard by a passing yacht and considered it possible that the jars came from a shipwreck site. I was skeptical. But when I learned that, since the mid-1960s, fishermen in the area had snagged at least fifty intact amphorae, each over 3 feet (1 m) in length, I began to think the museum director might be right. I found one diver who still had fourteen of the amphorae stored in his garage. The minute I saw them, I was sure they were Roman in origin. Subsequently, experts identified them as being from the third century A.D., and manufactured at Kouass, southwest of Tangiers, on the Atlantic coast of Morocco.

The amphorae were covered with marine growth. I borrowed one from the diver and took it to scientists at Brazil's two oceanographic institutions for study. I expected to be told that the growth was of Mediterranean origin. To my great surprise the scientists determined that all the marine encrustation was of a type found only in the vicinity of the Bay of Guanabara and that some of it had taken hundreds of years to grow on the ceramic.

Later, I sent ceramic shards with marine growth to Dr. Ruth Turner, the director of Harvard University's Museum of Comparative Zoology, and to Dr. Walton Smith of the University of Miami's Marine Laboratory. Both confirmed the Brazilian scientists' findings. Subsequent carbon-14 dating placed some of the growth at up to 1,500 years old. I had explored many Roman shipwrecks all around the Mediterranean, but I certainly never expected to dive on one in Brazil.

There is no written record that Roman ships ever came to the Americas. But that doesn't mean that there were not accidental crossings, such as the one for which Portuguese explorer Pedro Alvares Cabral was given credit for the discovery of Brazil. In 1500, while attempting to sail to the Indian Ocean, Cabral was becalmed off the

Co-author Robert Marx with a third-century A.D. Roman amphora recovered from a wreck near Rio de Janeiro, Brazil.

African coast. The ship was caught in a strong westbound current and carried across the South Atlantic to the shores of Brazil. In the 19th century alone, records indicate, more than 600 vessels were driven to the American coast by contrary winds and currents. A Roman ship could have suffered the same fate, entered the Bay of Guanabara in search of food and water after the long crossing, struck a submerged rock pinnacle and sunk.

I spent more than 200 hours in the murky water around this rock, surveying the plundered site over a period of several months. All the intact amphorae on the surface had been recovered, but I felt certain more would be found buried in the soft mud. I did locate several hundred shards, including the necks and handles of dozens of amphorae, and ceramic shards of smaller jugs and plates. Another find—a circular stone with a center hole, resembling a grinding wheel—may have been a small anchor.

In December 1982 I enlisted the services of the late Dr. Harold E. Edgerton of the Massachusetts Institute of Technology (MIT), inventor of the electronic strobe, the electronic flash and other electronic devices, including several types of underwater sonar. He conducted a three-day subbottom profiling sonar search of the area in an effort to pinpoint any wooden shipwreck remains.

In his report to the Brazilian government, Edgerton wrote:

> Two buried targets were located below the seafloor which produced sonar records such as can be expected to result from the disintegration of ancient wooden ships. If these two targets are indeed parts of a Roman sailing ship, it would appear that after hitting the dangerous high pinnacle of rock, the ship broke into two or more pieces. The scatter pattern of amphorae shards suggests that this occurred. The fact that intact amphorae have been found on the surface over the top of both buried targets indicates that the targets may possibly be a Roman ship.

What an opportunity to amplify our knowledge of history! Sadly, politics reared its head and prevented further study and excavation of what is one of the world's most intriguing underwater sites. Shortly after Edgerton's report appeared, the Portuguese and Spanish governments expressed great concern to the Brazilian government about the possibility that this discovery could displace Cabral as the discoverer of Brazil and Columbus as the discoverer of the New World.

We had begun to assemble an international team of archaeologists to excavate this unique site, but the Brazilian government decided that to do so would be too controversial. A dredge boat was employed to cover the entire site, and the area was declared a restricted zone. For now, the Roman wreck lies under a thick mantle of harbor sediment. But perhaps, one day, it will yield its secrets.

Most archaeologists have resorted to deep water to find Classical Period shipwrecks, believing that any found in shallow water have most likely been plundered by sport divers. All six archaeologists, scientists and cultural resource managers attending an international conference on deep-water archaeology at MIT in January 1999 were convinced that the future of ancient shipwreck exploration lay in deep water through the use of submersibles and ROVs, which are unmanned remotely-operated vehicles. One participant who reported on a deep-water project was Dr. Anna Marguerite McCann of Boston University, who had worked closely with Dr. George Bass and Robert Ballard, the underwater explorer who is best known for his discovery of the shipwrecked *Titanic*. Dr. McCann presented a paper on her work off Skerki Bank off the northwest coast of Sicily where she had discovered eight shipwrecks; five of them Roman from circa 80 B.C. to A.D. 400. On all five Roman sites amphorae and other artifacts were brought up for identification and dating purposes.

The absence of rivers depositing sediment over deep-water shipwreck sites has advantages and disadvantages for scholars. Usually the shipwreck remains are totally exposed and require very little excavation. On the other hand, the oxygen-rich waters of the Mediterranean provide little protection to the wooden ship hulls and other organic materials, so that there is scant information about ship construction—which to archaeologists is even more important than information gleaned from the recovery of a ship's contents.

About 7,500 years ago the Mediterranean Sea, swollen by melted glaciers, flooded over into the freshwater lake known today as the Black Sea. Some scientists believe that this event was the inspiration for the biblical story of Noah and his ark. As the deluge filled the lake, transforming it into a sea, it created a unique ecosystem, unknown in other areas of the world, an anaerobic zone below the upper 400 feet (122 m) of the Black Sea. In this oxygen-free abyss shipwrecks lie in inert frigid waters unaffected by any living creatures such as the wood-devouring *teredo navalis* shipworm.

Scholars for many years suspected that intact ancient ships could be found in the Black Sea, which was often used by the Phoenicians, Greeks, Romans and others on trading voyages throughout antiquity. However, it wasn't until 1999 when Dr. Robert Ballard and Dr. Fredrik Hiebert of the University of Pennsylvania proved this point. Using an ROV equipped with sonar, lights, cameras and several mechanical devices for retrieving small objects, they began their search off the Turkish city of Synope in the Black Sea. At a depth of 1,000 feet (366 m) in the anoxic dead-water zone, they located an intact Roman/Byzantine shipwreck dating from between A.D. 410 and 520. In the same general area they found three other shipwrecks dating from the fourth to sixth centuries. However, these vessels were located in shallower oxygen-rich waters and thus not as well preserved as the one in the greater depths. Dr. Cheryl Ward, a specialist in ancient ships at Florida State University, has taken over the project and should have good results once funding is found to carry on.

Italian archaeologist Stefano Bruni never imagined what he would find when he was summoned to Pisa. The Tuscan city was once one of the greatest Mediterranean ports and had two sheltered harbors. Ancient sources describe fleets setting sail from Pisa for Gaul and Spain during the Second Punic War (218–201 B.C.) During the Middle Ages it served as the port of Florence and other cities in Tuscany. However, by the end of the fifteenth century both harbors had been covered over by sediment from the nearby Auser River, and Pisa became landlocked.

In 1999 construction workers sinking a corrugated steel retaining wall during the construction of an office building in the middle of modern Pisa realized they had bisected an ancient ship, its wooden frame and planks still held together by copper nails. Soon afterward, while digging out the foundation pit about 300 by 150 feet (90 by 45 m), eight other Roman wrecks were found in remarkable states of preservation, dating from between the second century B.C. to the fifth century A.D.—covering the period from Pisa's reign as a Republican naval base to the end of the Roman Empire.

Dr. Bruni took charge and put together a large team of archaeologists and conservators, beginning the project immediately. Not only had the sediment preserved the wooden ship hulls but other organic materials as well. A wicker basket, a leather sandal, a coil of rope and the remains of olives, plums and cherries were recovered. From one of the wrecks the remains of 200 pork shoulder bones were found; for reasons that the archaeologists find mysterious, 180 came from the pig's right side. Other osseous remains found include what were probably the bones of several unfortunate sailors, a lion's jaw and dog bones. To date over 30,000 artifacts have been recovered from these hulls, and more knowledge about the construction of Roman vessels has already been obtained than from all of the other Roman ships found up until now on both land and underwater. Many of these interesting finds are already on display in a local museum.

ALEXANDRIA, EGYPT

Alexandria, founded by Alexander the Great in 331 B.C., became the capital of Egypt under the Ptolemaic Dynasty (323–30 B.C.) and one of the most important seaports in antiquity. Among its most magnificent buildings was the fabled Museion with a library containing over 700,000 scrolls and papyri of unique historical significance; all

destroyed when the Romans burned the library in 48 B.C. It was the meeting place of the greatest minds of the Ancient World such as Euclid, Aristarchos and Eratosthenes. Alexandria's wealth was beyond belief. The Roman historian Plutarch described how Cleopatra, summoned to visit Anthony, arrived in a gilded barge fitted with oars of silver and purple sails. He wrote "Instead of a crew, the barge was lined with the most beautiful of her waiting-women attired as Nereids and Graces, while an indescribable rich perfume wafted from the vessel to the river banks." In the harbor was Cleopatra's Island of Antirhodos, where she had her palace. Here was the stage for two of the most famous love stories in history: Cleopatra loved both Mark Anthony and Julius Caesar. When she took her own life in 30 B.C., the city declined under incompetent rulers. In A.D. 335 Alexandria was destroyed by an earthquake and tidal wave. Most of the city slipped beneath the sea and was soon forgotten. The famous lighthouse of Alexandria met a similar fate.

The turbid waters off Alexandria have long enthralled underwater explorers and divers because of the historic remains they conceal. Her secrets started to come to light only in the past century, and it took an amateur Egyptian diver named Kamel Abud-Saadat to stir up interest in the area, for which he has received very little recognition. In 1961 while spearfishing, he discovered a staircase surrounded by white marble columns; a cylindrical chair and a sarcophagus, both of marble; a red granite Roman statue and a gold coin from the time of Cleopatra.

Greek vase from sixth century B.C., found on a Greek galley lost off Majorca, Spain.

Egyptian archaeologists showed little interest in these finds as they were busy on numerous land sites for which funding was scarce. There is so much to be done; from Alexandria to the port of Sollum, 125 miles (200 km) away, over 125 other sunken cities referred to in classical text have yet to be found.

In 1996 Sorbonne-educated Jean-Yves Empereur was next on the scene. His goal was to get credit for the recovery of Alexandria's glittering Pharaonic and Hellenistic history; one of the central undertakings in contemporary Egyptology. On his very first dive in the murky waters of an area dubbed "Pharos City" because many think it is the location of the ancient lighthouse, Empereur encountered a regal red granite head of Ptolemy II, gazing out of the sediment. Since that time, he has been working continuously and is the arch rival of Franck Goddio, who has been doing incredible work in this area and receiving a great deal of publicity.

Goddio, who holds a degree in mathematics and statistics, decided in 1985 to become an underwater archaeologist and, despite the fact that he has no formal training in the field, the media touts him as one of the world's best. The same year, he formed L'Institut Européen d'Archéologie Sous-Marine and has been fortunate in funding for all his projects. He always works closely with local governments and scholars and brings in support personnel from all over the world. He cut his teeth in the Philippines on several shipwrecks and, when he's not working in Egypt, he continues working in Philippine waters, where he has located and excavated 14 historically important shipwrecks.

In late 1998 Goddio's claim to have found the barge of Cleopatra met with skepticism from the scholarly world. Soon afterward he announced he had discovered Cleopatra's palace. Marble floors on the seafloor with lumps of broken granite columns indicated that the site was likely one of the royal quarters of some ruler, but nothing connected it to the suicidal Cleopatra. In the same general area Goddio's team recovered two large stone sphinxes, including one modeled after Cleopatra's father, King Ptolemy XII, a statue of the priest of Isis holding a Canopic jar used in burials, and a shipwreck containing jewelry and other artifacts dating between 90 B.C. and A.D. 130.

Goddio has starred in several television specials focusing on his finds, but the fact remains that there is, thus far, no proof he found Cleopatra's palace. Empereur, who has no love for Goddio, stated: "If they found a skirt, they would call it the skirt of Cleopatra." The competition between the two Frenchmen has sparked a great debate in archaeological circles. Many contend that Goddio, who was then funded by the European-based Hiti International, a tool and building products company, was in the project only for the publicity value to the firm, and thus was pressured to make rather dubious claims. Critics believe that projects of this importance should be conducted only by qualified archaeologists such as Empereur. Nevertheless, although Goddio has no academic training in archaeology, he does use professional archaeologists and, with his unlimited budgets, he can carry on far more work than Empereur or other poorly funded archaeologists.

About 12 miles (19 km) from Alexandria Harbor lie the sunken cities of Canopus, Herakleion and Menouthis, which existed centuries before Alexandria. These ports were known only through Greek tragedies, legends and travelers' accounts. While Goddio's French team was working on "Cleopatra's palace," he sent another team to locate the wreck of the *Orient*, Napoleon Bonaparte's flagship lost during the famous Battle of the Nile. While conducting an electronic survey of Aboukir Bay, his men found all three of these long-forgotten cities. This was the first time that physical evidence proved their existence. The cities were known not only for their riches and art but also for temples dedicated to the gods Osiris, Isis and Serapes, making the region an important pilgrimage destination. Herakleion was once a customs port where commerce flourished until the founding of Alexandria. Greek mythology tells the story of Menelaos, king of the Spartans, who stopped in Herakleion during his return from Troy with Helena. Greek historian Herodotus also visited this port in 450 B.C. and wrote about its temple dedicated to Hercules. All three cities were believed to have been built during the waning days of the pharaohs in the seventh or sixth centuries B.C. Why they sank into the sea is not known. From the ruins of all three sunken cities hundreds of fascinating artifacts were recovered. These statues, gold coins, jewelry and more utilitarian objects bring the ancient past to life in a truly remarkable way.

2 SCANDINAVIAN SHIPWRECKS

The seventeenth-century Swedish warship *Vasa* is now housed in the Vasa Museum in Stockholm.

I IS HARD TO THINK OF SCANDINAVIA without thinking of the dragon-prowed ships of the Vikings, who ravaged coastal Europe from the eighth to the eleventh century. Their fleets of hundred-oared ships carried the Norsemen as far south as Spain and as far west as North America on raiding and settling voyages. Compared with Mediterranean peoples, the Scandinavians were slow to develop their prowess as seafarers and ship-builders; sailing vessels were not used until the seventh century in icy northern waters.

"Viking" means pirate or rover, and the Viking Age began about A.D. 800 when the Norsemen started raiding settlements along all the coasts of Europe. The Scandinavian sea rovers were proficient navigators and explorers. Their fleets penetrated the Mediterranean and, by about A.D. 1000, were making extended voyages on the open ocean, apparently reaching Newfoundland and other points on the North American continent.

The swift ships of the Scandinavian sea rovers have received considerable attention from historians and archaeologists. Thanks to unusual marine conditions, there are thousands of extraordinarily well-preserved shipwrecks, including countless Viking craft, in the Baltic and North seas. Although the water is salt, the saline content within diving depths is lower than in other seas. In addition, the water is very cold. Consequently, there are no coral-forming organisms and no sea teredos or other marine borers. This means that wood and other organic materials are not ravaged, even when unprotected by sedimentary deposits.

However, the cold water that helps preserve the shipwrecks makes excavating them especially challenging. Divers have located dozens of old ships standing as if they had sunk just the day before, but the frigid water restricts the length of time a diver can spend on the bottom, and visibility is seldom more than a few feet. Despite such difficulties, a number of important early Scandinavian shipwrecks have been excavated.

During the summer of 1956 a sport diver searching for lobsters among a pile of stones in Roskilde Fjord, Denmark, noticed evidence of the remains of a wooden ship buried under the stones. He notified the Danish National Museum's underwater archaeologists, who investigated the site. They thought the wreck might be one from a fleet of ships that, according to local legend, was sunk in the fourteenth century to defend Roskilde—then the capital of Denmark—from repeated pirate attack. Much to the archaeologists' surprise, the wreck was centuries older. Not only that, it turned out there were five complete ships under the rocks—all Viking ships from the eleventh century that had been deliberately scuttled to obstruct ships trying to attack a settlement there. To the archaeologists' disappointment, the vessels had been stripped and filled with rocks before being sunk. Even so, finding a fleet of Viking ships in such an exceptional state of preservation presented a unique opportunity for an underwater archaeological excavation.

One of the Roskilde Viking ships being restored.

Diving conditions in Roskilde Fjord are formidable: divers cannot see their own hands in front of them, and there are strong tidal currents at all times. It took three summers and more than 4,000 man-hours just to remove the stones covering the wrecks. Once the ships were exposed, archaeologists realized that the poor diving conditions would make it impossible for divers alone to excavate the wooden remains and bring them to the surface. In 1962 a cofferdam of interlocking steel sheets was erected around the site and the sea water was pumped out. On July 6 the excavation began, using dry-land techniques. A team of twenty archaeologists worked feverishly for the next fourteen weeks before the first winter storms struck. They removed all the mud covering the hulls and took thousands of photographs, so that the hulls could be reconstructed after the wood was preserved using the polyethylene-glycol process. During the excavation, each piece of the ships was labeled, packed in an airtight plastic bag and rushed to the conservation laboratory. In the laboratory technicians use repeated baths of distilled water to leach chlorides from pieces of wood. The wood is then immersed in a solution of polyethylene-glycol (PEG). The amount of time wood remains in the PEG solution depends on the size, condition and density of the piece being treated.

The five ships were all different, and their variety and excellent craftsmanship give a vivid picture of the scope of shipbuilding in the Viking age. The vessels included a light, a medium and a heavy merchant ship; a converted warship; and a "ferry" for transporting passengers in the surrounding seas. The converted warship, more than 100 feet (30 m) long, with thirty-six different rooms, was the largest of the vessels and represents the zenith of Viking ship development. Except for a few ceramic shards and animal bones, nothing except structural components was uncovered. These five magnificent ships have been reconstructed and are on display in a museum in Roskilde.

In 1981, another well-preserved Viking ship from the eleventh century was discovered by Dr. Catharina Ingelmen-Sundberg at the entrance to the port of Foteviken in

Sweden. This port, just south of Malmö, was a very important trading market during the Viking age. Like the five vessels scuttled at Roskilde, the Foteviken shipwreck was sunk in the middle of the port entrance and filled with stones to obstruct marauding ships.

Once again, archaeologists discovered that not one but five ships had been scuttled. The others were under a mound of stones farther inside the harbor, but their wooden remains were so poorly preserved that, after all pertinent archaeological data were recorded, the ships were covered over again with mud. Dr. Ingelmen-Sundberg's initial find was identified as a small warship about 36 feet (11 m) in length. All the wooden remains she had found were recovered and preserved, and eventually the hull was reconstructed.

THE VASA

The most ambitious underwater archaeological recovery ever made also took place in Swedish waters, with the raising of an intact seventeenth-century warship, the *Vasa*, in 1961. The War of Reformation had been going on for seven years when the Swedish king, Gustav Adolf II, decided to establish a powerful navy to protect his realm from eventual invasion. From Sweden's Dutch allies, the king obtained the services of master shipbuilders to construct a fleet of warships. The largest of the ships, the *Vasa*, was to serve as the flagship. In 1627 she left the ways and was moored before the king's palace in Stockholm Harbor, where she was outfitted with sails, rigging, and ballast stones. Ballast was essential to stabilize a ship in strong winds. By the end of the 18th century iron and lead ingots often replaced the use of stones. Her massive size of 1,400 tons made her the largest ship in the world at that time. The final touch was the placement of sixty-four large bronze cannon. She was also one of the most beautiful, with baroque carvings and elaborate decorations adorning her hull, which was 155 feet (47 m) long. From her keel to the top of her mainmast she measured almost 180 feet (55 m), surpassing most church towers in height.

On August 10, 1628, thousands of cheering spectators, including the king and his court, lined the wharves of Stockholm Harbor as the *Vasa* left the moorings and started

Once again sea-worthy in Stockholm's harbor, the intimidating size and power of the *Vasa* is clear.

off on her maiden voyage. Her crew, including officers, sailors and marines, numbered 433 men. As the splendid ship passed the fortress at Södermalm, her cannon fired a thundering salute, which was answered by the fortress's guns and jubilant cries from the people ashore. Minutes later, a sudden strong gust of wind from the surrounding mountains caused the ship to lurch sharply to one side. The captain ordered the sails cut loose and cannon from the lee side of the ship moved to the windward side in an effort to right her. But as the cannon were being shifted, tons of water entered through the lower cannon ports, which were still open, and the ship listed even further. She soon capsized and sank rapidly, carrying a large number of her crew, as well as many women and children who had come along to celebrate the great day. The captain and some of the other officers were rescued, only to be imprisoned and court-martialed. They were eventually exonerated, however.

In 1930, as a boy of six, Anders Franzén first heard the story of the *Vasa* from his father, an amateur historian, as they sat fishing from a wharf on Dalarö, one of the many islands in the archipelago of Stockholm. Even before his father had finished the story, Franzén resolved that one day he would find the ship. His persistent interest in the *Vasa* eventually led to the most important marine archaeological discovery of the century.

Anders's father took his son for a visit to the Stockholm Marine Historical Museum. There the boy stood fascinated before seven elaborately embellished bronze cannon, which allegedly had been recovered from the *Vasa* in 1920. The museum director told Franzén that a commercial fisherman had caught his anchor on something in an area where he had previously lost other anchors and

The gun deck of the *Vasa* after it was raised and preserved.

fishing nets. Luckily, he had noticed a salvage ship coming his way and stopped it, offering a bottle of brandy to one of the helmet divers to investigate the spot and recover his anchor. The diver landed on the remains of a large wooden ship and, after sending up the fisherman's anchor, decided to bring up the seven bronze cannon he discovered on the wreck. The Swedish government purchased the cannon for $12,500—a large sum of money in those days. Today, each of the cannon would fetch that amount. Unfortunately, the museum official told Franzén, the exact location of the wreck was not recorded, nor were the identities of the fisherman or salvors noted.

Franzén became an engineer and took up diving as an avocation, devoting many weekends to it. He continued to be fascinated by the *Vasa*. He learned that, from the moment she sank, there had been attempts to raise and salvage items from the flagship. People were still in mourning for those who had gone down with her when an Englishman, Jan Bulmer, presented himself at court with a letter identifying him as "Engineer to His Majesty, the King of England." Bulmer had witnessed the dramatic loss of the *Vasa* and confidently offered to raise it. King Gustav Adolf II gave him a contract, and the first part of Bulmer's project went well. The *Vasa* had almost completely righted herself before reaching the bottom. The main deck lay some 115 feet (35 m) deep. Divers were able to secure lines to the ship's submerged masts. The other ends of the lines were attached to horse teams on shore, and these were able to shift the wreck to an even keel.

Bulmer was then at a loss as to how to raise the ship and gave up. The king ordered the navy to try. Salvors snagged parts of the ship with grappling hooks attached to chains and ropes and made repeated attempts to lift the wreck, using other ships to pull on the lines and chains, but the massive vessel wouldn't budge. Over the next few decades many others, including French, Dutch and German would-be salvors, unsuccessfully tried the same method. They ripped open the decks and superstructures, leaving behind tons of chains, lines, anchors and grappling hooks.

Then in 1658, when all hope of raising the ship had been abandoned, a Swedish colonel, Albrekt von Treileben, who had worked with a German salvage expert, Andreas Peckell, obtained a salvage contract from the government. Treileben planned his project carefully. He induced Peckell to work with him, assembling many divers and procuring a newly invented diving bell. Work began in the autumn of 1663. The team quickly realized it was impossible to raise the whole ship and decided to concentrate on recovering the cannon and other valuable items. The divers worked in the icy waters for three years and managed to bring up fifty-three of the ship's cannon, as well as many other articles of value.

Franzén, who had spent years researching the *Vasa,* wanted to search for her. But Stockholm is a busy commercial and naval harbor, and amateurs are not permitted to dive there. He finally decided that if he could not search for the *Vasa,* he would search for wrecks elsewhere.

Franzén suspended his weekend diving trips and once again returned to the archives and libraries, devoting every spare minute to researching old ship losses. After many months, he had a list of more than fifty ships that had sunk along the east coast of Sweden. He selected the twelve most promising and went to the Marine Historical Museum to seek financial assistance. The specialists there listened with great interest to the enthusiastic young man. His persistence convinced them to conduct an exploratory search; but none of them thought he was correct in believing that a ship could be found intact.

Franzén chose the *Riksäpplet,* a Swedish warship, as his first goal. The ship had sunk in 1676, during a storm in the Bay of Dalarö, after the anchor cables parted and she was driven against a small rock island. The site of the wreck was only a few miles from where Franzén had spent his childhood dreaming of diving on ancient wrecks. There were two advantages to selecting this wreck: fishermen knew its approximate location from snagging their nets on the wreckage; and the depth of the water was only 55 feet (17 m), which would give the divers a reasonable amount of time to work on the bottom each day.

Franzén became very discouraged when he first dove on the wreck. Over the years, drifting ice and pounding surf had smashed it to pieces, so he recovered no more than a few oak planks and beams. But disappointment turned to elation when he discovered

The *Vasa* right after it was raised and on its way to dry-dock.

that the pieces of wood, although they had turned black, showed no sign of shipworm infestation and were as solid as the day they had been hewn. He was surer than ever that he could find an intact ship.

Franzén realized that he had to search in deeper water, where a shipwreck would be unaffected by ice or rough seas. Going over the other ships on his list, he found that all were either in shallow water, like the *Riksäpplet,* or in water too deep for safe scuba diving. He turned again to his first love, the *Vasa.* Professor Nils Ahnlund, a noted historian, helped him get permission from the government to conduct a search. Franzén also learned that the seven cannon recovered in 1920 were not, in fact, from the *Vasa,* but from another wreck, the *Riksnyckeln,* which had also sunk in 1628.

None of the thousands of pages of documents he read gave the precise location of the *Vasa.* Most simply stated that it was in Stockholm Ström, near the town of Danuiken. The waters are so muddy in that area that divers can't see their hands in front of their masks. With only a vague idea of the ship's location, it might take years to locate the wreck. But Franzén was determined, and he and many of his diving friends spent hundreds of fruitless hours on the bottom during the summer of 1953, discovering nothing more than a startling amount of modern debris.

The following summer Franzén resorted to another method of search, hoping to cover a greater area than the divers had the previous year. He towed grappling hooks on a long cable behind a small boat and searched many square miles of the bottom, but without success. His only finds were modern artifacts such as iron stoves, old bicycles, rusty bedsteads and skeletal Christmas trees. That winter in the archives Franzén discovered an eighteenth-century sea chart with an X marking a spot near the areas he had already searched. He suspected that it might mark the site of the *Vasa.* Franzén purchased a sonar device and invented a core sampler: a rocket-shaped lead instrument with a sharp-edged iron tube inside it, used to recover samples of material from objects located by the sonar set.

The well-preserved and intact hull of the *Vasa* being towed to dry-dock immediately after being raised.

He spent the summer of 1955 searching the new area with these instruments but found nothing. By this time Franzén had become the laughingstock of Stockholm. Even some of his own friends referred to him as the "mad treasure hunter." Once again he returned to the archives, hoping to find other documents that might give a more accurate location for the wreck. Months went by and nothing of importance turned up in the dusty documents. Then, about the time the ice began breaking up along the shores of the Baltic, he made a startling discovery. In a letter dated August 12, 1628, from the Swedish Parliament to the king, he read that the *Vasa* had gone down in about 120 feet (37 m) of water, near Beckholmsudden.

The previous summer, the sonar had recorded what looked like a large hill in that area, but Franzén hadn't investigated it because he didn't think the *Vasa* was near there. Some engineers to whom he later mentioned the sonar reading told him that it was nothing more than debris from the construction of a dry dock made there some years before. Unfortunately, Franzén hadn't marked the spot on a chart, so he would have to start from scratch. As soon as the last ice disappeared, he began searching. At the beginning of August 1956 he lowered the coring device and at 105 feet (32 m) it struck something hard. He quickly pulled it up and extracted the sample from the tube. It was a piece of oak, but it might be from an old rowboat, or even an old tree. He began sounding and pulling up more samples, all of which were pieces of oak, blackened by years underwater. Using this method, he was able to determine that it was an old wreck of the same dimensions of the *Vasa.*

Franzén was positive that he had discovered the *Vasa.* He felt that exploring and raising the wreck was too formidable an undertaking for an amateur like himself. He needed to raise money to hire professional divers and a proper salvage vessel. At first he was unable to raise any funds because very few people took his claim seriously. In desperation, he went to the commander of the Navy Diving School in Stockholm and told him the whole story. Although the commander was a bit skeptical, he agreed to conduct the navy's next training dive on the site.

Several days later Franzén joined both scuba and helmet divers at the site. The first diver to descend was the chief instructor, a helmet diver named Edvin Fälting, who had more than 10,000 hours of diving experience. Franzén was able to follow Fälting's descent over the telephone installed in the diver's helmet. The diver reached the bottom, reporting that he was standing up to his chest in mud and could see nothing. A few minutes later he said he was returning to the surface and Franzén's face betrayed his profound disappointment. Then suddenly he heard Fälting shout: "Wait a minute. I just ran into something solid. It feels like a wooden wall. No, it's a big ship, no doubt about it. Now I'm climbing up the wall…there are some rectangular openings…they must be cannon ports. …" The *Vasa* had been discovered.

In the days that followed, the navy divers inspected the wreck more thoroughly, and Franzén got busy trying to estimate the cost of raising and preserving the ship. He figured that it would cost at least several hundred thousand dollars, but his income as an engineer could cover only a small fraction of this amount. At first he had no idea how the money would be raised, but once the newspapers, radio and television announced his discovery, offers of assistance came from many sources. The Neptune Salvage Company, the largest commercial marine salvage company in Sweden, offered to raise the ship, and King Gustav Adolf VI ordered the navy to put all its divers and diving vessels at the disposal of the operation. It was arranged for Franzén to receive his engineer's salary from the navy, so he could continue to work full time on the project.

In the spring of 1957 the *Vasa* Committee was formed to investigate the technical and financial aspects of salvaging the whole ship. Many imaginative suggestions were presented to the committee, which was headed by Commodore Edward Clason. One man's plan entailed pumping refrigerant into the ship's interior. It would turn to ice and, since ice is lighter than water, the *Vasa* would, theoretically, rise like a giant iceberg. Another imaginative inventor recommended filling the ship's hull with ping-pong balls until the upward force exerted by the buoyant balls carried the ship to the surface. The committee members agreed with Franzén that the various schemes presented were too risky and that such an important find should not be subjected to experimental methods.

In February 1958 the committee issued a report recommending that the standard method of raising a ship be used. This meant that a network of steel cables would have to be attached to the wreck on the bottom and to pontoons on the surface. Many experts doubted that the ship's timbers would hold up under the pressure of the cables and feared that the wreck would collapse like an eggshell when an attempt was made to raise her. Franzén had many samples of wood from the wreck tested. The results proved that the wood still retained 60 percent of its original strength. This convinced the committee to take the gamble.

The next problem was money, but Franzén's fervor and the historical significance of the shipwreck elicited generous donations from industry, the Marcus and Amalia Wallenberg Fund, a Scandinavian charitable foundation, the king and many private citizens. By the time the ship had been raised, more than $3 million had been collected and spent on the project.

Chief diver Per Edvin Fälting with a lion's head from the Swedish national coat-of-arms. Fälting dug tunnels under the ship's hull so cables could be slung to raise the ship.

Franzén discovered that virtually nothing was known about preserving wood that had been immersed in the sea. The committee formed to investigate preservation concluded that it would be foolish to bring the *Vasa* to the surface before they knew how to preserve her. The first step would be to move her from the depths where she rested to a spot about 50 feet (15 m) deep.

Placing the cables under the keel of the wreck turned out to be very tricky and dangerous, because underwater visibility was so poor and because the keel had settled 6 to 9 feet (about 2 to 3 m) deep in the hard clay on the bottom. Franzén obtained powerful water jets and mud suckers, which work on the same principle as a vacuum cleaner, to dig shafts along the sides of the wreck and make tunnels under her keel. The water jet cut into the clay, and the mud sucker carried the clay to a barge on the surface. The mud along the sides of the ship was so soft that the shafts caved in on many occasions, temporarily burying the divers, who had to be rescued.

Once they reached the hard clay and began making the tunnels, the divers, crawling on their bellies, faced the possibility that the ship's planks might open, allowing tons of ballast stones to fall and crush them. Fortunately, the planks held, and there were no serious mishaps. No sooner had work begun on the first tunnel than the wreck began to reveal its treasures. One of the first finds was the ship's gilded figurehead: a carving of a ferocious lion weighing two tons. The iron bolts that had held the figurehead and other pieces of baroque carving in place had rusted through, causing the carvings to fall to the bottom. Figures of mythological and biblical characters were found, including Hercules, Cerberus, Nereus, and King David holding a lyre. Divers also discovered many of the cannon-port covers, bearing carvings of lion masks, the coat of arms of the royal house of Vasa, dragons, mermaids and knights.

The divers began bringing up dozens of priceless objects each day, and the National Marine Museum specialists in charge of preservation were hard-pressed to keep up. Finally, six tunnels were dug and 6-inch (15 cm) cables were slung through them and brought to the surface. Early in August 1959, the Neptune Salvage Company fleet arrived at the site, and the cables were attached to two large pontoons, which were flooded until they were barely afloat. The cables were tightened, and then the pontoons were pumped dry, raising the wreck about 20 inches (50 cm). Divers sent down to view the *Vasa* reported that the ship was showing no signs of strain, so this method was repeated again and again. Twenty-seven days later, the ship was moved to a new area in slightly shallower water, where her mast stump almost touched the surface.

At this point the salvors faced a tremendous obstacle. They couldn't use the same method to raise the *Vasa* to the surface because, as she came higher out of the water and put more weight on the outer cables, the cables would place a heavy strain on her. The two pontoons would be forced together and could crush the ship if she was caught between them. Franzén determined that the only safe way to raise the ship and get her into a dry dock was to have her float on her own keel. Experts agreed with his plan, and the navy divers were put to work again. The job took more than a year. The ship had to be made completely airtight. The divers worked with carpenters' tools, sealing all the cannon ports and passageways, and replacing thousands of rusted nails and rotten dowels holding the planking of the hull to the ship's frame. Four deflated rubber pontoons were placed under the stern castle, the heaviest section of the ship, and then filled with air.

On April 14, 1961, the Neptune Salvage fleet arrived for the second time, and the cables were made fast to the pontoons. While force was exerted on the cables, pumps with a capacity for removing 7,500 gallons (34,000 l) a minute were put into action. After only ten minutes the ship began to rise slowly. By May 4 the *Vasa* was riding high enough to be towed into dry dock and placed on a specially built concrete raft equipped with a sprinkler system to keep the timbers wet until they could be preserved. The raft alone cost more than $1 million.

While dock workers shored up the sides of the ship, dozens of volunteers removed the mud from her top deck and covered all exposed sections of the ship with plastic sheeting. Franzén was incredibly busy from the moment the ship was placed on the raft. With a small army of archaeologists and historians, under the direction of Per Lundström, he entered every accessible part of the ship, encountering a fantastic time capsule. Everything lay just as it had fallen three and a half centuries before: sea chests, leather boots, weapons, carpenters' tools, beer mugs, cooking implements, money and powder kegs. More than 10,000 artifacts were discovered inside the ship. The remains of some of the unfortunate victims of the disaster lay among the cannon carriages. Twelve complete skeletons, partially clad and still wearing high leather boots, were dug out of the mud. One of the seamen had a sheath knife attached to his belt and a leather moneybag with twenty coins in it. Anders Franzén's dream had become a reality; people no longer call him the "mad treasure hunter" but are grateful that his years of dedicated searching resulted in one of the most significant marine archaeological finds ever made.

Pewter and glass tableware belonging to the commanding officer of the *Vasa*.

A large aluminum housing was built over the raft and became a permanent museum for the ship. On shore, a second museum was built to display the recovered artifacts. The world's largest and best-equipped preservation laboratory was also constructed, and dozens of experts were employed to preserve the artifacts and the ship itself. Three million dollars were spent on preservation of the ship and artifacts during the first five years, bringing the total for recovery and preservation to $6 million. As time went on this figure rose to $30 million.

The unlucky *Vasa* was lucky in a way. She sank in glacier-fed waters not salty enough to support the ravenous *teredo navalis* shipworm; hence, she remained intact. In addition, the wreck lay in the path of the outfall from Stockholm's sewers and the putrid waters produced sulfur-reducing bacteria whose by-products penetrated the wooden hull and made it poisonous to underwater funguses and rot. Once the ship was out of the water, the problems began. It was found that when exposed to air and sunlight the wood began to crack, so in the beginning conservationists wrapped the beams and stanchions in plastic. Then the entire hull was sprayed with polyethylene glycol, a water-soluble wax, to prevent drying and cracking. The same procedure was applied to the more than 14,000 broken-off pieces of the hull that were found scattered on the

Shortly after the battle against the Danish and Dutch fleets began, the Swedish warship *Kronan* caught fire, exploded and sank.

bottom and throughout the ship when the mud was removed. These fragments were jigsaw-puzzle pieces that the archaeologists and conservators skillfully placed in their original places on the ship. Missing pieces had to be constructed, and today over 95 percent of the ship is original.

In 1978 it was discovered that the more than 5,000 rusted bolts—some 5 feet long (1.5 m)—were affected by the polyethylene preservative and had formed sulfuric acid in the areas where they were attached to the hull. The acid was destroying the hull, so all the bolts were replaced by stainless steel. Preservation problems still plague the *Vasa* but conservators are working diligently to solve them.

THE KRONAN AND THE LYBSKE SWAN

Franzén could have rested on his laurels after the *Vasa* project but, propelled by his insatiable appetite for finding shipwrecks, he continued to comb historical archives and the seafloor around Sweden, finding many wrecks. The most notable was the *Kronan,* another Swedish man-of-war that, like the *Riksäpplet,* was lost in 1676. The *Kronan,* designed by the Englishman Francis Sheldon, took seven years to build and in her day was one of the largest ships in the world, some 200 feet (60 m) in length and 2,140 tons in displacement. Her armament, unsurpassed in its time, consisted of 126 cannon, weighing 220 tons—larger than most merchantmen of the period. The weight of these guns made her dangerously top-heavy.

In 1675 Denmark and Holland jointly declared war on Sweden. The following year, Swedish King Karl XI appointed a rich nobleman, Lorentz Creutz, as admiral of the Swedish fleet. Creutz, who had little experience at sea, chose the *Kronan* as his flagship.

She carried a complement of 850 seamen and soldiers. On May 1, 1676, the opposing fleets met in the southern Baltic and engaged in a battle, but the outcome was not decisive. Most of the ships sustained damages. On June 1 the fleets engaged again off the island of Oland. Disaster struck before the first shot was fired.

As she maneuvered for a better fighting position, the *Kronan* was struck by a sudden gust of wind, and poor seamanship, combined with her instability, caused the ship to capsize. The powder room caught fire, and the great warship blew up with a tremendous explosion and quickly disappeared in 85 feet (26 m) of water, taking more than 800 men with her. In Franzén's words, "She took seven years to build and less than a minute to destroy."

The Dutch and Danes promptly attacked the remaining Swedish warships, and the Swedish navy suffered its greatest defeat of all time. Seven thousand men were slain, injured or taken prisoner.

Between 1682 and 1686, divers, using a primitive diving bell, recovered sixty of the *Kronan*'s large bronze cannon. There the salvage attempt ended, and over the centuries the once-mighty ship was forgotten, until Franzén revived interest in her. In 1979 he started a magnetometer search for the *Kronan*. In August 1980, the magnetometer found a target in an area where Swedish navy divers had reported sighting old wooden ship timbers some years earlier. Since the waters in these seas rarely exceed 40 degrees Fahrenheit (about 5°C), Franzén and his team were using an underwater closed-circuit television camera to check out each anomaly the magnetometer registered. This time they could scarcely believe their eyes. Scattered among ship's timbers on the seabed they saw bronze cannon. Since the ship had exploded as she sank, she wasn't intact like the *Vasa*. The main part of her starboard side was missing, but the rest of her wooden structure survived in a jumbled fashion on the bottom.

Survivors being picked up after the *Kronan* sank.

They began diving immediately and found that one of the bronze cannon was German and cast in 1514—a full century and a half before the *Kronan* was even launched. Other cannon proved to be from France, Austria, Denmark and Sweden. This was not unusual, since bronze cannon were very valuable and used for a long time.

The Kalmar County Museum, in the port of Kalmar on the Swedish mainland opposite Oland, has sponsored the ongoing excavation of the *Kronan*. To date, the team has recovered fifty-four of the *Kronan*'s cannon and excavated about two-thirds of the site. For the first three years they concentrated on mapping and digging test holes. In 1984 they found beautiful wooden carvings in their original positions lining the inner planking on the port side, and nearby discovered three chests. The first was a medical chest containing an assortment of filled medicine bottles and cups neatly arranged in rows. A brass breastplate with the Swedish royal crest on it was also in the chest. It had belonged to Peter Gripenflycht, the ship's surgeon, who perished in the disaster. Another chest held navigation instruments, including dividers, a protractor, a ruler, an adjustable pencil and a heavy lead inkwell. The sea chest of an unknown sailor held a large bottle of liquor, a handsome belt made of leather and silk, a pair of gloves and a length of silk ribbon once adorned with a flower—no doubt a memento from a lady. Scattered among these items were ginger root, garlic cloves and peppercorns, which were probably used to improve the taste of shipboard fare.

Franzén's project has yielded 22,000 artifacts. One of them was the ship's bell. It bore two still-legible inscriptions—*Soli Deo Gloria* ("Glory be to God"), and *Holmaie Me*

Funderbar John Mayer Anno 1670, which translates as "John Mayer cast me in Stockholm in 1670." More than 250 gold coins were also recovered; most had been minted in Sweden in the seventeenth century, but there were three Spanish coins minted during the reign of Ferdinand and Isabella in the latter part of the fifteenth and early part of the sixteenth centuries. Many of Admiral Creutz's possessions were excavated; the most poignant was a gold ring with his wife's initials. Dozens of bottles of vodka and aquavit were found with their contents; chemical analysis showed that three centuries on the bottom had dropped their alcoholic content to a mere 6 percent.

A large number of human skulls and other bones were found, including the lower half of the skeleton of a man of high rank, his shanks still clothed in stockings and leather boots. His personal possessions were nearby: gold and enamel cuff links, a gold charm in the shape of a skull, a gilded sword hilt, a pocket watch and a tortoise-shell snuffbox. Mixed in with the remains of several other skeletons were a trumpet, parts of two violins and fragments of a drum that had no doubt belonged to the *Kronan*'s musicians, who had been playing when the ship capsized. Limited funding and dependence on donations dictate a slow pace for the project, which relies chiefly on volunteer labor. It may take another twenty-five years to complete the excavation of this magnificent seventeenth-century shipwreck. The project continually battles with weather conditions, which limit work to about two months each summer. There are plans eventually to raise parts of the wooden hull and the stern section, which, like the *Vasa*'s, is ornately decorated. The wreck has its own museum in Kalmar, and over 100,000 people visit it every year.

One of the many ornate bronze cannon recovered from the *Kronan*.

In November 1990 Franzén did it again with the discovery of yet another important Swedish warship, the three-masted *Lybske Swan,* which was lost in 1525 near Stockholm. She was the flagship of King Gustav Vasa, who fought successfully to break the domination of the Danish kings over Sweden. In 1523, the Danes had surrendered aboard the *Lybske Swan* in a ceremony that marked the creation of the Swedish nation. Two years later, heavy with weapons and booty after a successful war expedition, she ran aground and sank in 150 feet (46 m) of water. Using side-scan sonar and a centuries-old chart he had found with an X marking the wreck site, Franzén located the *Lybske Swan* precisely where the chart indicated. Adam Tolby, the first diver to descend on the wreck, reported: "I saw a skeleton trapped under the stern, with even part of his clothes still on. I could have reached out and touched him." All the wooden remains were in an excellent state of preservation, but the 100-foot (30 m) ship was broken apart. She may have been damaged by Swedish navy depth charges fired against suspected Soviet submarines in the area.

Franzén had planned to spend the next ten to fifteen years on the *Lybske Swan* project. "Everything is there," he said. "You could raise her remains, reconstruct her and sail away to sea in her." Unfortunately, he died before he could undertake this new project.

THE VROUW MARIA

The most important recent find in the Baltic was the Dutch merchant ship *Vrouw Maria,* which had foundered in a storm in 1771 near the Island of Jurmo off Finland. The bulk of her cargo consisted of general merchandise, but she also carried a very valuable con-

The Dutch merchantman *Vrouw Maria* foundering during a storm in 1771, near the Island of Jurmo off the coast of Finland.

signment belonging to the Russian Empress, Catherine the Great. The ship was bound for St. Petersburg with additions to the Empress's famed collection of art in the Hermitage Museum. In Amsterdam she had purchased a number of paintings and other works of art. Supposedly there are many objects made of gold and silver; ivory figurines; porcelain and ancient Greek and Roman bronze statues on the wreck as well.

At that time Finland was part of Sweden, and Swedish officials quickly sent divers to the wreck site, which lay in 144 feet (43 m) of water. With the primitive tools then available they were unable to recover any of her treasures. In the 1970s historian Christian Ahlstrom found a number of documents in the Finnish and Danish National Archives and, like Anders Franzén, he became obsessed with finding this wreck.

In 1997 Ahlstrom teamed up with diver Rauno Koivusaari, and the following summer conducted a side-scan sonar survey in the area where the ship was believed to be. They did find a wreck from the same period as the *Vrouw Maria*—but it was the wrong ship. More archival research was conducted to narrow down the search area and the following year they located the wreck. Artifacts such as clay pipes, crockery and tools were bought up until local authorities halted the excavation to resolve ownership of the site. Under Finnish law the ship belongs to the nation; however, Sweden has also claimed the wreck since Finland was part of Sweden when it was lost. A legal battle rages over ownership while Ahlstrom and his divers anxiously wait to get back to the wreck and Catherine's treasures.

In 1999 a group of treasure hunters salvaged nearly 3,000 bottles of well-preserved champagne from a World War I wreck off Finland's west coast. Each bottle netted over $4,000 at auction. No government authorities made any claim on this wreck because they are primarily interested in protecting historical shipwrecks.

O GOVERNADOR AFFONÇO Đ ALBOQVERQVE·SVÇEDEO·NA J NDIA
A DOM·FRANCĪSCO·Đ ALMEIDA·EM NOVEMBRO·DE
509·TOMOV·DIAS VEZ·S [...] A CIDADE Đ GOA·FASĐ MALA
A Đ TEORVZ·E FEZ A FORTALEZ [...] A Đ CALECVTE FO J A PERÇĪA·E AO
ESTRETO·DE ORMVZ·E [...] MAR ROXO

GOVERNOV   ESTE   ESTADO·ATE
OANNOĐ·I·5I5   FEZ A FOR   TALEZA DA CIDADE
H GOA·E FA [...]   LECEO·NA   BARRA·DELLA

3 THE AGE OF DISCOVERY

ITH THE DECLINE OF THE ROMAN EMPIRE, the barbarian invaders from the north conquered most of the lands bordering the northern Mediterranean shores. To them the sea was an alien environment, and during the so-called Dark Ages they turned their backs on it, so that seamanship and navigation became lost arts for almost a thousand years.

During the Renaissance, Europeans threw off their fear and superstition about the sea, and the Age of Exploration dawned. Shipbuilding was revived and the art of navigation was relearned. Old trade routes were re-established and new ones sought. The Portuguese led in voyaging to hitherto unknown lands. The Spaniards followed soon after, and they and the Portuguese became the undisputed masters of the sea.

Before Christopher Columbus ventured westward, European nations were stagnating because of a severe lack of precious metals, the main ingredients in expanding mercantile trade. It was, in fact, the desire for precious metals that led to discovery of the New World.

COLUMBUS'S SHIPS

On the night of August 2, 1492, Columbus and his crew of about ninety men and boys attended a solemn mass in the small seaport of Palos in southern Spain. Then, full of the spirit of the great adventure before them, they boarded the three small vessels, the *Niña*, the *Pinta* and the *Santa María*, which were to carry them on an epic voyage of discovery. Columbus sailed aboard his flagship the *Santa María*, the largest of the three. As

The Portuguese conquistador Afonso de Albuquerque led a fleet of twenty-two ships that sieged and plundered their way from Lisbon to Malacca. His flagship, the *Flor de la Mar*, was possibly the richest shipwreck ever found.

Replica of the *Nina II*, which co-author Robert Marx sailed across the Atlantic in 1962. The *Nina II* is the nickname for the *Santa Clara*, the smallest of Columbus's three ships.

soon as the tide permitted, they dropped down the Rio Tinto and then set course "south and by west" in the Atlantic Ocean for the Canary Islands. Their goal was to reach Cathay, India and especially Zipango (Japan). There, according to Marco Polo's book, which Columbus carried aboard, there were palaces roofed in gold.

Thirty-three days after leaving the Canaries the little fleet made landfall, not in the golden lands of their quest, but on a palm-fringed isle in the Bahamas where they were greeted by tawny natives. They explored the islands of this archipelago, cruised along the north shore of Cuba and then coasted along the mountainous island of Cibeo, where native people they encountered along the shore informed them there was "plenty of gold." Later, Columbus named this island Española. Today it is called Hispaniola and is divided between the countries of Haiti and the Dominican Republic.

Still in search of the Orient, the fleet headed eastward along the north coast of Hispaniola. It was very difficult sailing. The ships had to beat against the trade winds, making long tacks to gain ground, and the men were exhausted. On Christmas Eve everyone aboard the *Santa María* was asleep, dreaming of great riches, except for a young boy who had been left at the helm. Columbus's own words describe what happened next:

> It pleased Our Lord that at midnight while I lay in bed, with the ship in a dead calm and the sea as peaceful as the water in a cup, all went to sleep, leaving the tiller in charge of a boy. So it happened that the swells drove the ship very gently onto one of those reefs, on which the waves broke with such a noise they could be heard a league away. Then the boy, feeling the rudder ground and hearing the noise, gave tongue…

Panic ensued aboard the flagship. The crew first tried to kedge her off, using several anchors and pulling with the longboat. When this failed, they began transferring her stores to the other two ships. As the tide dropped, the *Santa María* alternately lifted and fell on the large swells until she burst open at the seams, and within hours the ship was a complete wreck. A boy's inexperience had caused the first recorded shipwreck of a European vessel in the New World.

The crews of the three vessels dismantled the wreck, taking ashore all the timbers that remained above water and using them to build a small fort. Thirty-nine men were chosen to garrison the fort, called Fort La Navidad, until Columbus could return to rescue them. Columbus then headed northeast and, beating against the trade winds, made his way back to Spain and great acclaim.

The following December, when Columbus returned to the area, he found the fort razed by fire and all the men dead, presumably killed by Indians who resented the Spaniards' insatiable appetite for their gold and their women. All that remained was one of the ship's seven anchors. It was found in a nearby Indian village, whose inhabitants had vanished into the hills to escape the explorers' wrath.

The shipwrecked *Santa María* was forgotten until 1939, when American historian Samuel Eliot Morison retraced the route of Columbus's first voyage. Morison concluded that the *Santa María* had been lost near the present-day port of Cap Haïtien in Haiti. In 1955, a well-known American industrialist and underwater explorer, Edwin Link, and his wife, Marion, with whom he had explored shipwrecks in the Florida Keys, began a systematic search for the *Santa María* in the area Morison had identified. Peering through face masks day after day, they eventually found an iron anchor, which is believed to have come from the *Santa María*. It was of a design current at the time of Columbus, and analysis by the U.S. Bureau of Standards confirmed that the iron was consistent with that used to produce anchors during the period.

In 1967 Fred Dickson entered the picture. A businessman, amateur diver and member of the New York Explorers' Club, Dickson was obsessed with finding Columbus's flagship. He raised money and obtained the assistance of a team of specialists. After working for four summers, they located what they believed were the remains of the *Santa María*. The first evidence they found was ballast rock. Then they uncovered some wooden remains from the lower hull of a ship. Metal detectors led them to many ship fittings, nails and spikes of both iron and copper. Their most important find was a shard of Spanish pottery that the thermo luminescent process dated as being from the appropriate time. Sadly, Dickson drowned while diving on the site during the fourth year, and the project ended prematurely. A Florida-based group of amateur underwater archaeologists conducted an unsuccessful search for the *Santa María* during the summer of 1992 as part of the 500-year celebration of Columbus's first voyage. It's a mystery exactly what they expected to find as the ship had been almost totally dismantled and everything from it used to build Fort Navidad. Her lower hull would have long since been devoured by the *teredo navalis.* Proof of this was obtained through the excavations of the fort and surrounding area by Dr. Katherine Deagan of the University of Florida in the late 1980s.

In May 1502 Columbus embarked from Cádiz, Spain, on his fourth and last voyage of exploration. He sailed aboard his flagship, the *Capitana,* accompanied by three other caravels, the *Gallega,* the *Vizcaina* and the *Santiago de Palos.* After cruising along the northern coasts of Venezuela and Colombia they reached the coast of Panama, where they stayed for three months making repairs to the ships and trading with the Indians. Shipworms were a serious problem in those tropical waters, and two of the caravels were so badly damaged that they had to be abandoned and sunk. The *Vizcaina* went down off Porto Bello and the *Gallega* was scuttled at the mouth of the Belén River, where Columbus had planned to build an outpost until forced to retreat before hostile Indians.

In 1971 at the invitation of the Panama government, I began a survey of shipwrecks along the Caribbean side of the Isthmus of Panama. Over a three-year period I located many shipwrecks of various vintages. I met a U.S. sport diver who, while diving for placer gold deposits at the mouth of the alligator-infested Belén River, had found an "old anchor." He took me to the site, where I saw for myself a very old anchor indeed: one dating from the time of Columbus. Since no other ships are known to have been lost in this area, it probably came from the ill-fated *Gallega*. On this same site, we found scattered Spanish ballast stones, fish and animal bones and ceramic shards dating from the relevant period. Later, another American sport diver showed me a small cast-iron Lombard cannon that he had recovered some years before from the same site and that specialists identified as being from the period of the *Gallega*. Dr. Donald H. Keith, an underwater archaeologist who specializes in shipwrecks of the Age of Discovery, worked on the *Gallega* site. The main goal of Keith's nonprofit organization, Ships of Exploration and Discovery Research, was to locate the ship's wooden remains (as so little is known of ship construction of this period), some of which may have been preserved in the soft mud bottom of the river mouth. Unfortunately, the organization discovered little of note as others had been there before and had plundered the site.

In 1973 I was asked once again, this time under the auspices of the Organization of the American States (OAS), to return to Panama to investigate a shipwreck discovered by sport divers. It turned out to be Columbus's *Vizcaina* in 20 feet (6 m) of water only 35 feet (11 m) offshore in Porto Bello Bay. Artillery pieces of the period, three anchors, a ballast pile, numerous coral-encrusted objects and ceramic shards were visible. Realizing the importance of this find, I recommended that it be surveyed and excavated as soon as possible to prevent any damage by looters. My advice was not taken seriously by Panama government officials, and the wreck was soon forgotten.

In June 2002 it was announced that the *Vizcaina* had been located again. This time the find was made by a Florida-based salvor named Warren White, who claims he moved to Panama in 1995 specifically for the purpose of finding the *Vizcaina*. Many believe his main objective was to find treasure on the many Spanish treasure galleons lost in Porto Bello Bay. The Institute of Culture was alerted to the find and, instead of enlisting the assistance of professional archaeologists to take over the work on this historically important shipwreck, they issued White a standard salvage contract that gave the government 35 percent of any treasure found and the right to keep any of the finds if they choose, paying White half the value of the artifacts. (But how do you put a value on one of Columbus's cannon?) The cash-strapped Institute of Culture was not even able to assign anyone to oversee the salvage operation.

Without any archaeological supervision, White and his team brought up five cannon, stone cannonballs and a large amount of pottery shards. Luckily, when they found a half-decayed wooden chest containing swords, they put it back in the water to prevent it from drying out and disintegrating. Finally, thanks to outside pressure from scholars around the world, the excavation was halted in August 2002 and a twenty-four-hour watch put on the site to prevent looting. The Institute of Culture has called for assistance from abroad, and a major expedition is expected to be conducted during the summer of 2003.

Even with the little work that was done by White we learned some interesting historical information. It seems that the crew had to forage for victuals, as coconut shells, scallop shells and turtle bones were found mixed in with the ballast rock. Numerous archaeologists have been to Panama and from what was found by White they are all convinced that this wreck is the *Vizcaina*.

Co-author Robert Marx and assistant Louise Judge with ceramic shards they recovered from one of the Columbus wrecks in St. Ann's Bay, Jamaica.

In 1503, after leaving the coast of Panama, Columbus headed for the Spanish settlement of Santo Domingo on Hispaniola with his two remaining ships, the *Capitana* and the *Santiago de Palos*. They were badly rotted, and he planned to careen and repair them at Santo Domingo before sailing homeward. By the time he was off the north coast of Jamaica, however, both ships had gaping holes in their hulls and were on the verge of sinking, despite continuous pumping. Thus enfeebled, on June 25, 1503, Columbus entered St. Ann's Bay, midway along Jamaica's north coast, and ran both ships aground, "about a bow shot distance from shore." He dispatched a dugout canoe with a few men to the town of Santo Domingo, where there was a governor and assorted officials, to notify authorities there of his plight. The remaining Spaniards stripped both caravels, using what they could to construct crude shelters on the shore and abandoning the two worthless hulls, which eventually sank into the soft sediment of the harbor. It wasn't until June 29, 1504—a year and four days later—that Columbus and his 115 men were rescued by a ship from Santo Domingo.

In 1940 Samuel Eliot Morison explored the gently curving bay, which Columbus had called Santa Gloria, to determine where the *Capitana* and *Santiago* had been lost. Morison's estimate of the hulls' location was published in a chart in his Pulitzer Prize–winning book *Admiral of the Ocean Sea*. In 1968, the caravels' hulls were discovered a stone's throw from where he thought they were.

I had long been fascinated by the St. Ann's Bay shipwrecks. While excavating the sunken city of Port Royal on Jamaica's south coast, I put together a team of volunteers to look for the ships on weekends. We used Morison's chart as a guide, placing buoys on the two spots he had indicated and setting up a grid system of lines on the murky bottom of the shallow bay. We had no money for elaborate search equipment, so we probed the bottom sediment with long metal poles in an effort to locate solid objects that might indicate the presence of a wreck.

Though primitive, the system proved effective. After several days' search, we discovered a wooden beam. It was deeply embedded in the mud, and we spent six hours digging it out with our hands. In the same hole we also found numerous shards of Spanish pottery and pieces of obsidian, the black volcanic glass commonly found in Mexico and Central America, regions Columbus had visited before reaching Jamaica. It took several months for analysis to confirm that the pottery was from the late fifteenth century, and that the obsidian was from Central America. Meanwhile, we continued our weekend expeditions, discovering more shards in test holes and also finding ballast stones. Geologists confirmed that some stones were from southern Spain, where the *Capitana* and the *Santiago* had originally been loaded with ballast, and that others were from the Panama region, where more ballast must have been added to compensate for loss of weight caused by the consumption of the ship's stores and water supply.

Dr. Harold Edgerton, the distinguished physicist and electronics engineer from MIT (see Chapter 1), joined our volunteer team for a sonar survey of the site. He used subbottom profiling sonar equipment of his own design with which he had previously located shipwrecks and several submerged settlements in the Mediterranean. The sonar, which could "see" into the thick layer of sediment, revealed that two shipwrecks were concealed in the areas where we had made test holes. When Edgerton surveyed the rest of the bay without further sonar contacts, we were jubilant.

We notified the Jamaican government that Columbus's caravels had almost certainly been located, but because the government had no funds for work on the site, we went ahead on our own. Hoping to make a more certain identification, but not wanting to expose any wood or disturb the archaeological context, we decided to use a coring device to recover additional artifacts. Driving a 4-inch (10 cm) diameter coring tube into 20 feet (6 m) of sediment was not easy work. Extracting the tube was even more difficult, until we devised a way for divers in the skiff to help pull it up with lines. It took an average of three hours to pound the tube down with a 50-pound (23 kg) sledge hammer and another half hour to withdraw it. We sorted carefully through the mud from each sample, picking out the significant pieces and recording their stratigraphic depth. We made about thirty cores over a one-week period, finding interesting pieces in every core. They included many fragments of ballast stones, wood, bone and charcoal, ceramic shards, a bit of Venetian glass (later we learned it came from an hourglass) and a coral-encrusted sheathing tack. Subsequent analysis of the artifacts confirmed our conviction that the site was that of Columbus's shipwrecks. Despite their significance, however, these wrecks have still not been explored. Since what little remains of them is deep in fine sediment, normal underwater excavation methods are less effective than the procedure (used at the Roskilde Viking ship site in Denmark, see Chapter 2) of building a cofferdam around the site, pumping the water out and excavating as if on land. Columbus's caravels will remain safely ensconced in the waters of St. Ann's Bay until the money to excavate and conserve the remains can be raised.

A shipwreck found in 1977 may be Columbus's famous *Pinta*. According to documents, the *Pinta* and another caravel under the command of Spanish explorer Vicente Yáñez Pinzón were lost in 1500 "somewhere in the Caribbean during a hurricane." Caribbean Ventures, a Florida treasure-hunting firm, found a shipwreck dating from this period on Molasses Reef in the Turks and Caicos, a group of islands east of the Bahamas. Divers brought up six breech-loaded cannon called *bombardetas* and three swivel guns called *versos* but kept their find a secret while they chased after more lucrative treasure-bearing shipwrecks.

Underwater archaeologists carefully string gridlines over the Molasses Reef wreck site to ensure every inch is covered and to track the spread of the wreckage.

In 1980 the government of the Turks and Caicos learned about the find and invited Donald Keith, then a graduate student at the Institute of Nautical Archaeology at Texas A & M University, to explore it. Keith and his team worked on the site for four summers, recovering a wealth of artifacts. After first removing 42 tons of ballast rock they found that less than 1 percent of the wooden hull had survived on the site. They brought up more than 8 tons of cannon, tools, rigging and material from all parts of the wreck. Although the artifacts are from the turn of the sixteenth century, the wreck may not be the *Pinta,* since more than 115 small Spanish vessels, including nine of Columbus's ships from his four voyages, were lost in the Caribbean between 1492 and 1520.

Vicente Yañez Pinzón lost two of his caravels in 1500, and one of them may be the site known as the Highborn Cay wreck, located off the northern shore of Highborn Cay in the Bahamas. In 1965 three amateur divers accidentally located the wreck while spearfishing in 20 feet (6 m) of water. A small ballast pile covered by an assortment of cannon and two anchors were cemented in coral growth. The finders obtained a salvage permit from the Bahamian government and the following summer brought up the anchors, fifteen cannon, dozens of cannonballs, as well as pottery shards and iron fittings. Most of the artifacts were acquired by the Mariners' Museum of Newport News, Virginia, which had the artifacts taken to the Florida Bureau of Historical Sites and Properties for conservation treatment. One of the cannon was eventually put on display in the Smithsonian Institution.

Scholars realized the significance of the find, but the wreck languished for years due to a lack of funding until the Institute of Nautical Archaeology (INA) revisited the site in 1990. Noting similarities between the finds made on Molasses Reef with those of the Highborn Cay site, the INA team saw that the original finders had removed some of the ballast from both ends of the mound and had exposed hull timbers, a good indication that more of the hull's remains were hidden under the rest of the ballast mount. This proved correct, and two summers were spent carefully removing that ballast rock to expose the lower hull of the wreck. This shipwreck provided valuable information on ship construction of this early period.

CONQUISTADORS' SHIPS

More than 325 documented ships sank around the Cayman Islands, which were in the path of sailing vessels plying between Cuba, the last stop before setting out on the open ocean for Europe, and the Spanish Main. Over the years, amateur and professional divers have discovered a substantial amount of sunken treasure in the Caymans. One of the most valuable and historically important finds was also the most serendipitous. In 1970 a young couple from Dalton, Georgia, were snorkeling off the beach in front of the Holiday Inn Hotel on Grand Cayman Island when they spotted a metallic glint on the sandy bottom in water no more than waist-deep. To their great astonishment it turned out to be a gold cross covered with diamonds. They began fanning the fine white sand and within minutes had uncovered a few links of what proved to be a 13-foot (4 m) gold chain. In spite of their excitement, they managed to keep mum and rented scuba equipment so they could search the area more thoroughly.

What they pulled out of the gin-clear water that day ranks as one of history's most phenomenal treasure finds. Under a thin layer of sand they found a large bar of platinum dated 1521, seven bars of silver, many pieces of silver jewelry and a cache of more than 300 pounds (135 kg) of gold objects, still smooth and shining after centuries underwater. There were heavy gold discs, a gold bracelet in the form of a serpent covered with emeralds, more than fifty gold Aztec figurines and an impressive gold signet ring unmistakably of European origin.

Divers using a core sampler to determine the age of coral near a wreck site. Dating of this kind can help confirm the identity of a shipwreck.

The dazed young couple not only struck it rich but also solved a 450-year-old mystery. The signet ring held the answer to the question of what had become of the *Santiago,* a conquistadors' ship laden with Aztec plunder that disappeared in 1522 en route from Mexico to Spain. The coat of arms on the massive ring was that of the de León family of Spain, whose most illustrious member was Juan Ponce de León, the discoverer of Florida. The captain of the *Santiago* was his brother, Rodrigo, who accompanied Cortez to Mexico, and evidently lost his ship off Grand Cayman Island. The Georgia couple sold most of the treasure which they had smuggled off the island.

Another shipwreck associated with Cortez is *La Nicolasa,* which in 1526 sailed from Cuba for Veracruz, Mexico, with supplies for Cortez and his men. During a storm, the vessel was wrecked on a reef off Cancún Island on the coast of the Yucatán Peninsula. It too was discovered by chance. In 1956 a Mexican lawyer, José de Jesus Lima, and his sons were spearfishing when they came upon a large bronze cannon and two smaller iron cannon. Underwater explorer Edwin Link heard of their discovery and visited the site, which is covered by a thick deposit of coral. He found four more cannon and dozens of stone cannonballs. The following summer, the Mexican underwater club Conservation, Education, Diving, Archaeology Museums International (CEDAM) explored the shipwreck and recovered five cannon and two anchors. In 1984 a team of archaeologists from INA relocated the site but found very little of the wreck to study, confining most of their activities to examining the finds already made by CEDAM.

In 1527, a year after *La Nicolasa* sank, two other conquistador-era ships were wrecked farther down the coast of Yucatán near the Mayan ruins of Tulum, opposite Cozumel Island. In 1526 Cortez had dispatched his lieutenant Francisco de Montejo to conquer the Mayan inhabitants of Yucatán. De Montejo and a large expeditionary force of soldiers left Veracruz in the brigantine *La Gavarra,* accompanied by the caravel *San Jerónimo.* The ships anchored in sight of the cliff-top temple complex at Tulum, and the men went ashore. De Montejo anticipated a long and difficult campaign. To keep his force from deserting, he had the ships unloaded, set on fire and sunk, as Cortez had done upon reaching Veracruz. Thus the Spaniards had no choice but to subdue the Indians or die in the attempt. In fact, most of them were killed. The Maya resisted so fiercely that Yucatán was not completely pacified until 1546.

I lived on Cozumel Island between 1955 and 1959, pursuing countless shipwrecks, including de Montejo's. Armed with copies of original historical documentation from the Spanish archives, I was able to narrow down the area where the ships had been destroyed. Once I found the vestiges of the small fort the conquistadors had constructed on the coast, it was relatively easy to locate the wrecks. The first sign I found was an encrusted iron anchor. While digging it out of the sandy bottom I encountered ballast rock, ceramic shards and many pieces of charred wood. Less than 30 feet (100 m) from the first site I found the ring of the anchor from the second wreck protruding from the seafloor. I uncovered more ballast stones, shards and burnt wood there, as well as brass buttons, lead musket balls and a small silver crucifix. I submitted samples to experts, who identified them as belonging to the period 1500–1540. Carbon-14 analysis of a piece of wood dated it to approximately 450 years ago—compelling evidence of the *Gavarra* and the *San Jerónimo.*

MAGELLAN'S SHIPWRECK

In 1998 while visiting a museum in the Malaysian state of Sabah, on the north coast of Borneo, I saw an old iron cannon labeled as nineteenth-century British. I recognized it as Spanish from the early fifteenth century. I was intrigued and excited when museum

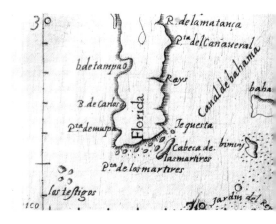

First known chart of Florida and part of the Bahamas—c. 1545. With such crude charts one can easily see why so many ships were lost.

Inca Indians pouring molten gold down the throat of a Spanish conquistador.

Tens of thousands of gold objects such as this Inca gold mask were plundered by the Spaniards from all over Mexico and South America.

staff told me it had been recovered by local divers from a nearby island named Magellan Island. Although people believe that Magellan was the first to circumnavigate the globe, the fact is that he was killed by natives of the Philippines and only one of the five ships that had sailed with him from Seville, Spain, in 1519 ever returned. Two were lost rounding the treacherous waters of South America, and after Magellan's death his men had to scuttle another ship near Cebu in the Philippines as too few men were left to man it. The two remaining ships were sailing uncharted waters off northern Borneo when the *Trinidad* struck a reef at night and was lost. Her survivors went aboard the *Victoria,* the remaining ship, which eventually reached Spain after further travails.

Under the auspices of the Sabah Museum, I mounted an expedition to locate the *Trinidad* with the assistance of local divers. The wreck was easy to locate off this small island, but unfortunately plunderers in quest of nonexistent treasures had looted the site. Craters pocked the entire reef, caused by dynamite used by fishermen, and little was left to find. I did recover ship's fittings, ballast stone, ceramic shards, stone cannon and lead firearm balls, and a weight belt lost by one of the plunderers. I suspected that more lay buried under coral growth so I applied for an excavation permit offering to give the museum everything recovered. Unfortunately, historical politics thwarted my project. The discovery had made headlines, and the Prime Minister of Malaysia declared there would be no excavation because it was with Magellan's voyage that foreigners began their exploitation of what is now Malaysia.

At the same time that I was working on the *Trinidad,* a very rich porcelain-carrying ship was discovered by the French Elf Petroleum Company working less than 100 miles (160 km) to the west and 32 miles (51 km) off the coast of Brunei. It was found by an ROV surveying the seafloor prior to laying pipe connecting an offshore oil platform to shore. For Brunei, a nation totally dependent on its oil revenue, this find gave new national pride, and the Sultan of Brunei himself took great interest in the wreck and provided the funds for its excavation.

The unidentified wreck, which lay in 200 feet (63 m) of water, was excavated over a period of two months under the direction of French archaeologist Michel L'Hour of the underwater branch of the French Ministry of Culture. More than 13,500 late fifteenth- and early seventeenth-century artifacts were brought up; very fine porcelain jars, bowls, plates and cups, most of Chinese manufacture. A dazzling variety of artifacts were found, including gold ingots and jewelry; objects of jade and ivory; brass gongs; bronze rifle bores; grinding stones; beads; glass and iron bracelets. These are now on display in the National Museum of Brunei, and the Sultan has hired a full-time seismic survey firm to find more shipwrecks in the country's waters.

Shipwrecks have a way of causing problems, and this find was no exception. Soon after the discovery was publicized, the Chinese government announced that the shipwreck belonged to them by virtue of it being found in the South China Sea. Four other nations that also claim sovereignty over the South China Sea joined the tussle, but the Sultan of Brunei has no intentions of giving up these priceless treasures of the past.

TRACES OF "ROBINSON CRUSOE"

In a remote part of the western Caribbean, 200 miles (320 km) off the coast of Nicaragua, lies Serrana Bank, a horseshoe-shaped coral reef few people have ever heard of. Yet four centuries ago, this dangerous reef, sprinkled with five desolate cays, was the setting for the remarkable eight-year saga of Pedro Serrano, a shipwreck survivor, on whose experiences Daniel Defoe may have based his famous book *Robinson Crusoe*. One day, while researching in the Spanish archives, I came across a stained and faded manuscript that turned out to be Pedro Serrano's story, written in his own hand. In 1528 he had been the master of a small vessel en route from Havana to the north coast of Venezuela. A hurricane blew it off course, and it was wrecked on an uncharted reef. The vessel quickly broke up, but Serrano and some others managed to reach a nearby cay. The tiny islet was utterly barren, so all but three of the survivors constructed a raft from driftwood and pushed off, never to be heard from again. A seaman who remained behind soon died, leaving Serrano alone with a cabin boy.

They drank the blood of turtles, seals and birds to supplement rare rainwater and brackish water that collected in wells they dug. For two months, they had no fire and ate raw meat and fish. Then, one day, Serrano dove on the wreck site and retrieved a flint from which he was able to strike a spark. During the third month, two survivors from another shipwreck floated onto the shore in a small boat. Eventually, one of them, along with the boy, left in the boat. They too were never heard from again. With his new companion, Serrano erected two stone towers. They kept a signal fire burning atop one of them, fueled by the driftwood that had been accumulating for eons.

After eight years, they were rescued by a passing ship and taken to Havana. The excitement proved too much for Serrano's companion, who died soon afterward. Serrano, however, reached Spain, where he became a celebrity. Wearing the garment he had fashioned out of sealskins, and with his hair and beard almost reaching his knees, he was exhibited at courts all over Europe. He managed to live for many more years, and when he died in 1564 he was a rich man.

In 1963 I organized an expedition to find which of the bank's cays had been Serrano's refuge. From historical documents, I established that he had most likely lived on Southwest Cay, the largest of the five. Within a few hours after setting up camp on this deserted island, we located the bases of the two stone towers he had built for signaling passing ships. Before the day was out, we had also found the site of a hut that Serrano or some other unlucky souls marooned on the cay may have built. Under a layer of sand we discovered thousands of fish, turtle and bird bones, as well as crude tools made from conch shells, fishhooks made from bone and a flint stone that may have been the very one Serrano mentioned finding on the wreck.

Finding his wreck was just as easy. It was less than 1,000 feet (some 300 m) off the island, buried in a very shallow coral reef. Using crowbars, chisels and sledge hammers, we extracted many artifacts: a big bronze bell, dozens of brass door hinges and a large silver crucifix—all of which had been destined for the newly built church on the island of Cubagua off the coast of Venezuela. We also found eleven cannon and hundreds of stone and iron cannonballs that were being transported to a fort on Margarita Island to protect the newly established pearl fisheries. Hundreds of other artifacts proved we had found the right wreck.

THE EMANUEL POINT SHIPWRECK

In 1990 the Florida Bureau of Archaeological Research, led by Dr. Roger Smith, initiated the Pensacola Shipwreck Survey, and they spent two summers locating 40 shipwrecks ranging from small fishing boats to a 450-foot long (160 m) battleship in Pensacola Bay. One of the Bureau's finds is the oldest shipwreck yet encountered in Florida waters.

Spain selected Pensacola as the base from which to launch its conquest and colonization of Florida. Command of the enterprise was given to Don Tristán de Luna y Arellano, who had first come to the New World with Hernán Cortez. Eleven ships sailed from Spain laden with colonists, officials, horses, livestock and everything required to construct a settlement. The small fleet anchored in the sheltered waters of

Pensacola Bay on August 15, 1559. On September 19, while many of the party were ashore searching for a settlement site, a hurricane struck, destroying all but three of the vessels. Many people lost their lives. Although relief vessels were sent from Mexico, the fledging colony was soon abandoned. It wasn't until 1693 that the settlement was established, which is today the city of Pensacola.

Between 1992 and 1995 Smith led a team of archaeologists conducting test excavations on the ballast mound they had encountered during the survey. They determined that the well-preserved lower hull of a large sailing ship lay underneath the ballast. From numerous artifacts they identified the wreck as one of the larger ships of Tristán de Luna's doomed fleet. Eventually they uncovered about 20 percent of the ship's lower hull—a remarkable find in such shallow water. The small amount of ballast on the wreck suggested that it had been heavily laden with cargo. Evidence of the shipboard diet was found in the bilge including cow, pig, goat and sheep bones and hazelnuts, cherry, plum and olive pits. All of the ship's ordnance must have been recovered at the time of the disaster, but the team found cannon and firearm projectiles, providing data on the types and sizes of the guns once on the ship.

In 1996 after the wreck was added to the National Register of Historical Places, Smith began a two-year excavation of the site using university students and other volunteers. Over 5,000 artifacts were brought up; among the most interesting were a cooking cauldron, a copper pitcher, pump wells and a large iron anchor. Lack of further funding has prevented the completion of the excavation.

THE BASQUE WHALERS

Far to the north of these tropical waters, archaeologists have discovered the remains of three Basque whaling ships from the Age of Discovery. Europeans began hunting whales in the Middle Ages, first for their meat and then for their oil, which was a superior source of illumination. Whale oil was also used for centuries in various pharmaceutical preparations, for making soap and as a protective coating for ships. Soon after French explorer Jacques Cartier's voyage to Canada in 1534, Basque whalers from northern Spain began whaling in this region. By 1540 as many as thirty whaling ships were plying the waters of Newfoundland and Labrador and possibly even farther southward.

In 1978 a team of underwater archaeologists from Parks Canada, the Canadian government agency responsible for national parks, discovered one of these Basque whaling ships in the harbor of Red Bay, Labrador. They had been led to the site by sleuthing on the part of historian Selma Huxley Barkham, who came across information in the Spanish archives regarding the loss in 1565 of a whaling vessel called the *San Juan*. The archaeologists found the wreck, which is Canada's oldest, on their first exploratory dive. The whole lower hull was intact. The frigid water had protected it from sea worms, which would have devoured a wooden ship in such shallow and exposed water conditions in warmer climates.

The following summer, the sleepy fishing port of Red Bay was invaded by a team of fifty underwater archaeologists and support staff, as excavation of the wreck began. Directed by Dr. James Tuck and Robert Grenier, the excavation continued for seven more summers. To survive in the icy waters, divers had to have hot water continuously pumped into their rubber suits from the surface. Though cold, the sea water was crystal clear, which greatly facilitated the collection of archaeological data. The Canadian archaeologists removed the mud and marl, which is a crumbly mix of clay and seashells, covering the site and found they had one of the best-preserved lower hulls in the western hemisphere. Instead of bringing material to the surface, they made latex

Conquistador Hernán Cortez presenting himself before the Aztec ruler Montezuma.

molds of all the wooden remains *in situ*. Later these molds were used to reconstruct a model of the ship. When the excavation was completed, the entire site was reburied and left intact for future study.

The *San Juan* furnished modern scholars with tens of thousands of fascinating six-teenth-century maritime artifacts, many of them rare, including half of a brass navigator's astrolabe, the ship's compass, intact wooden barrels for storing whale oil, and even the ship's whaleboat—the only one of its kind in existence. In general, after ballast stones, iron items account for the greatest quantity of artifacts found on old shipwrecks. However, the only iron objects on the *San Juan* site were an anchor and a small swivel gun. No one is sure why this is so, although the extremely low water tem-perature, which preserved the wreck's oak timbers so well that they still shone with a honeyed hue, may be a factor. Recent excavations in the pioneer field of deep-water archaeology, where the water is very cold and deeper than compressed air diving capa-bilities, have also yielded surprisingly little iron, probably because it was stripped from the hulks and used in the construction of other vessels. In 1983 and 1984 two other Basque whaling ships of the same vintage were discovered in Red Bay by Parks Canada divers. Preliminary investigation indicated that they are in an excellent state of preser-vation and they will be excavated when and if funds ever become available.

THE FLOR DE LA MAR

With the Treaty of Tordesillas in 1494, Pope Alexander VI had divided the non-Christian world between the two Iberian kingdoms. During the Age of Discovery, while the Spaniards were exploring and conquering the New World and ranging as far into the Pacific as the Philippines, the Portuguese were extending dominion over the remain-ing far-flung areas of the world. Portuguese ships, called carracks or *naus,* ranged around the globe, to the coast of Brazil, all over the Atlantic, the Indian Ocean, the China Sea and elsewhere in the Pacific. And they had their share of losses. The most renowned of these unfortunate vessels was the *Flor de la Mar,* commanded by Afonso de Albuquerque. This shipwreck, one of the most famous in history, is believed to be the richest ship ever lost anywhere.

In 1503, almost 500 years ago, Albuquerque set sail from Lisbon with a fleet of twenty-two ships on a mission to secure the riches of the East Indies for Portugal. He started his conquests at Mozambique on the southeast coast of Africa and systematically worked his way up the continent, attacking and plundering every place he stopped. The Portuguese preyed on settlements along the Red Sea, striking India and working their way along the coast to Thailand and Burma, which also fell to their swords.

After amassing a colossal amount of treasure, on August 8, 1511, Albuquerque's fleet anchored before the ancient city of Malacca on the Malay peninsula. Malacca was known as the emporium of the East, the richest city in the world. It was the Singapore of the period; the harbor was filled with ships from Japan, China, Arabia, India and Africa. From elephants to Ming Dynasty porcelains, every type of luxury and exotic object was traded at Malacca. Gold was so abundant that traders exchanged gold coins by weight rather than by count.

Albuquerque laid siege to the city. After twelve days of fierce battles, during which thousands of residents were slaughtered, the Malays surrendered. Because of Malacca's strategic position, Albuquerque established it as a Portuguese possession. It remained under Portuguese control until captured by the Dutch in 1641. The spoils the Portuguese took from Malacca staggered the imagination. More than sixty tons of gold booty in the form of animals, birds, gilded furniture ingots and coinage came from the sultan's palace alone. Albuquerque placed most of the sultan's gold on his flagship, the *Flor de la Mar*. It took up so much space that the crew had trouble stowing an additional 200 gem-filled chests. The diamonds, rubies, emeralds and sapphires in them, valued at more than thirty million crowns, would be worth billions of dollars today.

Interestingly, Albuquerque's greed led to the first minting of tin coins. He was adamant that all the gold and silver booty be returned to Lisbon, leaving no currency with which the Portuguese colonists who remained in Malacca could carry on commerce. The tin coins were minted to replace the plundered gold and silver.

By late December, Albuquerque was satisfied that the colony was flourishing. He set sail for Portugal with four ships crammed with eight years' worth of booty. The rest of the ships stayed behind to protect the city of Malacca and explore the surrounding region. Albuquerque promised to send supplies and reinforcements.

He never fulfilled his promise. Two days after he left Malacca a fierce storm overtook his little fleet. Two of the treasure-laden ships went to the bottom without any trace or survivors. Several hours later, the *Flor de la Mar*, with 400 souls on board, struck a reef off the northeastern tip of the island of Sumatra, near the entrance to the Strait of Malacca. Albuquerque jumped into the ship's longboat with five officers, promising to seek the remaining ship and return with assistance. Eventually, he and his officers were rescued by the fleet's other ship, but instead of returning to the stricken *Flor de la Mar*, Albuquerque sailed on to Portugal.

This gold and emerald-studded bracelet was one of the best objects recovered from the *Flor de la Mar*, believed to be the richest ship ever lost at sea.

Within a few hours, the *Flor de la Mar*, pounded by immense waves, broke into pieces. Only three of those on board reached shore alive. As soon as the storm abated, local divers and fishermen were on the site, salvaging what they could. Most of the precious cargo, however, sank in 120 feet (37 m) of water, where the main section of the hull settled after slipping off the reef. The pilot of the *Flor de la Mar* had gone with Albuquerque when he abandoned the sinking ship. Although he had made a chart indicating where the ship was lost, the shipwreck, lying in a remote spot on the globe, was soon forgotten.

In 1961 I located the chart as well as several accounts of the disaster in the Portuguese archives in Lisbon. I became obsessed with finding the wreck, which lies in Indonesian waters. I applied repeatedly and in vain to the Indonesian government for a search permit. Then in January 1989 I read that Indonesia had granted a permit to South East Asia Salvage, a Singapore firm. They spent a year and $8 million searching for the *Flor de la Mar* with three vessels and the latest in search equipment but didn't find it.

They then hired me as a consultant. They greeted my offer to show them the exact reef where the disaster had happened with some skepticism, but accepted. They had been searching in the wrong area, more than 100 miles (160 km) from where the chart showed she had been lost. In February 1990, on the second day of our expedition, we found the *Flor de la Mar*, or at least the reef where she had struck. Scattered ballast rock and a variety of artifacts proved this was the correct area. It appeared, however, that both sixteenth-century salvors and modern divers had plundered the site. The reef was pocked with hundreds of holes made by explosives. Later I learned that two American divers working for an oil-exploration firm had taken four bronze cannon from the reef, as well as an undisclosed number of gold artifacts. Fortunately, they left a little for us. We recovered several gold figurines, hundreds of the tin coins minted in Malacca, numerous intact pieces of Ming Dynasty porcelain and other interesting artifacts. A thorough sonar and magnetometer survey revealed that the main section of the wreck lies in an area the size of five football fields at a depth of 120 feet (37 m) under 50 feet (15 m) of concrete-like mud. Test holes were dug and more objects were recovered.

Politics thwarted excavation of the site. In the summer of 1990, just as a major project was to begin, the Malaysian and Portuguese governments contested Indonesia's claim to the *Flor de la Mar.* The question of ownership is currently before the International Court in The Hague. Once it is resolved, excavation of this richest of all shipwrecks will proceed, and the world will see an unparalleled hoard of the fabulous treasures of the Age of Discovery.

LA BELLE

One of the most important marine archaeological discoveries is the *La Belle,* which was serendipitously found by a fisherman in 1995, who brought up one of the ship's cannon in his net. The *La Belle* was the flagship of René-Robert Cavalier, Sieur de La Salle, one of the boldest explorers of the seventeenth century, who had earlier explored and charted the Great Lakes. Backed by King Louis XIV, he set off in 1686 with three ships to sail to the mouth of the Mississippi, which he had discovered some years before. The French king wanted him to sail up the river and establish a colony. La Salle overshot the mouth of the Mississippi by 400 miles and entered Matagorda Bay, Texas, with about 300 soldiers, explorers and colonists aboard. During the winter a storm struck, sinking the ship. Only a handful of people survived, among them La Salle, who was murdered by the survivors after the water supply ran out. They had been quenching their thirst with brandy and wine and were probably drunk when they killed their leader.

In 1996 soon after the discovery of the cannon, the Texas Historical Commission, led by Dr. Barto Arnold, joined forces with the Institute of Nautical Archaeology to survey the site. They established that a major portion of the hull was preserved under tons of harbor mud in the 20-foot (6 m) depth of the site's brackish water. Despite the great cost involved, a cofferdam was constructed around the entire site and dry land excavation techniques used because of the water's poor visibility. Once the water was pumped out from the cofferdam, the archaeologists recovered over one million artifacts, which are currently being studied.

In addition to the ship's wooden remains, the largest objects found were three bronze cannon, which had been cast in 1681 with the crest of Louis XIV on them, and a wooden gun carriage. Many of the artifacts consisted of trade goods for the Indians such as hawk's bells, glass beads and brass Jesuit rings. The most unexpected find was the well-preserved complete skeleton of a man lying in a fetal position next to a coil of rope and wooden cask. The bones will be shipped to France for a proper burial. Many large concretions were turned over to Dr. Donny Hamilton, President of INA, who runs the institute's conservation laboratory. Some of the concretions' contents were identified through X-rays, but it will take years before they are all taken apart and their secrets revealed. To date, excavation of this wreck, including constructing the cofferdam, has cost almost $6 million.

Thirty years before the *La Belle* was discovered, a shrimper had pulled up a cannon in his nets. He kept his find a secret until he read about the *La Belle.* He revealed the general location of his find to the National Underwater and Marine Agency (NUMA), founded by the famous writer Clive Cussler. Shortly after the *La Belle* excavation was completed, Cussler's group announced they had found a shipwreck. It was identified as the *Amiable,* one of La Salle's two other ships. The other, the *Joly,* had returned to France, but the *Amiable* remained in Matagorda Bay until it sank the following year. Cussler's team conducted a magnetometer survey pinpointing twenty-six sites where iron was detected on the bottom. On the sixth day of diving to identify these targets, the wreck was found. They brought up an encrusted pistol and musket that proved the identity of the wreck. Funding for this shipwreck is expected to cost twice as much as the *La Belle,* and the Texas Legislature has put the project on hold for the time being.

During a fierce storm in 1511, the *Flor de la Mar* struck a reef off the northeastern tip of the Indonesian Island of Sumatra and sank.

One of the first artifacts recovered from the *Flor de la Mar* was this ornately carved ivory Buddha.

4 THE SPANISH GALLEONS

THE EXPLORERS OF THE AGE OF DISCOVERY found the riches they had been seeking not in Zipango (Japan) but in the Spanish colonial mines of Mexico and South America. The treasure returning from the New World was important to all the European nations because it provided nearly 95 percent of the precious metals upon which their monetary systems were based.

Throughout the sixteenth, seventeenth and eighteenth centuries, galleon after galleon, some nearly keeling over from the precious loads, bore immense amounts of treasure home. But Spain had no industry and was dependent on other European nations for manufactured goods, so nearly all the gold and silver brought to Spain flowed out of the country and into the coffers of foreign nations. Between 1492 and 1803, more than four billion pesos in gold and silver reached Spain from the New World (a peso was not a coin but a monetary unit equal in value to 1 1/8 ounces of pure silver). An additional 10 to 15 percent of the gold and silver shipped never reached Spain. Pirates and privateers accounted for some losses, but hundreds of galleons were shipwrecked.

A diver's dream of shipwrecks laden with sunken treasure conjures up images of bulky galleons, their holds crammed with gleaming riches. Not without reason, since over the centuries more than 2,000 galleons were lost in the western hemisphere, and only a small number have ever been found. Many thousands of people perished in these shipwrecks or died from exposure or starvation after being cast ashore. Along the

Three gold bars recovered from the *Maravilla* lost in the Bahamas in 1656. Markings on the bars prove taxes were paid to the Spanish Monarchy and the Church.

east coast of Florida and down through the treacherous reefs of the Florida Keys, as well as in parts of the Bahamas and Bermuda, there is hardly a mile where some rich ship did not meet its doom.

As early as 1503, commerce with the Spanish American colonies was put on an organized basis. A virtual monopoly was granted to the merchants of Seville. A royal order created the House of Trade to control all aspects of commerce and colonization in the Americas, and hundreds of ships began sailing between the Old and New World on a scheduled basis.

The vessels leaving Seville carried a vast array of items for the Spanish colonies because colonists were forbidden to manufacture anything. For centuries a powerful coalition of Seville merchants had a monopoly on everything from pots and pans to musical instruments. Colonists were even forbidden to produce wine and olive oil, staples of the Spanish diet. Spain itself manufactured very little, so the ships were laden with goods from almost every nation in Europe: tools and weapons, cooking utensils, glassware and ceramics, cutlery, cloth and trimmings, hats, shoes, religious objects, furniture, window glass and even dressed stone and bricks for buildings.

On the return voyage, in addition to gold and silver specie and bullion—the main cargo in terms of value—the galleons carried chests of pearls, emeralds and other gemstones and agricultural products such as sugar, tobacco and dyestuffs. After 1565, when the Manila

Replica Spanish Galleon built by Bob Marx, for display in The Museum of Sunken Treasure in Cocoa Beach, Florida.

Galleons (see Chapter 6) began making the perilous voyage between the Philippines and Acapulco, on the west coast of Mexico, the exotic products from the Far East were added to the shipments destined for Seville. The oriental goods were unloaded at Acapulco and carried by pack animals across the mountains to the port of Veracruz on the Gulf of Mexico, where they were put aboard the transatlantic galleons.

A letter of September 1567 from the Venetian ambassador in Spain to the ruler in Venice, the Doge, illustrates the importance to Spain of the treasure from the New World:

At the time of writing my last dispatch to you, I informed you that there was great anxiety all over Spain over the delay of the arrival of the treasure fleets from the Indies and, when the Genoese bankers informed the King that unless the fleet reached port shortly, they would be unable to negotiate any further loans for him, Philip II fell into such a state of shock that he had to be confined to bed by his physicians. The King then ordered about ten thousand ducats, which was about all the treasure left in his royal coffers, to be sent all over his realm and distributed to various churches and monasteries for the saying of masses for the safe arrival of the treasure fleet. I am happy to inform you that news has just arrived from Seville that the fleet made port safely and there is now great rejoicing not only here in the Royal Court, but all over the land as well.

During the first half of the sixteenth century, Spanish ships made transatlantic voyages alone or in small convoys. A dramatic increase in attacks by pirates and privateers of the nations excluded from the 1494 Treaty of Tordesillas led to the establishment of a new convoy system. Starting in 1552, three separate fleets sailed each year. The New Spain or Mexican Fleet called first at Veracruz to load treasure and then made for Havana. The Tierra Firme Fleet picked up gold and emeralds from the Colombian mines at Cartagena and then went on to Panama. A great mercantile fair was held in Panama, in Nombre de Dios until 1596, the year it was attacked and leveled to the ground by Sir Francis Drake, and then Porto Bello was used. The treasures from Peru and Chile, consisting chiefly of gold and silver specie and bullion, were brought to Panama City on the Gulf of Panama and then transported across the isthmus by mule to the fair to await the arrival of the third fleet, which was called the Armada or the Galleons. After all the treasure was loaded on the Galleons, the Tierra Firme Fleet and the Galleons sailed together to Havana to join the New Spain Fleet and set forth for Spain. The combined homeward-bound fleet, which at times numbered more than 150 ships, must have been a stirring sight as it headed up the Straits of Florida.

The long ocean voyages were never easy. There was some safety in numbers from predatory attacks, but storms and navigational hazards were also to be reckoned with. Of the thirty-six ships of the New Spain Fleet that sailed for Veracruz in 1552 on the inaugural voyage of the organized convoy fleets, only two returned to Spain. Just as the fleet, loaded with three years' worth of accumulated treasure, was to leave Veracruz, a fierce "norther" struck, sending twelve of the galleons to the bottom. Departure was delayed until the following year, when the remaining twenty-four ships sailed for Havana. The fleet was buffeted by a vicious storm within six hours of leaving port, and ten more galleons sank in the Gulf of Mexico. The others limped back to Veracruz for repairs. In February 1554, four of the ships set sail for Havana. Somewhere in the Gulf of Mexico they all disappeared without a trace. Two months later, the remaining eight ships left Veracruz. When the galleons were halfway to Havana a hurricane struck, causing two to sink on the high seas and three, the *Espíritu Santo,* the *Santa María de Yciar* and the *San Esteban,* to be wrecked off the coast of Padre Island, Texas. One galleon limped into Havana, badly damaged, and the two survivors continued on to Spain without stopping in Havana. Most of the 300 souls who had been aboard the ships lost at Padre Island succumbed to Indian attacks, thirst and starvation. About twenty men managed to reach Veracruz after a month's trek along the desolate coast. Salvors sent from Veracruz worked on the site of the three shipwrecks and recovered a large part of the treasure.

Over the years beachcombers along the shore of Padre Island have found Spanish coins and artifacts after strong storms. In 1967 a treasure-hunting firm called Platoro pinpointed one of the wrecks in relatively shallow water. Archival research matched with evidence from the site proved that the ship was the *Santa María de Yciar.* Over a period of six months, divers from the Gary, Indiana, firm salvaged more than $1 million worth of treasure and artifacts. Then the State of Texas stepped in, with a claim that the shipwreck belonged to the state. The treasure hunters were accused of looting the heritage of Texas and prevented by injunction from further work on the site. The Texas legislature promptly passed the *State Antiquities Code,* providing for the creation of an antiquities committee to control and supervise all further work on shipwrecks in state waters.

Texas organized its own underwater archaeological team, led by Dr. Barto Arnold and Carl J. Clausen, to work on the shipwreck. Their project, which lasted from 1972 to 1975, was at the time the most comprehensive archaeological shipwreck excavation ever conducted in the western hemisphere. They recovered more than $10 million worth of treasure and artifacts, including gold bars, thousands of silver coins, dozens of silver and copper bars, a brass navigator's astrolabe and jewelry. They also excavated thousands of artifacts that enabled scientists to understand how the *Santa María de Yciar* had been constructed and what it carried, and revealed plenty about life aboard ship. The preserved artifacts toured Texas in a traveling display for five years and are now on display in the Texas State Museum.

THE ATOCHA AND THE MARGARITA

The name of Florida treasure salvor Mel Fisher is familiar to anyone who is fascinated by shipwrecked Spanish galleons. His discovery of two treasure galleons, the *Atocha* and the *Margarita*, in the Florida Keys generated immense international media coverage.

Mel Fisher holding a gold chain, gold bowl and silver candlestick from the *Atocha*.

Fisher, born in Hobart, Indiana, in 1922, was a pioneer scuba diver. He began his career at the age of ten when he fashioned a diving helmet out of a paint can. With time out for a decade of chicken farming, he prowled the seas in quest of sunken treasures, hitting the jackpot with the discoveries of the *Atocha* and the *Margarita*.

The story of these ill-fated ships began in September 1622 when a treasure fleet of twenty-eight galleons set sail from Havana for Spain. A few days out of port, a hurricane struck and eight of the ships were lost. Several sank on the high seas, and the others were dashed to pieces on the reefs of the Florida Keys. The *Atocha*, one of the richest galleons of the fleet, was carrying 550 people; only five survived. The souls on the *Margarita* fared a little better. Sixty-eight of the 330 people were rescued by other ships of the fleet. The loss of the ships was a heavy blow to Spain. Contemporary salvors spent four years searching for them before locating the *Margarita*, and another four years salvaging most of her cargo. But no trace of the *Atocha* was found, and she was forgotten for almost 350 years.

In the early 1960s Mel Fisher successfully salvaged a couple of galleons from the 1715 treasure fleet that had been wrecked in a hurricane off the east coast of Florida, south of Cape Canaveral. In 1966 armed with somewhat hazy data on their locations, he headed for the Keys in quest of the *Atocha* and the *Margarita*. He searched along the Upper and Middle Keys for four years, finding many other shipwrecks but not the 1622 galleons.

In 1970 Eugene Lyons, a noted maritime historian, went to work in the Spanish archives for Fisher, coming up with the news that Fisher had been looking for the two treasure ships more than 100 miles (160 km) north of where they sank. Lyons found a report by Captain Francisco Nuñez Melian, who had been in charge of salvaging the *Margarita* soon after it wrecked. Documents stated that both ships were lost within 4 miles (6.5 km) of each other off the Marquesa Islands to the west of Key West. Fisher believed that it wouldn't be too hard to find one of the galleons; it would then be easier to locate the other. His optimism was to be sorely tried as he launched what was to become one of the most frustrating, costly, yet ultimately rewarding search efforts ever undertaken at sea.

Whenever the weather permitted, Fisher kept two to four survey boats crisscrossing the search zone. They worked at a feverish pace from sunrise to sundown, dragging magnetometer sensor heads in the water to detect any concentrations of iron on the seafloor. By June 1971 they had logged more than 120,000 linear miles (192,000 km) and covered an area the size of the state of Rhode Island. It was Fisher's eldest son, Dirk, captain of one of the survey boats, who at last located one of the *Atocha*'s anchors. The magnetometer gave a strong reading, but divers could see nothing on the bottom, so they used a prop-wash to uncover the buried object. A prop-wash, a device first fashioned by Mel Fisher, deflects the wash of the propeller and blows away bottom sediment—in this case deep sand.

Don Kinkaid, the first diver to examine the hole, saw a large iron anchor. As he fanned sand from around it, he spotted something shiny. Kinkaid remembers:

> *There were a couple of links of some kind of chain sticking out of the sand and the sand around the hole kept falling back down trying to cover it over. In the green light it looked like brass at first, then suddenly I knew it was gold and I fought against the falling sand and dug frantically with my hands and ended up with an eight-foot gold chain, the first of tons of treasure to be eventually discovered on the fabled* Atocha.

The following euphoric day, Fisher's divers dug more holes around the anchor, bringing to light several heavy gold chains, hundreds of silver and gold coins, two small gold bars and two matchlock muskets. The coins were the most significant find: every one bore a date prior to 1622—a sure sign that the wreck was one of the 1622 galleons. A long dry period followed, during which the divers dug hundreds of holes in a mile radius around the anchor without finding a single trace of any other part of a wreck. Almost a year passed before they found treasure again. When they did, the spot yielded such phenomenal amounts that they dubbed it "the Bank of Spain." From the "bank" they withdrew 4,000 Spanish silver coins and one of three rare bronze astrolabes eventually recovered from the wreck, as well as several dozen other artifacts.

The treasure and artifacts they had found had spilled out of the ship as she broke up, but the main part of the wreck still eluded them. Famine followed feast as Fisher's team spent the next twelve months trying to pick up the trail of the galleon and pinpoint the mother lode. As many as six salvage vessels worked at a time, digging hundreds and hundreds of holes. The turning point in the frustrating search for the *Atocha* came almost a year to the day after discovery of the Bank of Spain, when Fisher's youngest son found three 80-pound (36 kg) silver bars.

When Eugene Lyons and underwater archaeologist Duncan Mathewson cleaned the bars, they found weigh and tally numbers on them that matched some found on the *Atocha*'s manifest. There was little doubt that they were on the trail of the *Atocha*. The search continued. Sometimes months passed with no trace of the wreck. Then an artifact would be found, and dejection would turn to elation. Dirk Fisher was thrilled when he located five of the *Atocha*'s massive bronze cannon in the summer of 1975. Tragically, a few nights later, he and two other members of Fisher's team died when his salvage vessel, *North Wind,* took on water through a faulty hull fitting and capsized while at anchor. Dirk, his wife, Angel, and diver Rick Gage were unable to get out of their cabins and drowned.

A grieving Fisher continued work after the tragedy, believing his son would have wanted him to. It wasn't easy. Bureaucratic interference was added to the normal challenges of shipwreck excavation. The wreck area was outside Florida's jurisdiction, but a number of state officials wanted a piece of the action. Fisher became embroiled in complex litigation with the state, spending more than $1 million before emerging victorious.

The search for the main part of the *Atocha* continued year after year. Fisher realized that the shipwreck was scattered over many miles of the ocean floor. During the search season in 1980, they found the *Margarita*. Although it had been salvaged by seventeenth-century Spanish salvors, Fisher felt there might still be some treasure on the wreck. He had hired Robert Jordan to do a magnetometer survey, and in a matter of days Jordan located the site.

Most of the treasures of the *Atocha* were buried under as much as 26 feet (8 m) of sand, but the *Margarita*'s were almost completely exposed. The diver Jordan sent down to see what had caused the anomaly on the magnetometer found a clump of four silver coins lying on top of scattered ballast. When the crew of ten saw that they had been minted prior to 1622, they raced one another to the bottom. Almost immediately, the men scooped up five large gold bars. At first they overlooked several silver ingots, as they dug by hand into the ballast, pulling out gold chains, coins, jewelry and other more interesting treasures. For the next few days they worked at a frantic pace, using metal detectors to find concealed treasure. The finds they brought up exceeded their wildest dreams. Staggering in amount, variety and beauty, they included forty-three elaborate gold-link chains measuring a total of 180 feet (55 m), fifty-six gold bars weighing a total of 118 pounds (54 kg), fifty-six gold coins, dozens of beautiful pieces of jewelry, 15,000 silver coins and eighteen large silver ingots. The most valuable item was a gold plate about 8 inches (20 cm) in diameter embossed with a neo-Moorish design and valued at $100,000. The overall find was valued at $5 million. This news gave Fisher a much-needed financial boost in his costly search for the *Atocha*.

After the *Margarita* had given up its treasure and artifacts, there was still a lot of archaeological work to do. The team located a large section of the ship's hull under the ballast. It took months to remove the ballast stones and to measure, map and photograph the timbers *in situ* before bringing them to the surface for preservation.

By 1985 Fisher had been after the *Atocha* for fifteen years, following a trail of *Atocha* materials and digging thousands of holes in the seafloor. That summer the team was working more than 12 miles (19 km) from the anchor area, but Fisher's faith never wavered. At the start of each day's search, he spurred his divers on with shouts of "Today's the day!" They thought May 25, 1985, would be "the day" when Susan Nelson, a twenty-six-year-old diver sent down to examine a new prop-wash hole, found the bottom covered with ballast rock, a sign that the hull of the *Atocha* was nearby.

Before then, they had found no more than the occasional ballast rock that had dropped out of the bottom of the broken ship as it staggered to its final resting place. When Nelson surfaced with four large gold bars she had found lying among the ballast there was a stampede into the water. By the day's end the divers had recovered thirteen gold bars, more than 6 1/2 feet (2 m) of a gold chain, sixteen emeralds, more than 400 silver coins and five intact silver plates. Surely, they had found the *Atocha*'s long-sought main hull.

Much to everyone's consternation, however, the next day they found nothing. Nor were the days and weeks that followed any more productive. It seemed that May's trove had been a fluke. Then on July 20, 1985, Kane Fisher's crew found the indisputable mother lode. They were digging holes about 1/2 mile (just under 1 km) from the May find. A diver exploring a hole found several silver coins and pottery shards. On his way to the surface, he noticed a gray linear mound not far from the edge of the hole. It was about 10 feet long and 3 feet high (3 m by 1 m), with the outlines of shapes resembling stacked bread loaves. They were silver bars, hundreds of them. Kane Fisher radioed his father at the company's headquarters in Key West. "Dad," he said with remarkable composure, "you can put away the charts. We found the pile!" By October

1986, most of the "pile" had been salvaged, and Fisher's divers had recovered 130,000 silver coins, 956 large silver ingots, fifteen gold chains, 115 gold bars, 315 emeralds, sixty-seven gold chains and twenty-two other gold objects, plus thousands of other priceless artifacts. The treasure's value was estimated at US $20 to $25 million. Fisher's perseverance had paid off handsomely.

Each summer since the wreck's discovery in 1985 salvage work continues on both the *Atocha* and *Margarita* sites, led by Kim Fisher, Mel Fisher's son. During this period, an additional $8 to $10 million in treasure and artifacts has been recovered. In July 2000, the team reported finding the galleon's stern castle—the part of the galleon where the aristocracy and clergy were quartered and stored their personal possessions and treasure. This new site was 12 miles (19 km) northwest of the main section of the wreck. On the first day of digging they found three gold bars; dozens of pieces of gold jewelry, including two large gold chains; as well as a large number of silver coins—total value over $500,000. As so often happens on shipwrecks the treasure then dried up and all they found was some hull wood and ballast stones. They are still searching for the rest of the stern castle, and there is little doubt they will eventually find it. Last summer (2002) one of the divers found a 40-carat emerald embedded in a conch shell.

In December 2002 Mel Fisher, the colorful character whose rallying cry "Today's the Day!" spurred his team on during the long *Atocha* search, succumbed to cancer at the age of 76. In a moving ceremony, his family and friends spread his ashes where he found the first silver coins on the wreck back in 1971. Fisher was not only the most famous but also the most controversial person in the shipwreck business. Known for writing agreements on barroom napkins, he spent a great deal of his life running afoul of the law. During his last year, he faced two serious problems that cast a cloud over his life's considerable accomplishments. He was fined $589,331 for destroying over an acre of protected sea grass during excavation and ordered to surrender artifacts his son had illegally brought up from an unidentified shipwreck in the Florida Keys National Marine Sanctuary. Then State of Florida officials seized 25 counterfeit gold coins from his museum's gift shop and fined him $67,000.

Everyone in the shipwreck exploration business misses Mel Fisher. He did more than anyone to generate excitement in the general public about Spanish galleons and their fabulous history.

THE SECRET OF SILVER SHOALS

One treasure-laden galleon that Fisher sought but never found was the *Nuestra Señora de la Concepción,* lost in 1641 on Silver Shoals, about 90 miles (150 km) north of Santo Domingo. Also known as the *Almiranta,* the ship was the one that William Phips of Boston salvaged in 1686 (see Introduction). Although Phips netted $50 million in treasure, the largest sum recovered from a single wreck until the present century, he didn't get it all. Some of the salvors who visited the site within a few decades of Phips were successful in varying degrees. But the exact location of the wreck was eventually lost and the galleon forgotten until

When the *Concepción* was first discovered, it was completely camouflaged by a coral reef.

the advent of scuba diving. Then, beginning in the 1950s, many millions of dollars were spent looking for the *Concepción.* Twenty major expeditions, including Fisher's and one led by Jacques Cousteau, hunted in vain for the wreck.

In 1978 Burt Webber, a part-time bookseller, mason and welder, succeeded where so many had failed. Webber was passionate about shipwrecks. As a boy, he had read about Phips and the *Concepción,* and he dreamed of some day having the resources to go after it. For years, he would work for six months of the year in Pennsylvania and then wreck hunt in the Florida Keys for the remaining six, leaving his family in Anneville. He located quite a few shipwrecks, but they had all been picked over by earlier salvors and he rarely realized enough to cover expenses.

The *Concepción* was never far from Webber's thoughts. His conviction that he could find it was contagious, and by late 1976 he had attracted investors who put up half a million dollars for an expedition. He organized a team, and in January 1977 they sailed for the Caribbean and the bank of Silver Shoals. He had no idea how difficult the wreck would be to find. The target lay somewhere in the 1,000 square miles (250,000 ha) of the bank, but Silver Shoals is one of the wildest, most remote expanses of ocean on earth. Thousands of coral heads rise from the seafloor almost to the surface, and the waters swarm with sharks. The expedition began with a magnetometer survey of the area. Six months later, when the money ran out, they had searched the entire area and found thirteen shipwrecks, but not the elusive *Concepción.*

Webber retreated, but didn't give up. His big break came when he read a recently published book about the Phips expedition. English author Peter Earle had located the logbook of Phips's salvage vessel, the *Henry,* in a private English archive. Webber went to London accompanied by treasure hunter Jack Haskins, who had experience in archival research. Reading the logbook of the *Henry,* they found the missing pieces of the puzzle, allowing Webber to pinpoint the wreck within a mile or two.

A year later Webber had $2.5 million in funding, a larger vessel, better detection equipment, and a team of thirty men. They sailed for Silver Shoals in November 1978, vowing not to return until they found the *Concepción.* On the second day of the expedition, divers spotted a trail of ballast rock, which later proved to be where the galleon had struck before being carried by large seas farther into the reef maze. For three more days they pursued this trail of ballast rock, iron fittings and pottery shards until, on the last day of the month, a diver found the first silver coin, which set them all shouting with joy.

What started with a single coin quickly became a steady flow. They found coins by the bucketful in a depression in the sand that they dubbed the "money hole." Haskins noticed that the surrounding high coral heads were discolored and discovered that thousands of coins were embedded in them. Using hammers and chisels the divers began tearing the reef apart, sometimes bringing up conglomerates weighing more than 200 pounds (90 kg) that contained as many as 3,000 coins.

They removed over 45 tons of coral to clean out the area of the "money hole," finding more than 60,000 silver coins, numerous gold chains, several gold coins and thousands of other priceless artifacts, including three astrolabes and a collection of fragile Ming Dynasty porcelain. They worked seven days a week for eleven months before the wreck was completely salvaged. The entire find from the *Concepción* was valued at $10 million, proving that Phips had indeed left plenty of treasure behind. Webber returned to the wreck again in 1995 and recovered another $1 million in treasure—mainly silver coins. All of the artifacts and a substantial portion of the treasure is on permanent display in the National Museum of Santo Domingo.

"MARX'S PHANTOM WRECK"

Nuestra Señora de las Maravillas was another seventeenth-century treasure wreck that long eluded modern-day salvors. The *Maravilla,* as she is called, was the lead galleon of a large convoy sailing up the Straits of Florida, also known as the Bahama Channel. She was laden with an immense amount of treasure from Mexico and South America—five times what the *Atocha* went down with, in fact—and included cargo that had been recovered from the *Jesus María de la Limpia Concepción,* a galleon lost in 1654 off Chanduy, Ecuador. In addition to more than five million pesos in treasure, the ship also carried a life-size, solid-gold statue of the Madonna and Christ Child.

Shortly after midnight on New Year's Day of 1656, most of the ship's 700 passengers and crew were sleeping off a night of carousing, when the lookout realized that the ship was in perilously shallow water. A cannon was fired to warn the other ships of the danger. Confusion reigned as drink-addled crews tried to maneuver their vessels. Another galleon collided with the *Maravilla,* tearing a gaping hole in her bow below the waterline. Her commander, Admiral Mathias de Orellanas, headed for even shallower water, and the ship struck a reef. She broke into two sections, the bow settling near the reef and the main part of the hull drifting southward. At daybreak the other ships found only fifty-six survivors clinging to debris.

When Spanish salvors arrived several months later, they found that winter storms had scattered the *Maravilla's* remains over a wide area, and shifting sands had covered most of her treasures. Over a period of three summers, when seas are calmest, government divers managed to recover about one-quarter of her riches. They returned for a fourth summer, but could find no further traces of her. Nevertheless, her cargo was so valuable that the search continued for another twenty years before it was abandoned.

In 1960 I was living in Seville, researching shipwrecks in the General Archives of the Indies. Delving into primary documents, I found more than 15,000 pages dealing with the *Maravilla*. There was a copy of her original cargo manifest, which listed and described every item aboard (save contraband) when she went down. Most remarkable of all, I came across a 144-page book published in Madrid in 1657 by one of the survivors, Doctor Don Diego Portichuelo de Ribadeneyra, who had been the director of the Spanish Inquisition in South America. He had written a detailed account of everything he observed from the time he left Lima until he was shipwrecked. His memoir was so vivid that I felt as if I had been on board with him.

I was determined to find the *Maravilla*. It wasn't treasure alone I sought, but proof that the galleon existed and the satisfaction of finding her. Since the introduction of scuba diving in the early 1950s, almost everyone of note in the treasure-hunting business had made a stab at locating the wreck, mistakenly searching in the Florida Keys. I had searched for several summers with no better luck, although I knew the general area in the Bahamas where she had gone down. Many treasure hunters began to doubt that the *Maravilla* existed. Because of my unflagging fascination with her, they referred to her as "Marx's Phantom Wreck."

In 1972 I teamed up with well-known oceanographer Willard Bascom to find the *Maravilla*. Our company, Seafinders, Inc., was financed by eleven Wall Street tycoons. We made an agreement with the Bahamian government that it would receive 25 percent of anything we recovered from the wreck; the remainder would be ours. For four grueling months, working from dawn to dusk, we scoured the Little Bahama Bank, towing a magnetometer sensor head from a small boat and living aboard the *Grifon*. Persevering through almost daily summer lightning storms and early autumn storms, we located seventy shipwrecks ranging from a late-sixteenth-century British merchantman to modern yachts.

This piece of eight was recovered off the *San Miguel Arcangel* lost in 1659 off Jupiter Inlet, Florida. It was recovered from the *Maravilla* by contemporary divers and lost again.

Ironically, although we were using the latest in technology, we discovered the bow section of the *Maravilla* by a totally unscientific fluke. Late one afternoon when the *Grifon*'s anchor was pulled up, we found two Spanish-type ballast stones stuck in it. I quickly threw a marker buoy overboard and descended, to find the reef below us teeming with fish. Even before I reached the bottom I saw the glint of a gold coin. After twelve years of frustration, I had found the *Maravilla*. Grabbing the shimmering coin, I made out the date—1655—and knew, beyond the shadow of a doubt, that this was my golden galleon! I had found treasure almost every year during the previous twenty-five years, but this was the most thrilling moment of my life.

Pandemonium broke loose aboard the *Grifon* as the crew celebrated with me. During the long, tedious search phase of our operation we had been beleaguered by myriad problems and frustrations: equipment breakdowns, waterspouts, hurricanes, poor visibility, encircling sharks and barracudas, and physical discomforts from strained muscles to painful jellyfish stings. But all that was instantly forgotten the moment we began bringing up armloads of a treasure that had last seen the light of day more than three centuries before.

The following day we located four of the ship's huge iron anchors and two very ornately decorated bronze cannon bearing the coat of arms of Spain's King Philip IV. As we moved farther away from the reef, the sand, white and very fine, got deeper and deeper, and we soon had to remove as much as 33 feet (10 m) of it with the prop-wash. This was difficult and time-consuming, but well worth the effort. The second day's work produced more than 600 silver coins, three large silver bars, many silver plates, cups and pitchers, and numerous other artifacts. We found a clay smoking pipe, dating from the middle of the eighteenth century, which most likely had been lost overboard from an early salvor's boat.

Our fifth day was the most memorable. We brought up an incredible amount and variety of treasure: more than five tons of silver bars, around 50,000 silver coins, twelve gold discs weighing 11 pounds (5 kg) each, more than one hundred gold coins, many exquisite pieces of gold jewelry, hundreds of uncut emeralds, a large ivory tusk and about half a ton of other artifacts were found. At least six divers worked at a time, sending up treasure as fast as those on the surface could haul it aboard the *Grifon*. To me, the most stirring find was a silver plate bearing the coat of arms of Dr. Ribadeneyra, author of the book that had led to my discovery of the *Maravilla*.

With the exception of a few days lost to bad weather, we continued bringing up treasure at a frantic pace. We didn't consider it a good day unless we had found at least $250,000 worth. By October 6 the decks and the rest of the boat were crammed with treasure and artifacts. Many artifacts we stored in containers filled with fresh water that leaches out the chlorides in the objects prior to preservation. Our food and water were exhausted; and so were we, after working nonstop for six electrifying weeks. It was time to head for Fort Pierce, Florida, our home port.

On this last day I wanted to look for the main section of the wreck, where the gold Madonna most likely was. I calculated the trail the main section had probably taken after the great galleon broke apart and set off alone in a skiff, towing the magnetometer head. After three barren hours, the magnetometer indicated an anomaly on the bottom. I dived to investigate and saw the fluke of an anchor barely protruding through the sandy bottom. Digging around it with my bare hands, I found dozens of silver coins and several large silver bars. I was ecstatic, because I was convinced that this was the main section and that it would be only a matter of time before we found the bulk of the treasure and the golden statue. I was also cautious. A premonition led me to remove the anchor that marked the area, and when I returned to the *Grifon* I didn't mention my find to anyone, because it was the end of the season and I wanted to protect it from poachers.

There is a time-worn saying that "treasure is trouble," and the *Maravilla's* treasure proved no exception. Soon after reaching port I was notified that the Bahamian government had rescinded our salvage permit. I rushed to Nassau and learned that news of our find had leaked out, and other treasure hunters wanted to cash in. Rumors, which inevitably plague any treasure operation, were circulating that we had found more than five tons of gold, as well as the Golden Madonna, and had spirited it all away so as to cheat the Bahamians. No amount of reasoning persuaded the Bahamian officials otherwise. Unable to produce what we had not found, we were forbidden to continue work. We not only lost our rights to the rest of the wreck but also had to wait more than four years to get our share of what we had already found.

Every year thereafter, one treasure-hunting firm or another received a permit for the *Maravilla* and set out to find the main section. Inevitably, after weeks and months of futile search, each group resorted to reworking the area of the bow section where we had recovered treasure. Some were more successful than others. Maritime Archaeological Research, Ltd., a firm headed by Tennessee businessman Herbert Humphreys, worked for ten seasons around the bow section, and the "hot spot" from which I removed the anchor years earlier. The team's efforts were generously rewarded. In 1988, they recovered an emerald of over 100 carats. Valued at $1 million, it is the largest emerald ever found on a shipwreck. The following year they found 5,000 silver coins, 13 feet (4 m) of gold chain, dozens of gold lockets, rings, pendants and several gold bars. The 1991 season was the best of all, with the discovery of twenty-nine gold ingots—the largest weighing over 35 pounds (16 kg)—4,000 silver coins and dozens of silver bars. During the summer of 1992, divers recovered almost as much treasure, as well as a complete elephant tusk.

The 1993 and 1994 seasons were lean ones, producing several hundred silver coins and a few artifacts. However, they did locate a large ornate English cannon on another unidentified mid-sixteenth century shipwreck, which was mixed in with the scatter pattern of the *Maravilla*. On this wreck they also recovered about a ton of wedge-shaped bars of *tumbaga,* an alloy of copper, silver and gold. As they prepared to work on this new wreck, however, their agreement with the Bahamian government was terminated for undisclosed reasons. All of the treasure salvaged from the *Maravilla* by contemporary divers was taken back to Havana for shipment to Spain.

Diver holding a gold coin next to three 80-pound silver ingots on the *Maravilla.*

Centuries ago, the line of communication between Spain and her New World possessions depended on small vessels called *avisos*—advice boats—which carried the mail. A law prohibiting them from carrying treasure was never heeded. One such vessel was the *San Miguel el Arcangel,* which was carrying a substantial amount of treasure recovered from the *Maravilla* in 1659. En route to Spain, the vessel encountered a fierce storm and was wrecked near present-day Jupiter Inlet, several miles north of Palm Beach, Florida. Only thirty-three of the 120 persons aboard survived. For the third time, the treasure sent from Peru was lost. Attacks from coastal Indians prevented Spanish salvors from recovering any of the treasure.

This wreck is unique in that it has been "lost" and "found" at least seven times since the 1950s. In July 1987 Peter Leo, a Jupiter municipal lifeguard, woke up with a wicked hangover and decided to clear his head with an early morning swim. The water was clear, and he spotted cannon on the bottom. Later that day he and a friend recovered several hundred gold and silver coins. The State of Florida got wind of the find and laid claim to the shipwreck and its contents. Leo launched a costly, time-consuming battle and eventually won the rights to the "Jupiter Wreck." Several subcontractors excavated the site, including Marex International Ltd., and by the end of 1996 over 10,000 silver and one hundred gold coins, two gold bars, a 78-pound (35 kg) silver bar and numerous artifacts had been recovered.

Diver looking for objects under a bronze cannon on the *Maravilla*.

It had been almost ridiculously easy to work on the wreck, which lay under a foot or two (0.3 to 0.6 m) of fine sand, until the County of Palm Beach forged ahead with a beach replenishment project and dumped 10 to 15 feet (3 to 6 m) of sand on the site. David Foster, a commercial diver who had been involved with the wreck since 1991, convinced Leo that he could find suitable salvage boats to blow away the heavy sand overburden. First he procured a 75-foot (23 m) oceanographic vessel named *Ocean Star,* which had two large powerful propwashes to operate in deeper water offshore and hopefully find the main section of the wreck. However, months of digging produced only a few coins, and they soon abandoned the project.

Foster also convinced Allan Gardner, a successful businessman who had relatively little experience working on shipwrecks, to use his newly constructed vessel the *Ella Warley* to work the inshore area where Peter Leo and the subcontractors had found treasure. Over the next three years Gardner and team recovered over 3,000 silver coins and a few artifacts. He moved on to other projects in the Bahamas and Haiti because he had completely covered the inshore area and his prop-washes weren't powerful enough to dig in deeper water to find the main section of the wreck.

The mystery of the "Jupiter Wreck" is why so few artifacts have been found. But, for hard-working salvors, there are still a great number of those coins that sank three times waiting to be found!

The *Maravilla's* treasure included cargo recovered from the *Jesus María de la Limpia Concepción,* which sank in 1654 off Chanduy, Ecuador. The wreck was immediately salvaged. Divers brought up about four times as much treasure as had been listed on her cargo manifest, although frustrated officials believed even more lay below. She was eventually covered by a protective mantle of sand and forgotten for centuries.

In 1997 a team of U.S. treasure hunters led by Rob McClung, ex-police chief of Vail, Colorado, who had worked on the pirate shipwreck *Whydah*, and Herman Moro, an

Arlington, Virginia, gardener, explored the site after local fishermen reported finding a section of the wreck uncovered as a result of a bad storm. The government of Ecuador hired another U.S. citizen, John De Bry, an underwater archaeologist with over 30 years experience working on Spanish galleons, to oversee the operation. Before they even began, a rival group laid claim to the wreck and a lawsuit ensued, eventually giving the Americans the rights. After the group had recovered over 6,000 silver pieces of eight, several gold and silvers bars, and a large number of artifacts, the government halted the operation, claiming that divers employed by the American group had smuggled a large amount of treasure out of the country. The matter was never resolved, and the rest of the treasure is still down on the bottom under about 20 feet (6 m) of sediment, waiting to be discovered.

While the Americans were working at Chanduy, an important find was made off Santa Clara Island about 100 miles (160 km) away. In 1680, the small Spanish merchant ship *El Salvador* was sailing between Calláo, Peru, and Panama with over 100,000 pieces of eight aboard and other general cargo. Several pirate vessels commanded by the English pirate Bartholomew Sharpe had been causing havoc in those waters for months when they sighted the *El Salvador* and gave chase. The Spanish captain deliberately ran his ship aground in the shallows of this island, and the crew escaped ashore. It is not clear if they set the ship ablaze or not. The pirates were unable to find any of the treasure as the underwater visibility was bad and because of very strong currents in that area.

As so often happens this wreck was discovered when a local fisherman brought up a chest crammed with pieces of eight. Ecuadorian businessman Roberto Moran jumped at the chance to fulfill his boyhood dream of finding the treasure. He put a team together of locals and divers from Key West, Florida, who had previously worked for Mel Fisher. The team was led by American archaeologist Joel Ruth and although the diving conditions are deplorable, the team managed to recover over 60,000 Spanish silver coins of different denominations. However, that's about all that they found with the exception of a few pieces of pottery. To date, no trace of the ship has been located; not even her cannon, anchors or ballast stones, not to mention the thousands of other artifacts normally associated with an old shipwreck. Ruth is obsessed with finding the actual ship, not so much for the rest of her treasure but to be able to write a complete archaeological report on the site. The coins that have been recovered were probably flung overboard while the Spaniards were being chased by the pirates.

The largest number of Spanish colonial silver coins found to date came off the Spanish galleon *El Cazador,* sunk in a storm in the Gulf of Mexico while en route from Veracruz to New Orleans in 1784. There were no survivors.

At the end of the American Revolution in 1783, King Charles III of Spain determined that the only way to save the economy of Louisiana and keep it from falling into the hands of the French was to redeem all the paper currency as quickly as possible, replacing it with silver coinage. Orders were sent to Mexico to dispatch the *El Cazador* with as much silver coinage as possible. The loss of the ship and its cargo of 450,000 silver coins changed the course of history as Spain ceded Louisiana back to France in 1800, and three years later the United States purchased Louisiana for $15 million.

In August 1993 the fishing boat *Mistake* was trawling about 50 miles (80 km) south of New Orleans when her nets snagged on an obstruction. The captain and crew couldn't believe their eyes when hundreds of gleaming coins fell on the deck as they pulled the damaged nets aboard. The boat captain formed the Grumpy Partnership with maritime lawyer David Paul Horan of *Atocha* fame. Marex International Ltd. was contracted to salvage the shipwreck. They used ROVs and divers breathing trimix (a mixture of nitrogen, helium and oxygen, which allows extended diving time) in their scuba tanks and recovered three and a half tons of coins and other artifacts. The following year, Oceaneering International took over the operation and brought up another two and a half tons of coins. In August 2002 a new group used an ROV and a mechanical clam-shell bucket to recover an additional 15 tons of silver coins and some interesting artifacts.

THE 1715 FLEET

In 1700 Charles II of Spain died, leaving no heirs to the crown. In his will he nominated the grandson of Louis XIV of France to succeed him as Philip V. Other European powers looked on this extension of Bourbon power as an intolerable threat and launched the costly War of the Spanish Succession, which continued until 1714. During the course of the war, the Dutch and the English concentrated on disrupting the flow of treasure between the Spanish American colonies and Spain. In 1702, a combined Anglo-Dutch fleet in Vigo Bay, Spain, totally destroyed a large convoy of returning Spanish treasure galleons and the French warships escorting them. Following this disaster, Spain suspended its annual sailings of treasure fleets to the Indies.

During the War of the Spanish Succession only three other attempts to bring back treasure to the mother country were made, and two of them failed. The English destroyed one treasure fleet off Cartagena in 1708, and another was lost in a hurricane off the north coast of Cuba in 1711. So little treasure reached Spain during the war years that the Spanish crown was on the verge of bankruptcy. As the war drew to a close, Philip V ordered that "as much treasure as possible must be brought back from the Indies without any regards for the costs or the dangers involved."

At sunrise on July 24, 1715, a convoy of twelve ships set sail from Havana Harbor for the long voyage back to Spain. More than 12 million pesos' worth of registered and contraband treasure was aboard the heavily laden galleons. Six days later, during the night of July 30, as the convoy was making its way up the Straits of Florida, it was struck by a fierce hurricane; three of the ships sank on the high seas and the others were dashed to pieces on the shores of the east coast of Florida between St. Augustine and Stuart. More than 1,000 people lost their lives, including Captain General Juan Esteban de Ubilla, who commanded the convoy. About 1,500 persons reached shore by swimming or floating on pieces of wreckage, but some of them perished from exposure, thirst and hunger before aid could reach them from Havana and St. Augustine. Salvage efforts on the shallow-water wrecks began immediately, and by the end of December about half the treasure had been recovered. Some of it was lost to pirates from Nassau, who raided the salvage camp the Spaniards had set up on the shore. During the winter, storms spread the wreckage and treasure over a large area, and shifting sands prevented most of the remainder from being found.

In 1948 a building contractor named Kip Wagner was walking along the beach near Sebastian Inlet, about midway between Fort Pierce Inlet and Cape Canaveral, when he found seven Spanish coins. Intrigued, during the next ten years he continued beachcombing whenever he could, finding hundreds of coins, both silver and gold. He found them in four different areas and, noting that none was dated later than 1715, assumed that they must come from four wrecks. Wagner wrote to the director of the Archives of the Indies in Seville and learned the whole story about the ill-fated convoy. The State of Florida granted him an exclusive permit to find and salvage the wrecks, and he began his search by paddling on a float and peering at the bottom through a face mask. He discovered a large ballast pile off the beach near Sebastian Inlet. Since

Wagner wasn't a diver, he put together a team to help him with his wrecks. Lou Ullian, Del Long, Dan Thompson and Harry Cannon all worked in the space program at the Cape and all were avid sport divers.

Wagner didn't know any of them well, so he decided to test their mettle—as divers and as men—on another ballast pile north of Fort Pierce Inlet, rather than on the site near Sebastian, which he had a hunch contained a great deal of treasure. He set them to work on weekends, whenever weather permitted, moving ballast. For months they moved ballast rock, tons of it, without finding more than a few ceramic shards and iron fittings. Then, just when everyone was thinking of giving up, Thompson found a large clump that looked out of place in the ballast pile. He brought it to the surface, broke it open and found more than 1,500 Spanish pieces of eight. By the end of the day the other divers had found an additional 600 loose coins. This was the big strike the men needed. They knew a find of $80,000 worth of silver coins wouldn't happen every day, but they were certain a lot more treasure awaited them.

For the next five weeks the water was too rough to dive at all. When at last they could resume work, they found that sand had covered most of the ballast pile. Using an underwater dredge, Ullian sat on what he thought was a large piece of coral, and soon began finding silver coins. Thompson came over and pointed to his "stool," and Ullian realized that he had been using an expensive seat; it was a conglomerate containing more than 2,000 pieces of eight. Over the next year, the men found thousands of coins and then hundreds of wedge-shaped silver ingots weighing up to 10 pounds (4.5 kg) each. They named the site the Wedge Wreck.

After recovering more than $1 million in treasure from this wreck, they decided to treat the matter as a business, and formed the Real Eight Company. By the end of 1960, they had completely excavated the Wedge Wreck, and Wagner, now confident of his team, decided to tackle the Sebastian wreck. Diving conditions during Florida's winter months are poor to terrible, but having savored the sweet taste of treasure, the men were raring for more. On January 8, 1961, in spite of rough seas and bone-chilling winds, they risked going to the new wreck site. The waves were so high that their boat almost capsized several times.

Cannon was the first diver on the bottom, and within minutes he had found two clumps of silver coins weighing 75 pounds (34 kg) each. The rest of the men jumped in, and by the end of the day they had brought up about half a million dollars in silver coins—not bad for a bunch of weekend warriors. By September, when Real Eight called a halt to the year's work, the men had recovered more than 100,000 silver coins. They had also found an interesting array of artifacts, including muskets, a bronze apothecary mortar, a gold-plated pewter jewel box and silver forks and plates.

The best find was actually made on the beach. During a November storm, Wagner and his nephew, Rex Stocker, were on the beach with metal detectors, picking up dozens of silver coins that had been thrown ashore by the storm. Suddenly Stocker gave a shout. When Wagner rushed over, he found his nephew holding an intricate gold chain almost 13 feet (4 m) long with a whistle pendant in the form of a dragon. The back of the cleverly wrought creature opened to reveal a toothpick, and the tail could be used as a spoon, probably for removing ear wax.

Kip Wagner's hunch about the Sebastian Inlet wreck was correct. It proved to be

Spanish silver pieces of eight and gold doubloons on a chart. Recovered from the flagship of the 1715 fleet.

the richest ship in the 1715 fleet, Captain General Ubilla's flagship, the *Nuestra Señora de la Regla, San Dimas y San Francisco*. She had broken up after hitting a reef about 650 yards (200 m) from shore, and her remains were scattered along a 3-mile (5 km) stretch of beach and offshore. This wreck, known as the "Cabin Site," has the distinction of having had more man-hours spent on excavating her than any other shipwreck in history. Real Eight worked the flagship until 1972. Every summer since then, from two to eight salvage boats, working under contract from the State of Florida, have been digging on her scattered remains. This shipwreck remains a prime target because, although she has yielded more than half a million silver coins, few of the gold coins listed on her manifest and little of the bullion and jewelry have been found.

In December 1962 Lou Ullian met Mel Fisher on a trip to California. Hearing of his interest in shipwrecks, he invited him to come to Florida to work with Real Eight. Fisher formed a company, Treasure Salvors, Inc., with his wife, Delores, who was a diver, and five other men willing to move to Florida with him. Rupe Gates, Walt Holzworth, Dick Williams, Fay Fields and Demostines Molinar agreed to try shipwreck salvaging in Florida for a year. Fields, a magnetometer expert, had built several magnetometers of his own design, which Fisher had used to locate a number of wrecks off California. Wagner first put the Treasure Salvors team on the Wedge Wreck to acquaint them with local diving conditions. They worked there for a month, finding nothing more than one silver wedge and several small ceramic figurines. Wagner then moved them up to a site just south of Vero Beach where silver coins had been found on the beach and where six months of hard work had produced only 1,200 silver and three gold coins.

To remove the tremendous amount of sand that covered this site, Fisher devised the prop-wash, still the main excavation tool in use today. It consists of an elbow-shaped metal tube. One end fits over the boat's propeller; the other points vertically toward the seafloor. When a boat is held stationary by four anchors, the stream of water created by the turning of the propeller is deflected downward and can blow away tremendous amounts of bottom sediment.

When the Wedge Wreck was finished, Fisher moved to Douglas Beach, a site several miles south of Fort Pierce Inlet where beachcombers had been finding 1715 coins, both silver and gold. At first it was disappointing. By the end of the 1963 season the only find was a single cannon. April Fool's Day marked the start of the 1964 season. Treasure Salvors started diving just seaward from the cannon and found three more cannon and scattered ballast. By this time the men had been in Florida for almost a year. Several, disenchanted with the project, were planning to return to California. The recovery of 100 silver coins during the first week of excavation raised their spirits somewhat, however. They felt even better on May 8, when Molinar discovered two 22-carat gold disks, each weighing 7 1/2 pounds (3.5 kg).

As often happens in shipwreck work, weather conditions worsened and they had to wait, jittery and impatient, for ten days before they could resume operations. Then, just thirty seconds after Molinar jumped in, he surfaced holding a gold doubloon dated 1698. Three others were found that day. Several disappointing days followed when nothing was found. On May 21, they salvaged 200 gold coins, and then had two more unproductive days.

On the morning of May 24 Fisher announced that he had one of his famous "feelings." If they moved about 500 yards (150 m) farther seaward, he was sure they would make a strike. Though the others thought it ridiculous to abandon an area that had proved so lucrative, they agreed to shift position. With the prop-wash, they cut a hole about 15 feet (4.5 m) in diameter, and three divers went down to check the hole. They stared in awe at a literal carpet of gold coins that had been uncovered. All day long, the divers stuffed coins into gloves and dumped them in glistening cascades onto the deck of the boat, until the total came to 1,073. The next day they brought up 900 coins, the day after that 600 more. By summer's end the "Colored Beach Wreck" had yielded more than 3,500 gold and 6,000 silver coins, several more gold disks and a number of gold chains, medallions, rings and other pieces of jewelry. The payoff for Fisher's "feeling" was the most valuable treasure recovery from a shipwreck up to that time.

The wreck was identified as the *Patache,* the smallest vessel in the 1715 fleet. It provides a good example of the amount of contraband these galleons had on board. According to the ship's manifest, it was carrying 44,000 pieces of eight and no gold; and yet more than 20,000 gold and 100,000 silver coins and several million dollars in gold jewelry have been recovered from the site. Like the Sebastian Inlet wreck, the *Patache* is still being salvaged today. During the summer of 1990, one lucky salvor recovered more than 900 gold coins in an area that had been worked repeatedly by others.

One of the most spectacular finds in recent years took place on the Cabin Site during the summer of 1993. Bob Weller, a veteran treasure hunter, subcontracted from Mel Fisher and me as we both had rights to the site at that time. About 100 feet (30 m) offshore in an area that had been searched repeatedly over the years, one of Weller's divers, Chris James, found fabulous jewelry and gold objects valued at several million dollars. One of the large gold pendants had 250 diamonds in it, another had 128 and a pair of earrings had about 80 diamonds between them.

The following year a young boy was surfboarding in that area. During the winter strong northeasterly storms had removed a great deal of sand from the site. As he came ashore he looked down and saw the glint of gold. The incredibly lucky lad plucked 53 large gold doubloons worth over $200,000 from the shallow water.

Two large silver bars and gold jewelry, buttons, chains, rosary and two manicure sets from the flagship of the 1715 fleet.

In 1996 another subcontractor, Historical Research and Development, led by professional treasure hunter Moe Molinar, hit it big on the same wreck, finding amazingly beautiful jewelry. They were digging in 8 feet (2.8 m) of water just north of the Bob Weller and surfer finds and recovered five ornate large gold rosaries; two beautiful gold manicure sets, each with its own 5-foot (1.8 m) long gold chain; two gold buckles; twenty-two gold filigree buttons; and ten gold rings with animal engravings. The following summer they were back in the same area and found three more of the stunning gold rosaries and other gold objects.

The seven galleons from the 1715 fleet that have been found and excavated have yielded substantial amounts of treasure; but five more of the wrecks remain hidden beneath the sea, awaiting discovery.

CUBAN SHIPWRECKS

Throughout the colonial period Havana played a very important role in the shipment of New World riches back to Spain. Each year some 300 Spanish ships came to this port—both those in the organized treasure fleets and those sailing alone or in small groups. This was the last stop where victuals and fresh water could be obtained before the long haul across the Atlantic. Although the Spaniards at that time knew the hurricane season as well as we do today, most of the ships set sail for Spain between July and September, the peak of the hurricane period. During the colonial period over 1,200 ships were lost in Cuban waters; the majority from hurricanes and other storms, but some also due to faulty navigation and enemy attacks.

Although Fidel Castro is a very keen diver himself and interested in old shipwrecks, very little has been done to date to locate any of these valuable shipwrecks. Castro did form Caribsub, a treasure hunting company, but it accomplished very little for two decades, partly because the company's divers, with monthly salaries of about US$10 and no bonus for finds, were more interested in filling the family larder with fish and lobsters than in bringing up treasure. In addition, there was scant funding for shipwreck work in economically depressed Cuba.

As a journalist, I broke no U.S. laws making six trips to Cuba between 1964 and 1998. On each of these occasions Caribsub took me to dive on various shipwrecks, all located accidentally by fishermen. We found thousands of gold and silver coins and a great collection of artifacts on three seventeenth-century shipwrecks. Every evening when we came into port, the drill was the same: the salvage boat's rudders, propellers and compass were removed and the vessel was guarded by the army to preclude anyone's jumping aboard and heading for Florida as so many Cubans have. Not even the Caribsub divers were trusted, and we always had a few soldiers with us when we were diving.

In 1998 Castro finally opened up salvage to outsiders who would be supervised by the Caribsub people. First to appear on the scene was Franck Goddio. Within a week his team had found the first treasure consisting of over 12,000 silver coins, gold bars and jewelry, a bronze astrolabe and thousands of other

A Spanish galleon under sail, leaving the port of Havana, Cuba. Fierce storms were the main danger to ships off the Cuban coast, and left nearly 1,200 shipwrecks during colonial times.

artifacts. They came up from an unidentified Spanish galleon dating from around 1550 lost off Cape San Antonio, the western tip of Cuba, which every ship had to pass close to en route to Havana or Europe. Goddio anticipated spending years working in Cuba, but when the government accused him and his divers of smuggling out some of the treasure they found, he left in a rage without even collecting his share of the finds. The Cubans realized later that the accusations were false, but Goddio has no intention of working in Cuba again.

Two Canadian salvage groups, Visa Gold and Terrawest Industries, and Africub Ltd., a South African group, worked the past few years in Cuba, but their finds have been meager compared to Goddio's. Despite the plethora of shipwrecks there, salvors are not flocking to Cuba because the government now receives 75 percent of all finds, the reverse of other nations, which generally take only 25 percent. The most recent news from Cuba was in April 2002 when a Canadian ocean engineer, Paulina Zelistsky, claimed to have discovered the sunken continent of *Atlantis* in 2,000 feet (650 m) of water off the northwestern coast of Cuba. The claim has been proven inaccurate and the sonar records show that the "sunken buildings" are geological outcroppings.

THE EL MATANCEROS

Modern hunters of Spanish galleon wrecks have concentrated their efforts in the waters of Florida, the Bahamas and Bermuda, where treasure-laden ships were lost en route to Spain. Very little has been done to locate galleons that sank while sailing from

Spain to the New World with trade goods for the Spanish colonies. One outward-bound galleon that has been salvaged, however, is the *Nuestra Señora de los Milagros* (*Our Lady of the Miracles*), nicknamed *El Matanceros.*

In 1739, England's commercial conflict with Spain erupted in the War of Jenkins's Ear. This war, which forced Spain to suspend the treasure convoy system, was precipitated by an English captain who waved a shriveled bit of flesh before a committee of the House of Commons claiming that Spanish privateers had boarded his ship and sliced off his ear. In fact, the event occurred when Jenkins, who dabbled in piracy, had his ship boarded by a Spanish *guarda costa,* or patrol ship, after raiding a Spanish salvage party on Pedro Shoals, south of Jamaica, where divers were recovering treasure from the wreck of the galleon *Genovese.* With the treasure convoys no longer sailing, the volume of shipping between Spain and its New World possessions decreased dramatically, and vessels began sailing alone to reduce the risk of enemy capture. Very few ships reached the Spanish colonies, which were desperate for supplies at any price. Taking advantage of the situation, Francisco Sanchez Marques, a wealthy Madrid merchant, chartered a galleon and filled it with trade goods for the New World.

The overloaded *El Matanceros* sailed from Cádiz on November 30, 1740. After an uneventful crossing to Puerto Rico, where it discharged some cargo, it went on to Santo Domingo and then sailed for Veracruz. But during the night of February 22, 1741, faulty navigation caused the galleon to run aground on the desolate east coast of Yucatán. It broke up quickly in the surf. Most of the crew drowned or were killed by Indians, but a few men managed to battle their way through hostile jungle to the settlement at Campeche on the other side of the Yucatán Peninsula. Although a salvage vessel was sent to the wreck site, very little cargo was recovered because of the difficulty of trying to work in the crashing breakers. Then the *Matanceros* slipped into obscurity for more than two centuries.

One day in 1956, while I was living in Cozumel, I was poring over a chart when I noticed that the coast opposite the island was called Punta Matanceros, which translates as "Slaughter Point." That made me think that perhaps a ship had been lost there and the survivors massacred by Indians. I might never have investigated the area if I had known then what I later gleaned from the archives: the vessel's nickname came from Matanzas, Cuba, where it was built. I went to the isolated area and spoke to a few local fishermen. When they told me that ancient shoe buckles, buttons and small crucifixes were often found on the beach after particularly severe storms, I could hardly wait to get into the water. I put on snorkeling gear, jumped in and almost immediately saw two coral-encrusted cannon. Nearby were six more cannon and two immense anchors, 15 feet (4.5 m) long.

At that time very little was known about old shipwrecks. The books and movies that had kept me spellbound in my childhood encouraged people to imagine sunken ships lying intact on the bottom with a skeleton at the wheel. Fortunately, by this time I knew better and realized that no wooden remains would be found on a wreck that had broken up on a reef in pounding surf. Still, I was surprised not to find any ballast or other traces of a shipwreck in the area where the cannon and anchors lay. Maybe, I reasoned, a ship had run aground, the crew had thrown the cannon and anchors overboard to lighten ship and then the ship had pulled itself off to safety. The more I thought about it, however, the more I thought that the ship itself had disappeared and its cargo was buried under the coral reef.

In September 1957 I returned to Punta Matanceros with two American friends, journalists Clay Blair, Jr., and Wally Bennett. This time we had a supply of scuba tanks.

The seas were boisterous. Huge waves were breaking over the reef, so we anchored our small boat well offshore and made our way to the wreck underwater armed with crowbars, hammers and chisels. Each time a big wave approached, we had to dive and hold onto a piece of coral on the bottom to keep from being swept away and thrown on the rocky beach. During one of these dives, Blair spotted an intact green wine bottle. It took us more than an hour to gingerly extract it from the coral. Next, we found a bit of wood protruding through some coral growth. Digging around it we uncovered an intact teakwood chest. This convinced me that we were definitely on a wreck. We pried the lid off and gasped as we saw the contents. Amid a chest full of silver buckles and ivory-handled knives were dozens of gems. These glowing "diamonds" and "emeralds" later proved to be paste jewelry.

Just then the sound of our boat's engine starting signaled that there was trouble, and we surfaced to find that the anchor line had snapped in the choppy seas. We had to run to safety, outracing menacing storm clouds that were only minutes away. After waiting in vain for three weeks for the seas to subside, Blair and Bennett had to return to their jobs in the States. We formed a partnership to work the wreck together, and I agreed to wait for them to return on their vacations the next year.

The following June, when we returned to the site, the seas were almost as rough as they had been the year before. We mapped the site, which covered about 2 acres (0.8 ha), and then began excavation. This time, rather than try to extract individual objects embedded in the reef, we hacked out chunks of coral about the size of basketballs and threw them in a potato sack. We brought up about 500 pounds (230 kg) of the conglomerates the first day and then broke them apart. Inside we found several dozen brass crucifixes, twenty silver shoe buckles, two copper Spanish coins, chunks of beeswax, fragments of rope, musket balls, pewter buttons and thousands of glass beads—characteristic trade goods from an eighteenth-century merchantman.

We expected to spend a month on the *Matanceros* and were delighted that the second day dawned with a flat, calm sea. The first hour in the water we netted three pewter plates and two silver spoons, all perfectly preserved and bearing hallmarks, and about twenty silver religious medallions. Then, as the three of us were digging around a large copper cauldron, we were summoned to the surface by our boatman and found a Mexican customs boat tied up alongside ours. The customs officials announced that we were under arrest for disturbing an archaeological site. I produced letters from government ministries in Mexico City stating that no permission was required to work on shipwrecks, but it did little good. The officials confiscated our finds and ordered us back to Cozumel for questioning. That marked the end of the season's excavation, for nothing is quickly resolved in the "land of *mañana*."

Not long after, I was contacted by Pablo Bush Romero, a wealthy Mexican businessman who was very interested in shipwrecks. He offered to assist me in resolving the question of a permit for the *Matanceros*. He was president of CEDAM, a newly formed underwater archaeological club in Mexico, and he proposed that we work together on the site. We planned a joint expedition for the following summer. Bush was a capable organizer, and our 1959 expedition was a full-scale military maneuver compared to our previous expeditions. CEDAM volunteers arrived with three boats, a helicopter, a plane and $1 million worth of equipment and supplies. It was like the Normandy invasion.

There was just one problem, but it was a major one. Bush had too many friends, and the laws of Mexican hospitality demand that you have "open house," even, apparently, on an expedition. At times during the three-month expedition we had as many as 200

Co-author Robert Marx (left) and Clay Blair, Jr. (right) with some of the thousands of brass crucifixes found on the *El Matanceros* shipwreck.

people at our campsite on the shore near the wreck—film stars, television and radio personalities, members of the press, government officials and just plain friends. Fewer than thirty were divers, and only three or four of them did much of the actual excavation.

Some areas of the site were more lucrative to dig on than others, but it seemed impossible to dig on the reef without finding something. The coral was so thick that in some places we had to dig 6 or 7 feet (2 m) into the reef to recover artifacts. Ashore each evening, everyone assisted in breaking apart the coral conglomerates to see what treasures would be found inside. There were so many spoons, knives, buckles, plates, bottles, cups, crucifixes, medallions and glass beads that we sorted them into piles without comment. Our excitement was reserved for unusual discoveries. One day it was paper packages of needles with the manufacturer's name (Johanes Esser von Ach, from Aachen, Germany) still legible; another day it was dozens of pewter plates with English hallmarks; and still another it was the lead packing seal of a French manufacturer.

During the first six weeks we had found the occasional silver coin, and everyone wondered if we would ever find any treasure. Then one day, in a single hole, we found six pounds of gold leaf, probably destined for gilding a church altar, a gold chain with several rubies on it, several dozen silver spoons, a large silver platter with a coat of arms on it, a small gold cross, five gold coins and several silver coins. We had such a celebration that night that I had a difficult time getting divers into the water the following morning. I was diving alone when I spotted a small glint of gold in the coral. I began extracting what turned out to be a perfectly preserved gold pocket watch. When we opened it we found the name of the maker, "William Webster, Exchange Alley, London," engraved on the lid. Also inside were several pieces of English newspaper, cut neatly to fit between the watch and its case. They were dry and perfectly legible.

We had mixed feelings when the *Matanceros* expedition ended. Those of us who had been diving were physically exhausted. Several of us had been spending ten hours a day on the bottom, fighting the surging seas and digging into the coral. Our fingers were severely lacerated and we had all lost weight. But it had been well worth the effort. We had recovered more than 50,000 artifacts, in addition to countless pins and needles and thousands of beads and paste jewels. There must have been an insatiable market for trinkets in the Spanish colonies. We had also found more than 5,000 crucifixes; 2,500 holy medallions; 6,000 belt and shoe buckles; 4,000 buttons; 2,000 knife handles; several thousand pieces of costume jewelry such as earrings, rings, necklaces, cuff-links and bracelets; besides bottles, glasses, plates, spoons, forks and knives. Added to these were several thousand musket balls, cannonballs, thimbles, flints, keys, tools, mirrors, two pairs of gold-rimmed eyeglasses and countless other objects. The ship must have been stuffed to the gunwales with cargo.

As exciting as excavating the *Matanceros* had been, the most satisfying aspect of the entire adventure came the next year when I went to Seville. Spanish colonial shipwrecks are especially fascinating because the Spaniards were such meticulous record-keepers that it is often possible to flesh out the bare bones of a wreck to bring it to life. In Seville, I was able to verify the identity of the *Matanceros*. Sifting through mountains of crumbling documents in the archives, I found copious information not only about the shipwreck event itself, but also about the ship, its cargo, the people who sailed in her, and Sanchez Marques, the ambitious eighteenth-century merchant who gambled on getting his goods to market in the colonies and lost. Casa Botín, a renowned Madrid restaurant, is owned by descendants of Marques, and I felt that the story of the *Matanceros* had come full circle when I gave them two pewter plates, a couple of ceramic jars and a bottle from their ancestor's shipwreck.

5 THE INVINCIBLE ARMADA OF 1588

The escutcheon on a cast taken from one of the *Trinidad Valencera*'s siege guns. It is painted according to the description given in the lading documents and shows the arms of Philip II of Spain and those of his wife, the English queen, Mary Tudor.

HE GREAT NAVAL BATTLE BETWEEN SPAIN AND ENGLAND in 1588, one of the most important in history, is often called the Battle of the Invincible Armada. What an ironic misnomer! The mighty fleet of warships that Philip II sent to invade England was so badly defeated that Spain could never again rule the oceans. How was it possible that this fleet, which had awed all Europe with its size and strength, was unable to defend against the forces of a much smaller and less powerful enemy?

Spain was at the height of its power, and its devout king was fired by an almost lunatic zeal to restore a Catholic monarch to the English throne. As a more worldly aim, he was also eager to rid the seas of Queen Elizabeth's raiders, who had been wreaking havoc on Spain's shipping and New World possessions. Ranged against Spain's might and superior numbers of both ships and men were the smaller but faster English ships and such daring "sea dogs" as John Hawkins, Francis Drake, and Martin Frobisher, comanded by the queen's distant cousin Lord Howard.

In May 1588 the greatest assemblage of naval power the world had ever seen set sail from Lisbon under the command of the Duke of Medina Sidonia. The Armada comprised 130 vessels of various sizes and types—a total tonnage of 57,868 tons. The Armada vessels carried more than 2,500 cannon, nearly twice the number of the English fleet. But the guns were small—four-, six- and nine-pounders—and more suitable for repelling boarders from the galleys of Barbary pirates than for destroying the strongly built English vessels with their long-range cannon. This imbalance in firepower was the key factor in the battle's outcome.

It took two months for the Armada to reach the English Channel. The two fleets first sighted one another on July 30, 1588. Fighting for the first few days was sporadic, consisting of skirmishes rather than fixed battles. The English ships stayed out of range of the enemy guns, blasting the Spanish ships with their longer-range cannon. Many Spanish ships were damaged, but only two were sunk. The English captured two ships without suffering any losses.

Poor planning and the damage to Spain's vessels scuttled plans to transport an invasion force of Spanish troops from The Netherlands to England. The Armada anchored off Calais, licking its wounds. After the English made an unsuccessful attempt to destroy the fleet using fire ships, Medina Sidonia knew that the "Enterprise of England" had failed. There was no hope now of invading England. Spain's ships were no match for the English, and the wind was blowing them into the North Sea. So Medina Sidonia decided to return to Spain. Getting there wasn't easy, however. To pick up favorable winds, the Armada had to sail completely around the British Isles and down the west coast of Ireland.

Humiliated, hungry and thirsty, the Spanish sailed northward with the English close behind. Many of the wounded died each day. On August 12, as the Armada began rounding the northern coast of Scotland, the English fleet abandoned pursuit. The Spanish, their ships in deplorable condition, were in unfamiliar waters, without charts or knowledgeable pilots. The weather turned foul. South of the Orkneys the fleet was struck by a gale that scattered the ships. More than half of them never rejoined the main body. Some sank on the high seas, and others were dashed to pieces on the coasts.

The crippled Armada limped down the west coast of Ireland, racked by one gale after another. The miserable ships began sinking and wrecking in large numbers. In a September letter, Lord Deputy Fitzwilliam at Dublin Castle wrote:

> *Whereas the distressed fleet of Spaniards, by tempest and contrary winds, through providence of God, have been driven upon this coast, and many of them wrecked in several places in the province of Munster, where there is to be thought hath not only been much treasure cast away, now subject to the spoil of the country people, but also great store of ordnance, munitions, armours and other goods of several kinds … we authorize you to apprehend and execute all Spaniards found there, of what quality soever. Torture may be used in prosecuting this inquiry …*

Only sixty or sixty-five of the Armada's 130 ships made it back to Spain, and many of them sank after making port. Less than one-third of the more than 30,000 men who had embarked on the Enterprise of England got home alive. The majority, weakened by wounds, disease and deprivation, died in port. By the end of the year there were fewer than 3,000 survivors, including a small number of shipwreck castaways hiding out in Ireland who managed to escape death at the hands of the Irish.

THE DUQUE DE FLORENCIA

The remains of at least sixty of the famous Armada ships lie off the British Isles. In the past thirty years, fourteen have been discovered; most by fishermen or sport divers. The location of one has been known since the day she was lost, her position handed down from generation to generation. The *Duque de Florencia* was a 486-ton galleon, with fifty-two bronze cannon, commanded by Captain Dominic Fareija. Seeking safety from the elements, she entered Tobermory Bay, a natural harbor on the Isle of Mull, Scotland. According to legend, local residents set fire to the ship, blowing her up, after the Spaniards refused to pay for the food and water they had been given. Legend also

The Spanish Armada setting sail from Cadiz Bay, Spain, on its way to England.

Spanish and English ships fighting off the south coast of England.

has it that she was the pay ship for the entire Armada and went down with a prodigious treasure; however, historical documents do not support this tale.

Over the centuries the amount of treasure reputed to be on this wreck has grown to staggering amounts, and there have been no fewer than fifty attempts to find it. The first took place in 1608 while the galleon still lay exposed on the seafloor, but nothing of value was recovered. In 1665 salvors used a diving bell and raised nine cannon. Over the years, others found another twenty or so of the cannon, some silverware, a large silver bell and about one hundred gold and silver coins—just enough to whet the appetite. The seafloor is always changing, and by 1955, when the last attempt was made on the wreck in Tobermory Bay, more than 30 feet (9 m) of mud blanketed the site. Although salvors spent about half a million dollars to uncover and excavate it, to find only a few timbers and cannonballs, the tale of great sunken treasure persists.

THE SANTA MARÍA DE LA ROSA AND THE GRAN GRIFON

On September 21, 1588, three storm-tossed Armada galleons sought refuge in Blasket Sound, County Kerry, on the southwest coast of Ireland. Even today this is an area mariners dread because of its notorious riptides, ever-changing eddies and the sinister pinnacles of rock that lie just below the surface. While they lay at anchor, a fourth galleon, the *Santa María de la Rosa*, limped in and dropped her one remaining anchor. Her sails were in tatters and she was barely afloat. Even as the crew fired her guns to signal for help she foundered and sank in full view of the other ships. More than 500 men went down with her, including the young Prince of Ascoli, who was the illegitimate son of Philip II. The raging storm prevented rescue efforts and only one man survived, by swimming 4 miles (6.5 km) to shore. The 1,000-ton *Santa María de la Rosa* was a vice admiral's flagship in one of the Armada's squadrons and one of the largest ships in the Armada.

An English cannon foundry casting cannons used in the 1588 battle.

In 1962 a fisherman snagged a small bronze cannon in his nets. It was identified as an Armada gun, and throughout the summer of 1963 a Dublin sport diver, Des Brannigan, and several friends searched for a wreck to go with it. The following year, another group, led by Welshman Sydney Wignall, also started searching the area, which is so hazardous that diving is restricted to slack tide. The third summer, still another group, led by Englishman John Grattan, joined the search. The three groups were working on a shoestring and had no money for electronic equipment. Poor underwater visibility and difficult diving conditions slowed the search, which went on for six seasons. In 1968, Wignall and Grattan joined forces for a three-month expedition. After a month they found four anchors, but no sign of the wreck. Another month's search still failed to turn up any signs, and Grattan's team pulled out. Wignall persevered and, as so often happens, on the last day of the expedition his divers came upon a ballast pile 100 feet (30 m) long. Scattered among the ballast rock were hundreds of iron cannonballs, lead musket shot and large lead ingots. No cannon were in evidence. Apparently the upper section of the galleon's hull where the cannon were carried had broken off and drifted away.

The following summer, Wignall's divers began digging into the ballast pile. They found a number of arquebuses (matchbox guns) and muskets and, under a large pewter platter, made the gruesome discovery of leg, pelvis and rib bones. One of the first finds—two pewter plates, inscribed "Matute"—allowed Wignall to identify the shipwreck. Again thanks to the Spanish passion for record-keeping, he was able to determine that a Francisco Ruiz Matute was an artillery officer on the *Santa María de la Rosa*. Apparently, the local inhabitants had salvaged the ship soon after she sank, because Wignall found very few artifacts and no treasure of any kind.

Sydney Wignall participated in another Armada project with Dr. Colin Martin, director of the Institute of Maritime Archaeology of St. Andrews University in Scotland. Their target, the *Gran Grifon,* a galleon of 650 tons and thirty-eight guns commanded by Admiral Gómez de Medina, had been lost off Fair Isle, in the wild waters between the Orkney and Shetland Islands off northern Scotland. Diving conditions so far north are even harsher than in Blasket Sound. When their team of four began a two-week visual search in June 1970, the water was just above freezing. Among the Fair Isle residents were descendants of islanders who had seen the ship strike a submerged rock and sink, and they pointed out where tradition placed the wreck. The team found the *Gran Grifon* on the second day in 50 feet (15 m) of water. Lying at the base of a submerged rock were five iron and two bronze cannon, one with an iron cannonball still lodged in its bore. Lying among the guns were hundreds of cannonballs and dozens of lead ingots, which would have been melted down and used to make musket and pistol shot.

BBC Television helped fund excavation of the site, and the British government supplied HM Fleet Tender *Brodick,* plenty of diving and excavation equipment and sixteen divers from the Naval Air Command Sub-Aqua Club, led by Commander Alan Baldwin. The divers worked in shifts eight hours a day for three months using an airlift until the project was completed. The finds were scant: one Spanish silver coin, some artillery and other weapons, a large copper cooking cauldron, ship's rigging, tools and a few personal items, such as buttons. The huge North Atlantic seas that pounded the site had obliterated all other traces of the *Gran Grifon*.

Kitchen utensils found on the *Gran Grifon* wreck.

THE GIRONA AND THE TRINIDAD VALENCERA

The greatest single loss of the Armada debacle was the *Girona,* sunk with nearly 1,300 souls. Those who perished included men from some of Spain's noblest families and survivors from four other Armada ships that had wrecked earlier. Only five men reached shore alive. The *Girona*'s manifest shows that she carried the largest amount of treasure, a great deal of which local residents most likely salvaged.

As a boy in Belgium, Robert Stenuit was fascinated by tales of diving and sunken treasure. He became a professional diver, specializing in deep diving in the offshore petroleum industry in the North Sea, but he never lost his interest in sunken ships. In 1956 he had his first taste of treasure hunting when he joined an American group searching for a Spanish fleet lost in Vigo Bay, Spain, in 1702. Although the expedition met with little success, Stenuit got hooked on old shipwrecks and decided to pursue them full time.

He spent several years in methodical research, amassing data on hundreds of shipwrecks worldwide. The *Girona* was his first target, and he spent six months hunting for clues in archives all over Europe. Although the galleon's position in historical documents was vague, even contradictory, he narrowed her location to three areas on the north coast of Ireland near Bushmills, in County Antrim. The names Spanish Rock, Spanish Cave and Port na Spaniagh on old charts indicated a tie to the ill-fated Armada ships. Stenuit believed that one would be the *Girona*'s resting place.

In June 1967 Stenuit initiated his quest in the stormy seas off Port na Spaniagh. Working out of a small rubber boat with four friends, he found the *Girona* on the very first dive. The remains of the once-proud galleon lay in 30 feet (9 m) of icy water, strewn among huge boulders and covered with dense kelp. Stenuit started fanning away the sand and uncovered a Spanish two-escudo gold coin and several pieces of eight. Nearby were two small bronze cannon. Under one he found a beautiful gold ring. By the end of the day, Stenuit was numb from the cold, but he knew he had made a major discovery. He decided to keep it a secret until he could return with adequate salvage equipment.

In April 1968 he returned with six divers to make a photographic record—an archaeological map—of everything on the bottom. As he expected, no wood remained after close to four centuries of constant pounding by Atlantic waves. Working in a chaotic submarine environment of waves crashing against cliffs, crevices and stone-filled basins, it took the men a month to gather the pertinent archaeological data. Then excavation began. For the next three months they worked with hydraulic jacks to break up hundreds of tons of rock and used buoyancy lift bags to move them. They removed sand with high-pressure water jets and scanned with metal detectors to ferret out artifacts like coins and pieces of jewelry hidden in small crevices.

The bitterly cold water presented a real challenge. Scuba divers generally insulate themselves by wearing a wetsuit, a close-fitting garment of neoprene rubber, which traps a thin layer of body-warmed water. One diver wore three wetsuits at once, and at times the men were literally paralyzed by the frigid water. But gold has a way of warming one's body and soul. On May 2, when two divers moved a boulder, they uncovered a bed of gravel in which lay two four-escudo gold coins, several ornate gold buttons, silver forks and hundreds of silver and copper coins. An hour later Stenuit also struck it rich. He found so many gold and silver coins that, after filling a jam jar, a mustard pot and a pickle jar, he had to stuff many more in his gloves before surfacing.

Gold jewelry found on the *Gran Girona*.

From then on, rarely a day passed without a major find. At times the water was so black that they had to rely on the metal detectors to be their eyes. Just as they were getting bored with gold and silver coins, more interesting objects began to appear. First was a navigator's brass astrolabe, followed by a small quartz perfume bottle with a silver stopper. Many pieces of jewelry, including gold and silver crosses, rings, medallions, pendants and gold chains, were soon coming aboard the salvage boat. The best pieces turned up during the last few days of the season: two baroque brooches of beautifully worked gold with pearl borders, a lapis-lazuli cameo of a Roman emperor in profile, and a gold cross of the Knights of Malta, probably the property of Fabricio Spinola, the captain of the *Girona*.

There is no keeping secret such a big find. As the team were preparing to leave, two groups of divers appeared on the scene, having heard that Stenuit had found 200 tons of gold ingots on the site and smuggled them out of the country. Stenuit's divers held the would-be poachers at bay while Stenuit rushed to Belfast, where he was granted exclusive salvage rights by the High Court. By the time he returned, the weather was so bad that everyone gave up, including the rival divers; keeping the location of any shipwreck safe after it has been discovered is virtually impossible. Policing a site is financially prohibitive; not even a government that has issued a lease and stands to lose its share of treasure and artifacts can afford to constantly guard a site. Some sites, such as the *Maravillas,* lost in the Bahamas more than 40 miles (65 km) from the nearest land, are particularly vulnerable because poachers can go undetected. Even shipwrecks such as the 1715 galleons lost close to the heavily populated beaches of Florida's east coast are plundered, generally at night but sometimes even in the daytime.

The next summer, Stenuit spent four months on the *Girona,* completing the excavation for a total of 8,000 hours of diving in the two seasons. The divers found fewer coins the second summer, but recovered a great deal more jewelry—the best collection of Renaissance jewelry ever found on a shipwreck. One of the most spectacular pieces was a textured gold salamander, set with rubies. The salamander, credited in mythology with the power to extinguish flames, was a charm against the ever-present danger of fire aboard ship. One of the most intriguing pieces was an Agnus Dei reliquary, a little gold book whose cover opened to reveal a series of little compartments, two of which still contained wax tablets. Men's rings were very popular during the Armada period, and Stenuit recovered many. One was inscribed "Madame de Champagney MDXXIIII" (1524). Stenuit's archival sleuthing revealed that the ring had belonged to the woman's grandson, Don Tomás Perrenotto, who perished on the *Girona*. One of the twelve gold chains found was particularly impressive. Resembling the elaborate chains worn by gentlemen in Renaissance portraits, it was over 8 feet (2.5 m) long and weighed more than 4 pounds (almost 2 kg).

The *Girona* excavation produced an interesting assortment of coins: 405 gold, 756 silver and 115 copper. They represented fourteen different mints in six different countries. Originally, there were tens of thousands of coins on the wreck, but the vast majority, like most of her artillery and other treasures, were salvaged soon after the disaster by an Ulsterman named Sorley Boy MacDonnell. The Northern Ireland government bought the entire collection from Stenuit's excavation of the *Girona*, and it is displayed in the Ulster Museum in Belfast.

In February 1971 two members of the City of Derry Sub-Aqua Club were on a training dive in Kinnegoe Bay, County Donegal, in Northern Ireland, when they stumbled upon two 10-foot (3 m) bronze cannon bearing the coat of arms of Philip II and the legend "Philippus Rex." They realized that they had found the *Trinidad Valencera*, an Armada wreck that divers had been seeking for years. Club members were thrilled at the prospect of having their own Armada shipwreck to explore. Resolved to undertake a valid archaeological excavation, they recruited Colin Martin to lead them. The *Trinidad Valencera* project was a model of cooperation between sport divers and professional archaeologists. Members spent the summer of 1971 mapping and surveying the site under Martin's direction. They also removed five immense bronze cannon to prevent theft. Like the ship, three of the cannon were made in Venice; the other two were of Spanish manufacture. The divers excavated 20,000 square feet (1850 m²) of seafloor without finding any more guns. Since the ship had been wrecked in less than 33 feet (10 m) of water, local salvors had almost certainly "fished" for valuables soon after her demise.

The *Trinidad Valencera* was a galleon of 1,100 tons and the fourth-largest ship in the entire Armada. She had sailed under the command of Don Alonso de Luzon, with 360 seamen, 281 soldiers and forty-two bronze cannon. Most of the men made it ashore, where they were massacred after being tricked by villagers into laying down their arms.

Fortunately most of the materials on the wreck site were either exposed on the surface or covered by just a few inches of sand and gravel, eliminating the challenge of removing vast amounts of bottom sediment. Only a few planks of the hull remained but, interestingly enough, quite a number of artifacts made of organic materials survived in the very cold water, including wooden bowls, dishes, platters, blocks from the rigging, cordage and even textiles, such as fragments of garments made of silk, wool and velvet. There were also two traditional Spanish wineskins, and several leather boots and shoes. Under one cannon, a bay leaf was found.

Members of the expedition were fascinated by the recovery of hundreds of personal items that shed light on life aboard ship. They found a tambourine, a great assortment of pewter plates, bowls, flagons, cups and candlesticks, as well as earthenware utensils and a porcelain bowl from China. They even found the skeleton of a rat that didn't leave the sinking ship in time.

An original gun from the *Trinidad Valencera* is mounted on this modern restoration of one of the ship's siege carriages.

OTHER DISCOVERIES

Three Armada ships that were wrecked off County Sligo, on the northwest Irish coast, were discovered in 1985 thanks to detective work by Colin Martin, who read a vivid account of the disaster written by one of the few survivors, Francisco de Cuellar. De Cuellar was an artillery captain who was held prisoner by the Irish for two years before being ransomed by his rich family. The *Juliana,* the *Lavia* and the *Santa María de la Vision,* seeking safe harbor during a raging gale, found a lee shore off Steedagh Strand, a sandy beach flanked by high mountains. The ships stayed for four days, hoping to land men to secure badly needed supplies and water, but the surf was too high on the beach. On the fifth day, the storm veered and the full fury of the gale bore down on them, bringing seas "as high as heaven." One by one their anchor cables parted, and the ships were driven ashore and pounded to pieces. More than 1,100 men drowned, and most of the 300 who made it ashore were slain by hostile inhabitants.

Underwater view of one of the unidentified 1558 Spanish Armada wrecks discovered in Sligo Bay.

Colin Martin convinced a team of sport divers, led by Englishman Stephen Birch, to look for the three wrecks. In contrast to the other Armada sites, the bottom was sandy, and as they expected that the wrecks were deeply buried, they used a magnetometer to detect hidden iron concentrations. They found the first galleon on the seventh day and the other two the following week. To their surprise, ship's timbers protruded from the sand on all three sites, and two had anchors on the surface. They decided to concentrate on the first wreck and used a dredge to uncover three bronze cannon, four siege-train wheels, cannonballs and a pewter plate. Colin Martin plotted these finds *in situ,* after which they were raised. It was then that trouble started.

With the 400th anniversary of the defeat of the Armada only three years away, Martin assumed that it would be relatively easy to find funding to excavate all three wreck sites and that the Irish government would be pleased with the project. But officials turned out to be anything but supportive. Concerned that the divers were all nonprofessionals and that there were no conservation facilities available, the government seized the finds and ordered operations to cease. A 1987 law was enacted prohibiting anyone from excavating shipwrecks in Irish waters. This was a blow not only to Martin and the divers who had found the three Armada shipwrecks but also to many other divers, whose hopes of finding shipwrecks were dashed. Some time in the future, perhaps, this law will be rescinded so that the three Armada wrecks can be excavated and the search for other shipwrecks of historical significance can continue.

Another unidentified galleon from the Spanish Armada was discovered in 1998 close to shore at Kinlochbervie, south of Cape Wrath in Scotland, by an amateur diver named Roy Hamming. Unlike most of the other Armada finds in shallow water, this site was around 90 feet (27 m) deep. On his first dive Hamming brought up a stunning collection of fine Italian Renaissance pottery. After he reported his find to the receiver of wrecks, the government's Archaeological Diving Unit was sent to work with him. They located four large iron cannon, four anchors, a sounding lead, iron and stone cannonballs, and more pottery. Due to the fact that the site lies on a rocky seafloor no traces of the actual wooden hull have survived. Hamming applied to the Scottish Parliament for an excavation permit. To date it has not been granted, despite the assistance of several qualified underwater archaeologists who have offered to work closely with Hamming.

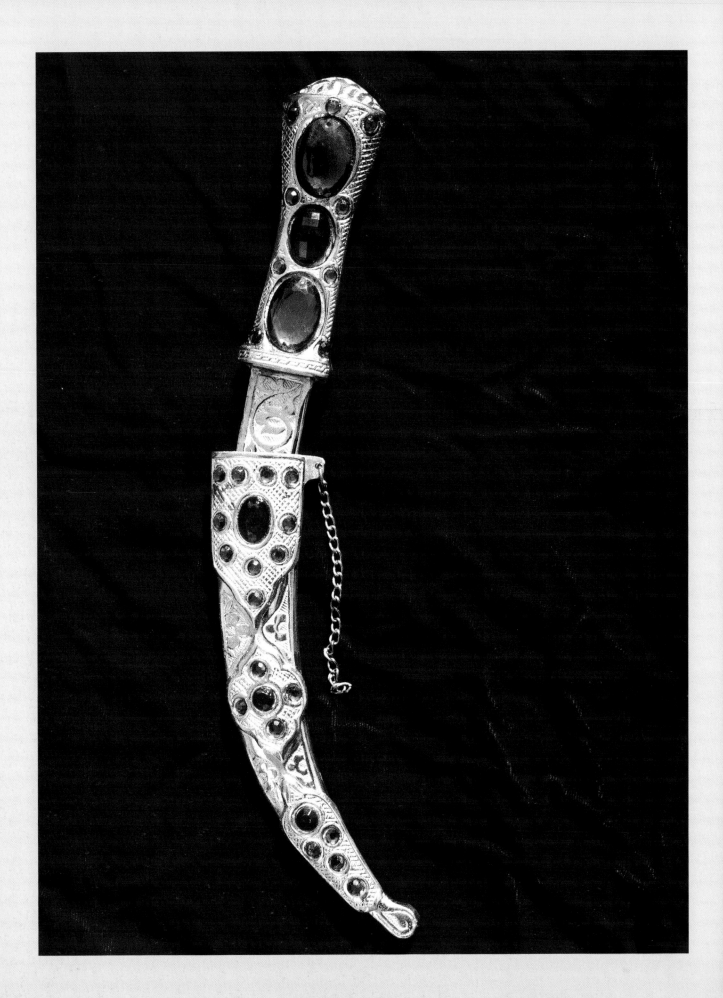

6 THE MANILA GALLEONS

THE GREAT WEALTH OF THE ORIENT LURED THE SPANISH to the Philippine Islands soon after the first contact by Magellan in 1521. Spain established a royal shipping line, the Manila Galleons, to link the mother country to the new colony. For 250 years, between 1568 and 1815, the Manila Galleons made annual crossings between the Mexican port of Acapulco and the Philippines. They were the largest ships afloat during the Spanish colonial period and plied the longest route, sometimes sailing for six or eight months without making landfall. During the heyday of the Pacific galleons, Manila was the entrepôt for oriental trade. Its strategic location made it the "Queen of the Orient," attracting ships bearing cargoes from as far away as Arabia and the east coast of Africa.

People find the Manila Galleons and their voyages endlessly fascinating. Writers of fiction imbue them with romance and high adventure. Scholars and underwater archaeologists focus on their influence on international commerce and the colonial history of the Spanish Empire. The galleons were massive vessels, some as huge as 2,500 tons. Neither sleek nor graceful, they were short, broad, cumbersome ships characterized by a half-moon shape with high fore and stern castles. They had four decks and carried as many as one hundred bronze cannon. The sails were enormous, marked with the blazing insignias of Royal Spain and the Roman Catholic Church. Most of the Manila Galleons were constructed in the Philippines of durable hardwoods, but a few were built in Cambodia and Thailand. The Philippine hemp that provided excellent

Gold jewel-studded dagger recovered from a Manila Galleon in the Philippines.

cordage for the Spanish ships soon gained worldwide acceptance. But the galleons had an Achilles heel—they drew as much as 10 feet (3 m) of water, which caused many of them to wreck on shallow reefs and shoals.

The galleons embarked on their westward voyages from Acapulco sailing in convoys of from two to five. They carried colossal amounts of treasure for commerce in the Orient. A single galleon might carry more silver than an entire Spanish treasure fleet sailing between Veracruz and Spain. On average, they carried between one and three million pesos as registered cargo as well as large amounts of unregistered gold and silver. The ingots and chests of coins were stored over the keel in the main hold. Sometimes the ships were so laden that they needed no ballast rock to stabilize them.

An estimated one-third of all the silver and gold mined in the Spanish New World

made its way to the Far East aboard the lumbering Manila Galleons, which also carried supplies to colonists in the Marianas and the Philippines. Slipping down to about 12 degrees of north latitude to pick up the easterly trade winds, they rarely encountered foul weather during the four to six weeks it took to reach Guam or one of the other Marianas Islands, where they stopped for "refreshments" and to deliver supplies to the colonists. It took another six weeks to reach the Strait of San Bernardino on the eastern end of Luzon in the Philippine Archipelago. The straits kindled anxiety in the most seasoned mariners—both outward and inward bound. Of the approximately 130 Manila Galleons lost over the centuries, almost 100 met their doom within a 50-mile (80 km) radius of the entrance to that treacherous passage.

The treasure the galleons unloaded in Manila was used to buy the varied products of the East. Spanish coinage spread throughout the Orient and remained legal tender there long after the end of the Manila Galleons' era. The Spanish government made repeated efforts to slow the drain of silver and gold to China and other Asian countries by imposing harsh trade restrictions, but Europe's insatiable hunger for exotic oriental

Diver using an airlift to excavate one Chinese porcelain jar and an earthenware storage jar.

goods made the exodus of capital impossible to control.

The bulk of the cargoes aboard Acapulco-bound ships were silks, porcelains and spices, but the most valuable were the myriad objects fashioned by eastern artisans in gold, silver, copper, ivory, jade, sandalwood and onyx, and the chests of jewelry and gems—pearls, diamonds, emeralds, rubies and sapphires.

Finding crews for the galleons was never easy, for few men wished to make a career of the hazardous voyages. On the eastward voyages, which averaged about seven months, shipwrecks, epidemics, thirst and starvation generally claimed more than a fifth of the men. On one such voyage, in 1657, all 450 souls perished when a smallpox epidemic swept through a ship, which was found drifting unmanned off the Mexican coast by fishermen. For an individual, the key to profit lay in contraband, and once a man had completed a couple of voyages and feathered his nest, he usually preferred to retire while still in good health.

Even successful voyages were not pleasant for the 300 to 800 passengers and crew a Manila Galleon carried. Their provisions consisted mainly of weevily biscuit, rice, beans, salted fish and salted meat. Water was carried in large earthenware jars or sealed bamboo tubes. Rainwater was also collected by hanging mats from a jackstay stretched along the bulwarks. Water was reserved for essential needs. Bathing was not reckoned among them, so the stench must have been powerful. Life aboard was hectic and difficult. Cabins, passageways, storerooms and decks were stacked with bales and chests, so gear and stores were often inaccessible or misplaced, and there was very little space for working the ship.

The following graphic description was given by an Italian traveler, Gemelli Careri, who sailed on a galleon in 1697:

> The Ship swarms with little Vermine the Spaniard call Gorgojos, bred in the biskit so swift, that they in a short time not only run over cabins, beds and the very dishes the Men eat on, but insensibly fasten upon the Body. There are several other sorts of Vermin of Sundry Colours, that suck the Blood. Abundance of Flies falls into the Dishes of Broth, in which there also swim Worms of several sorts. I had a good share in these Misfortunes; for the Boatswain, with whom I had agreed for my Diet, as he had Fowls at his Table the first Days, so when we were out at Sea he made me fast after the Armenian manner, having banish'd from his Table, all Wine, Oyl and Vinegar; dressing his Fish with fair Water … [serving] Steaks of Beef, or Buffalo dry'd in the Sun or Wind; which are so hard that it is impossible to Eat them without first they are well beaten.
>
> At Dinner another piece of that same sticky Flesh was boil'd without any other sauce but its own hardness, and fair Water. At last he depriv'd me of the Satisfaction of gnawing a good Biskit, because he would spend no more of his own, but laid all the King's Allowance on the Table in every Mouthful whereof there went down abundance of Maggots, and Gorgojos chew'd and bruis'd.
>
> On Fish Days the common Diet was old rank Fish, boil'd in fair Water and Salt; at noon we had Mongos, something like Kidney Beans, in which there were so many Maggots, that they swam at the top of the Broth, and the quantity was so great, that besides the Loathing they caus'd, I doubted the dinner was Fish or Flesh. This bitter Fare was sweetened after Dinner with a little Water and Sugar; yet the Allowance was but a small Coco Shell full, which rather increas'd than quench'd drought.

The Acapulco-bound voyage, which unceasingly tested the endurance of the passengers and crew, also tested the vessel. It was one of the longest and most perilous routes ever plied by sailing ships. Embarking from Manila, the ships passed through the dreaded Strait of San Bernardino, which separates the China Sea from the Pacific. Then the galleons were forced by contrary winds and currents to much higher latitudes, where they picked up the westerlies for the long haul across the Pacific. During the crossing they were inevitably buffeted by many severe storms, which, if not full-blown typhoons, were gales of frightening strength. Frequently, large amounts of deck cargo had to be hurled overboard to lighten the ship, and many seamen were swept into the raging seas.

The galleons attempted to make landfall around Cape Mendocino on the coast of California, but were sometimes forced to sail as far north as the Aleutian Islands, southwest of the Alaskan peninsula, before being able to beat their way down the west coast of North America toward Acapulco. Once the ships reached safe harbor there, they were unloaded and their cargoes carried overland by mule train, the majority going to Veracruz to be taken by Spanish galleons to Seville, and some going to Panama to be shipped to Peru.

A TANTALIZING PROSPECT IN DRAKES BAY
The saga of the Manila Galleons was periodically marred by tragedy. Approximately 130 of these great ships were lost in storms, wrecked on unmarked reefs and shoals, sunk

In the sixteenth century, Spain established a royal shipping line, the Manila Galleons, to transport wealth from the Orient. The Manila Galleons were often at sea for six or eight months without making landfall.

under the direction of incompetent navigators or destroyed by British or Dutch privateers. One of the most notable casualties was the *San Agustín,* lost in Drakes Bay in 1595,
one of five Manila Galleons sunk on the west coast of America. Drakes Bay, 25 nautical
miles (46 km) northwest of San Francisco, is one of the most beautiful sections of the
California coast. The great, sweeping bay, framed by soaring bluffs, takes its name from
Sir Francis Drake, who careened the leaking *Golden Hind* there in June 1579 during his
circumnavigation of the world. For centuries Drakes Bay served as a refuge for countless ships—and a graveyard for many.

On July 5, 1595, four galleons were dispatched from Manila en route to Acapulco,
their holds crammed with treasure. The smallest ship was the *San Agustín.* Conflicting
contemporary accounts place her size at between 200 and 700 tons; sources agree that
she carried 130 tons of precious cargo in silks of various types,
Chinese porcelain, spices and objects made of gold, silver, ivory,
jade and ebony.

A late sixteenth-century Manila galleon
sinking while another rescues survivors.

The three largest ships were to proceed directly to Acapulco.
The *San Agustín,* meanwhile, had orders to sail along the coast of
California scouting for safe havens where other galleons could
stop to make necessary repairs and take on fresh water and fire-
wood before continuing on to Acapulco. The *San Agustín* carried
a prefabricated launch on deck to be used for exploration of the
coast in shallower water. Although the convoy was buffeted by
numerous storms, it made one of the fastest recorded crossings,
reaching California 106 days after leaving the Philippines. Sailing
south from landfall at Cape Mendocino, the *San Agustín*
anchored at Drakes Bay on November 6, 1595. The weary crew
were delighted by the beautiful bay and by the local Miwok
Indians, who rowed out to greet them, bearing gifts. Captain
Cermeño, the ship's Portuguese captain, took an armed party ashore to explore the dramatic cliffs and austere scrublands of the coastal terrain. Toward the end of November,
Cermeño and most of the crew were on the beach when a fierce squall struck. Within
minutes the galleon had disappeared beneath the waves with about ten men aboard.
Only a few pieces of the *San Agustín*'s rigging washed ashore. The survivors had no
more than the clothes on their backs and the launch. After scrounging for provisions,
they set sail for Acapulco, 2,000 miles (3200 km) to the south, reaching the Mexican
port of Chacala two months later.

My fascination with the galleon began in 1950 when I was a teenager in Los
Angeles, diving every chance I had. Diving gear in those days was primitive. To brave
the cold waters we coated ourselves with axle grease. Our diving tanks were fashioned
from fire-extinguisher bottles, and our regulators and connectors were cobbled
together out of aviators' oxygen equipment. Once I'd had my fill of spearfishing and
grabbing abalone, I joined other early divers looking for gold in the rivers of northern
California and for shipwrecks off the coast. When I found a few gold coins from a Gold-
Rush-era wreck I decided I was ready for bigger adventures.

I haunted libraries, researching California history and shipwrecks. I was especially
intrigued by what I read about Drakes Bay and the *San Agustín.* I headed north, inspired
by Hollywood visions of finding an intact ship, fish nets tangled in the mast and rigging, skeletons on deck and, of course, a giant octopus guarding chests brimming with
treasure. I thought the *San Agustín* was a secret. To my amazement, the dairy farmers
and fishermen on the sparsely populated Point Reyes peninsula not only knew about

the galleon but also showed me shards of blue-and-white Chinese porcelain they had found on the beach.

My hopes were naively high as I started to explore off the section of beach where shards had washed ashore. I dived for three days in frigid, murky water without finding my dream galleon. No skeletons, no treasure chests. But I did find several shards, which I later learned were Ming Dynasty, and a handful of musket balls, and I vowed to return one day to find the elusive *San Agustín*.

Today the *San Agustín* offers a unique resource for studying Pacific maritime history. Her approximate location has been known for a long time, because of the porcelain shards and other artifacts that still wash up on the beach and that archaeologists have excavated from local Indian middens. I worked on many shipwrecks over the years, but I never forgot the galleon in Drakes Bay. In 1986 I applied to the state of California for permission to find and salvage it. In contrast to my teenage attempt, I now had the benefit of decades of underwater archaeological experience, advanced technology and the necessary resources. Years of research in Spanish and Mexican archives led me to documents that detailed the bearings Cermeño had made when his ship sank, and I narrowed down the wreck site to a small area.

Since then, I have been mired in what amounts to a jurisdictional dispute over who controls the waters of Drakes Bay—the state of California or the federal government. The federal government claims control of the *San Agustín* site because Drakes Bay lies in both the Point Reyes National Seashore and a National Oceanographic and Atmospheric Administration (NOAA) Marine Sanctuary. On the other hand, the state of California claims rights to the wreck. A tug of war has been going on, and my project is caught in the middle of a maze of permitting procedures and public hearings. In 1989 I did get permission from the state of California to conduct a magnetometric survey of the bay. The NOAA also consented, stipulating that the seabed itself must not be disturbed. The National Park Service, while not permitting us to "mag" within a quarter-mile of shore, let us launch our small boat from an area in the park. We chartered a larger search boat from San Francisco. Scott Ellis, *San Agustín* project manager, friends Don Beacock and Ken Castle and I were ready to begin in June, one of the area's windiest months.

As I was to begin the search for the remains of the *San Agustín*, I empathized with what Sebastian Rodriguez Cermeño, the ship's captain, must have felt as he stood on the shore, watching helplessly as a sudden storm capsized and sank his anchored galleon. I stood on the same stretch of beach at Drakes Bay, braced against 40-knot (45 mph, or 70 kph) winds, and scanned the horizon for my search vessel, which was overdue from San Francisco.

I was apprehensive as we prepared for the search. In addition to worrying about rough seas, high winds and the fact that the search vessel was late, I was concerned about a critical piece of equipment—the proton magnetometer, which would indicate where masses of iron lay on or beneath the seabed. The magnetometer was new, and I had allotted a couple of days to test it. However, the airline carrying it from Toronto, where it was manufactured, to San Francisco, mislaid it for a week. It finally turned up in Tokyo, and we received it too late to test it beforehand. Fortunately, when the search vessel finally arrived and we began working, the magnetometer worked like a charm. In fact, within half an hour of beginning the survey, I was convinced we had located the long-lost galleon. I hadn't been so excited since finding my first gold coin thirty-nine years earlier.

The magnetometer indicated that the wreck lay exactly where Cermeño's account had placed it, and where I had found musket balls and shards in 1950. We continued magging the area around the hot spot, but found nothing significant. I believe the

Gold pendant with a dragon motif found on the *San Agustín* wreck in Drakes Bay, California.

wreck is buried anywhere from just under the seabed to 50 or 60 feet (16 or 19 m) below it. We used hand-held metal detectors to scour the bottom in water where the visibility was a dismal 6 inches (15 cm). We got a number of "hits" with the detectors but, lacking permission to disturb the bottom, we couldn't follow up to see what they were. California officials are eager for the project to proceed and are currently working to resolve conflicts with NOAA and the Parks Service. We hope to continue with the project before long.

Although the delicate-colored silks and pungent spices packed in the galleon's hold will have long since disappeared, the wreck will yield other precious cargo, not the least of which may be knowledge of galleon construction and fitting, as well as an abundance of maritime and personal artifacts.

In 1997 the National Park Service, faced with limited funds, mounted a two-week expedition to work on the wreck. They were unable to relocate the wreck and their only find was a cow bone that proved to be of recent vintage. They vowed to return again the following summer but to date haven't been back to the *San Agustín* again.

WRECKS OF THE MARIANAS ISLANDS

The first of the Manila Galleons was the *San Pablo,* which left Manila for Acapulco in 1568. The *San Pablo* was also the first of the Manila Galleons to be shipwrecked. The northern route hadn't yet been established, and during the night the ship was wrecked on the west side of Guam—to the great joy of the native people, who lost no time in plundering her cargo. Over the next two centuries nine other galleons were shipwrecked in the Marianas Islands—then called the Islas de los Ladrones (Isles of Thieves), because the inhabitants were notorious for grabbing anything not nailed down. On one occasion they swam out at night and cut the anchors of a moored ship so they could later retrieve them.

The most famous Manila Galleon ever lost was the *Nuestra Señora de Pilar y Zaragosa y Santiago,* commanded by Admiral Juan de Echavarria. In 1690 she was sailing from Acapulco to Manila with a cargo of more than a million and a half pesos in registered silver, plus a large quantity of contraband. The galleon was headed for the port of Umatac on the south shore of Guam, to deliver supplies and take on fresh water and provisions, when she struck a shallow reef off nearby Cocos Island.

Using kedge anchors, the crew managed to pull the ship off. But in attempting to round the point of the reef, she was driven back onto another section of reef by a strong current and remained stranded. Another galleon sailing with her, the *Santo Niño,* was unable to help because strong winds forced it to continue on toward Manila. During the next three days, small boats from Umatac managed to rescue all the passengers and crew, as well as some of their personal possessions and a certain amount of treasure. But before the bulk of the treasure could be brought ashore, a violent storm came up and the once-proud galleon slid off the reef and sank in waters about one-quarter mile (400 m) deep.

Not all the ships lost in the Marianas were westward bound. Occasionally, when a ship was severely damaged en route to Acapulco and unable to reach Mexico or return to the Philippines, it would make for the Marianas. In 1754, for example, the *Nuestra Señora de Buen Viaje,* after surviving three typhoons that sheared off three of her four masts, attempted to reach Umatac Harbor. She anchored off Pago Bay on the eastern and windward side of Guam. A storm drove her up on a barrier reef. Most of those aboard managed to get safely ashore, but the ship sank in deep water before any cargo could be recovered.

Until recently, underwater archaeologists focused on relatively shallow sites around the world, primarily because these were the wrecks reported to them by fishermen and divers and also because of the formidable challenges of deep-water excavation. But natural forces dictate that wrecks in shallow water can provide only a limited amount of data about ship construction. Soon after wrecking in shallow water, a vessel breaks up. Its wooden remains are carried away and scattered by currents or storm-whipped seas; or they succumb to the ravages of *teredo navalis*, the shipworm, so that there are few clues about its construction and how equipment, stores and cargo were carried.

Every underwater archaeologist longs to find an intact, well-preserved shipwreck. But such finds are extremely rare. To realize this dream in the open sea it is necessary to delve beyond the reach of scuba equipment into extremely deep water, something that was impossible until very recently. Exciting technological advances in the past few years, including the development of deep-diving submersibles and remote-operated vehicles (ROVs), signal the dawn of a new era in underwater archaeology. The recent discoveries of the *Titanic* and the *Bismarck* by Robert Ballard of Massachusetts's Woods Hole Oceanographic Institute show that we can find shipwrecks in almost any depth of water.

The two Manila Galleon wrecks off Guam—the *Pilar* in a quarter-mile (400 m) of water and the *Buen Viaje* at about twice that depth—are virgin historical time capsules. Their recovery, though costly, would be well worth the effort in light of the archaeological information they can provide. Over the years I have amassed hundreds of pages of original documentation from archives in Spain, Mexico and Manila on both these ships. Their locations were easy to fix within one-quarter mile (400 m). I began by looking for the places on the barrier reefs where they first struck. In 1985 I started searching the waters around Cocos Island for traces of the *Pilar*. I sighted iron fittings and pottery, and even found a Spanish silver coin. With the assistance of Bob Saylor and Jimmy Rogers, two divers who collect tropical fish for a livelihood, I began searching the seaward side of the reef. It wasn't difficult to find the spot where the *Pilar* had scraped aground. We found ballast stones and artifacts scattered around and embedded in the reef, indicating that she had been stove in there.

Following a trail of ballast and artifacts that included silver coins, ceramic shards, ship's fittings and cannonballs, we traced the route of the ship as she attempted to round the point of Cocos Reef and found the place on the barrier reef where she struck again and remained fast for several days. From there we followed still another trail going off into deeper water and surveyed it using scuba equipment to a depth of 300 feet (90 m). The slope bottoms out at a quarter-mile (400 m), where I am certain the *Pilar* lies in thousands of feet of water. Don Baker, a diver and excellent draftsman, and I mapped the entire shallow-water portion of the site.

I also looked for the *Buen Viaje*. This was easier because the galleon lies right off the shore of Pago Bay, where the University of Guam has a marine laboratory. I enlisted the aid of some of the scientists there, who told me that, after storms, brass spikes, porcelain shards and other artifacts have been found on a beach very close to the laboratory. Just a week before I started to search, a staff member found a brass trigger guard from a musket, a handful of lead musket balls and an intact wine bottle dating from the time of the galleon's sinking. Ten minutes into my first dive in Pago Bay I found a galleon anchor embedded in a coral reef surrounded by hundreds of broken porcelain shards and other artifacts also from that time. While digging around a large conglomerate of cannonballs and iron tools, one of our divers found an ornate gold sewing thimble; minutes later another diver recovered three gold buckles and a small gold crucifix. Searching visually and using a metal detector we were able to follow the trail the ves-

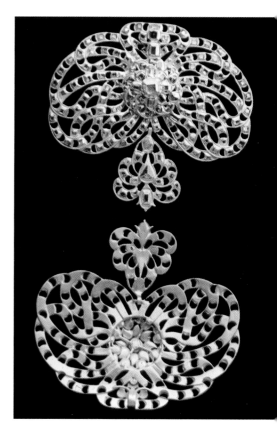

Beautiful gold jewelry, with more than 300 diamonds between both pieces, brought over to Acapulco and later lost on one of the 1715 shipwrecks off the coast of Florida.

Large Chinese porcelain plate recovered from a Manila Galleon found in Acapulco Bay, Mexico.

sel had left as she was lifted off the reef by a subsequent storm and plunged into deep water. We carefully plotted and mapped the trail leading from the anchor, finding many artifacts in the process. At 175 feet (53 m) the ledge abruptly dropped off into the very deep water so common in this area of the Pacific. Back in the 1970s on this same ledge a retired U.S. Navy diver discovered the single most valuable and interesting object from any Manila Galleon; on one deep dive he located over 500 pounds (226 kg) of pieces of worked jade. It took him days to bring them all to the surface and many more months to reassemble them into their original form. The end result was a complete jade Chinese carriage that could hold two people. Experts dated the carriage from the mid-fourteenth century, so the priceless artifact was actually around 300 years old when the ship was lost. It was most likely destined as a gift for the King of Spain. The unique carriage has been valued at US$25 million, but the finder refuses to sell it and keeps it in his home to enjoy. He paid a heavy price for the exquisite carriage; on his last dive on the wreck he suffered from the bends and has been incapacitated in a wheelchair ever since.

The federal government maintains that, since Guam is a U.S. Trust Territory, its waters are under federal control. The Guam government is contesting this claim, and the battle could continue for years. Once the issue is settled, however, I would like to return to excavate both these deep-water galleons using ROVs or submersibles.

In the meantime the government of Guam granted a search permit to a group of Australians to find the *Pilar*—which I had already found! The only treasure reaped to date by the Aussies has been the hundreds of thousands of dollars invested by their disappointed backers. They refuse to believe that the wreck lies in great depths and have been searching in the shallow-water area, where they find an occasional silver coin or artifact, always hoping that the mother lode is nearby.

An American shipwreck explorer, Bill Mathers, discovered another Manila Galleon, *Nuestra Señora de la Concepción*, off Saipan, to the north of Guam. Saipan, an island in the chain of the Commonwealth of the Northern Marianas, had been ceded the rights for shipwrecks by the U.S. government, and it granted Mathers a permit to search for the *Concepción*. The galleon was on her way to Acapulco when she was damaged in a typhoon. Seeking the safety of the Marianas, she struck a reef on September 20, 1638, and then slipped off into deep water.

In March 1987, armed with information gleaned from historical documents, Mathers began his search. His team included archaeologists, divers and electronic technicians from several different countries. During the first season they were able to locate the impact point on the reef where the galleon had first struck because damage to the reef was still visible and two bow anchors lay on the spot. The first five months of excavation yielded only a small amount of ballast rock and a few ceramic shards. Then, just as the season was drawing to a close, they recovered a tangled mass of thirty-two gold chains—each about 5 feet (1.5 m) in length. Spurred on by this exciting discovery, Mathers and his team continued following the trail of ballast and other debris from the galleon into the deeper water. Using metal detectors they found more than 1,300 pieces of gold jewelry in small sand pockets along this trail. The jewelry sold for $5 million. They eventually reached the limits of conventional diving equipment, but without finding the main section of the galleon. Then during the summer of 1990, using an ROV equipped with closed-circuit television, they located a pile of 156 intact clay storage jars at a depth of 270 feet (83 m). Mathers is convinced that the main hull of the *Concepción* lies a mile or more (1600 m) deep, and he is trying to raise the necessary capital to continue his pursuit with specialized equipment.

Chinese porcelain recovered from an early seventeenth-century Manila Galleon off the Philippines.

Unfortunately, with today's sophisticated equipment, ship-wreck projects, particularly those in deep water, are incredibly costly. Financing them has become increasingly difficult because of spiraling costs and the rather bleak global investment climate, and also because, in recent years, shipwrecks have become discouragingly entangled in governmental red tape. The one bright note is that the longer it takes to fund the *Concepción* project, the more advanced technology will be, making it easier to locate, salvage and preserve the wreck and its contents.

THE SAN DIEGO

In 1600 the Dutch had just began to contest Portugal and Spain's claims to the riches of the Orient. This was the year that a Dutchman invented the first crude telescope and Shakespeare wrote *Hamlet.* In 1598 four Dutch merchant vessels, commanded by Admiral Olivier van Noort, set sail from Holland to seek plunder and trade routes to the Orient. Unfortunately two sank in a storm crossing the Atlantic. After some minor successes off the coasts of Chile and Peru, the surviving *Mauritius* and *Eendracht* were forced to replenish their stores with eggs from birds and penguins, which they salted before sailing across the Pacific to the Philippines. Their goal was to capture small ships coming to Manila with trade goods, but they were in for a surprise.

A solid jade Chinese carriage recovered from the *Nuestra Señora de Buen Viaje* off Guam.

Two Manila Galleons, the *San Diego* and the *San Bartolomé,* were put into action to fight the Dutch. They gave chase, and the *San Bartolmé* soon captured the *Eendracht* and took her into Manila Bay. It should have been an easy victory for the Spaniards since they had over 500 men against 90 malnourished Dutchmen. However, the cannon on the *San Diego* were useless as the ship was so overloaded with cargo destined for Acapulco that her gun ports were below the waterline. Undaunted, Antonio Morga, the Lieutenant Governor of the Philippines, who was in command of the *San Diego,* ordered the ship to ram the *Mauritius* under full sail. As a result the *San Diego* sprung a fatal leak and began taking on fatal amounts of water. While hand-to-hand fighting was going on aboard the *Mauritius,* the *San Diego* suddenly plunged to the bottom, taking over 350 of the crew members down with it. There were only twenty-two survivors, who had been fighting aboard the Dutch ship. The Dutch ship sailed away with an unexpected and extraordinary victory.

As a result of intensive research in both Dutch and Spanish archives, researcher Patrick Lizé was able to provide Franck Goddio with the approximate location of the *San Diego.* In 1991, after four weeks of searching with both magnetometers and sonar, he located the wreck in 170 feet (52 m) of water. Diving at these depths is both dangerous and time consuming because the bottom times for divers are very limited; each diver could only make two thirty-minute dives a day.

During the following two seasons the team recovered over 5,000 wonderful artifacts, including 800 large ceramic jars from Burma; 1,200 blue-and-white pieces of Ming Dynasty porcelain; coins; gold and silver jewelry; an ivory chess set and all of the cannon aboard the ill-fated ship. After removing 150 tons of ballast they found that the lower section of the hull was intact, and this was brought up for conservation. After conservation and study by an international team of experts most of the recoveries were assembled in a traveling expedition and put on display in Paris, Madrid and New York.

7 BERMUDA, GRAVEYARD OF SHIPS

OVER THE PAST FIVE CENTURIES, more than a thousand ships have been lost around Bermuda. A nineteenth-century historian aptly dubbed the island a "graveyard of ships." The waters around Bermuda conceal more shipwrecks than any other area in the western hemisphere, with the possible exception of the Florida Keys. There are several places where two, and, in one case, three ships from different periods lie on top of one another on the seafloor. On modern maps, Bermuda appears as only a small dot in the Atlantic some 570 miles (912 km) off Cape Hatteras, North Carolina. It played a key role in early navigation, however, and is shown disproportionately large on old maritime charts. One of the largest of the three hundred isles, islets and rocks that make up the British colony of Bermuda, the island was also known as the Isle of Devils because of its perilous waters.

All Spanish ships, as well as those of other European nations sailing in New World waters, attempted to pass within sight of Bermuda on their homeward voyages, using it as a checkpoint in their haphazard navigation. Most of the ships bringing colonists to North America either made a stop there or passed within sight of the island. Because the Bermuda islands are low in elevation and are often concealed by mist or haze, sighting them was not easy, and large numbers of ships ran up on the reefs that encircle them, some of which stretch out 10 miles (16 km).

Exactly when the first European saw the islands is not known, but they were already marked and named on a Spanish chart dated 1515. Credit is generally given to

A coral-encrusted navigational astrolabe from a seventeenth-century Spanish ship.

The lower hull of a late sixteenth-century Spanish galleon found off Bermuda. Archaeologists are drawing the wooden remains.

a Spaniard named Juan de Bermúdez, who had made several voyages to the New World prior to that date. The first settlers arrived there as a result of a shipwreck. In 1609, the *Sea Venture,* an English ship under the command of Sir George Somers that was carrying colonists to the Virginia Plantation, was wrecked off the Bermudas. In May 1610, the survivors reached Virginia, but some returned to Bermuda, and a colony that was part of the Virginia Company was founded there in 1612 with sixty settlers. In 1684, the islands became a crown colony.

From earliest times, Bermudans engaged in salvaging shipwrecks around their islands and throughout the West Indies. When William Phips first reached the *Nuestra Señora de la Concepción* on Silver Shoals, he discovered that Bermudan wreckers had already beat him to the galleon and recovered a substantial amount of treasure. As late as World War II, salvaging wrecks was still an important occupation for Bermudans. They recovered thousands of tons of scrap iron from wrecks for the war effort, including untold numbers of cannon and anchors from older ships. Their efforts made later detection of wrecks difficult in the many cases where the remains of a ship are buried beneath the seabed.

TEDDY TUCKER: THE SAN PEDRO AND OTHER FINDS

The first major treasure recovery from an old wreck in this century was made in 1955 by Teddy Tucker, a Bermudan descended from the island's first governor. Tucker learned to dive at the age of twelve from an old helmet diver working in Hamilton Harbour, Bermuda's main port. The boy was so fascinated with the underwater environment after his first dive that he ran home and constructed his own diving helmet. He placed a glass window in half a small boiler tank and attached one end of a garden hose to the top and the other end to a hand pump on the surface. With this contraption, young Teddy and several school chums explored the miles and miles of coral reefs and the seafloor around Bermuda and made plenty of money selling sea fans, shells and coral to tourists.

When World War II broke out, Tucker joined the British navy and served in the Far East. After the war he spent three years as a commercial diver in the Far East and the Indian Ocean, salvaging ships lost during the war. On returning to Bermuda, he started a commercial salvage firm, and when the salvage business was slow, he and Bob Canton, his partner and brother-in-law, engaged in commercial fishing.

One day in 1950 he was using a glass-bottomed bucket to search for one of his fish traps when he spotted two iron cannon in about 28 feet (8.5 m) of water. Several days later he and Canton returned to the spot, which was about 10 miles (16 km) offshore from Hamilton Harbour. The two men raised both cannon, as well as a large copper kettle full of lead musket balls. They planned to sell the cannon as scrap iron, but members of the Bermuda Monuments Trust Commission heard of the discovery and offered them a great deal more than they would have received by selling them for scrap. They went back to the wreck site and recovered four more cannon, an anchor and a pewter plate. The wreck was interesting, but they had families to support and decided to stick with commercial salvage.

One summer afternoon five years later, after a severe storm had passed the area, the two men stopped at the wreck site and Tucker jumped in wearing a face mask. The underwater visibility was excellent, and he noticed that the storm had removed a great deal of sand from the area. Reaching the bottom, he saw a piece of metal and pulled it out. It was a beautifully decorated bronze apothecary's mortar bearing a date of 1561. Excited by the find, he returned to the boat, started the air compressor, and then jumped back in wearing his Desco shallow-water diving mask (a mask that completely covers the diver's face and is connected by a rubber hose to an air compressor on a boat). Using a small piece of board, Tucker began fanning the sand where he had discovered the mortar, and in five minutes he had a handful of blackened silver coins. He then dug a trench about 18 inches (45 cm) deep and saw a gleaming object fall out. It was a gold cube weighing two ounces. Tucker was so intoxicated by this find that he bumped his head on the bottom of the boat while surfacing.

Portuguese silver ingots recovered from a sixteenth-century Spanish trading ship.

On the spot, Tucker and his brother-in-law resolved to abandon their bread-and-butter commercial salvage operations, and hunt treasure full-time, working the wreck systematically and secretly. The next day, with several trusted friends to serve as diving tenders and deckhands, they began excavating. There were ominous signs of a storm brewing, but nothing could have kept them off the wreck that day. Their first goal was to remove all visual signs of the shipwreck to keep others from finding the site in case word of their discoveries leaked out.

The coins and gold cube had come from a sand pocket of about 65 feet (20 m) in diameter in the coral reef. In the reef itself, which rose to within 13 feet (4 m) of the surface, they located dozens of iron cannonballs and several muskets embedded in the coral growth. They chopped these out with axes. Attached to them they discovered more than 200 coral-encrusted silver Spanish and French coins. The most recent date any of them bore was 1592.

Tucker began fanning away the sand with a ping-pong paddle in the same area where he had discovered the gold cube. Enlarging the trench, he discovered three gold buttons, each studded with three large pearls. The men were elated, but the impending storm bore down on them and they were forced to run for shelter. The storm continued for three days, but the minute it abated Tucker and Canton got underway for the wreck site. During the first hour on the bottom, Tucker discovered a round gold disc bearing the stamp of the Spanish crown. The rest of the day, which yielded another of the gold-and-pearl buttons and a number of ceramic shards, was something of an anticlimax.

A strong northeaster was blowing the following day. It lasted two more days, keeping them from the wreck. All Tucker's daytime thoughts and nighttime dreams were of treasure. In one dream he was working about 20 feet (6 m) from the spot where he had found the buttons and cube. Above his head on the reef was a bright yellow brain-coral formation. He began fanning directly under it and discovered a round gold ingot and two smaller pieces of gold. When he recounted the dream to his wife, Edna, she said she was sure it was an omen.

When Tucker got back to the wreck he swam around until he found a piece of brain coral that looked like the one in his dream. He began fanning the sand under it. In less than ten minutes he proved the dream was not altogether accurate. Instead of finding three pieces of gold he found only two: a bar of 24-carat gold over 10 inches (25 cm) long and weighing over two pounds (about 1 kg), and another small gold cube. The bar was marked with the Spanish royal tax stamp and tally number and the word "PINTO," which he later learned was the name of the Colombian mine the gold had come from.

On the fifth day of diving, Tucker discovered a number of interesting artifacts, and on the sixth, another small gold bar and a number of silver coins. Then for several days foul weather prevailed. The hurricane season had started, when large seas can break on the reefs for months on end, and for a while the team feared that they might not get back to the wreck until the following summer.

They had a reprieve, however, and the seventh day on the wreck was the most thrilling day of Tucker's life. Racing against time, he decided to use a water hose to blast away the sand on the bottom. He excavated a large hole, then turned the jet off to let the sediment settle. With just a few inches of visibility, he stuck his head into the hole and saw a magnificent, emerald-studded gold cross, containing seven emeralds, each about the size of a musket ball. When he surfaced with the dazzling cross, his wife and others aboard the boat put a damper on his enthusiasm, saying that the green stones must be glass and couldn't possibly be real emeralds. Not until a year later, when the cross was sent to the British Museum, were the stones positively identified as emeralds. Tucker felt he had an important find, but he had no idea that eventually the cross would be valued at $200,000. It is the most valuable item ever recovered from an old shipwreck and is thought to have been a gift for the Queen of Spain.

Diver surfacing with Spanish gold ingot.

Before bad weather halted that year's work, Tucker and Canton had three more days of diving. More gold-and-pearl buttons were recovered, as well as an intriguing array of finds, including a ceremonial spear made by Carib Indians, other Indian artifacts, several pewter plates and porringer bowls, hand grenades, swords, muskets, a breastplate, small brass weights used by the ship's surgeon, a pair of navigational dividers, hourglasses, a pottery cruet for oil or vinegar, buckles, buttons and hundreds of cannonballs and musket balls. After removing all the coral encrustation from the bronze mortar, they discovered the name "Peter Van den Ghein" engraved on it. Van den Ghein was a member of a prominent family of mortar founders in Mechelen, Belgium.

Mendel Peterson of the Smithsonian Institution spent months doing historical detective work and was able to identify the wreck as the Spanish merchant vessel *San Pedro,* which had been lost in 1596 while sailing between Mexico and Spain. The documents did not indicate the type of cargo nor the amount of treasure she carried, or if any attempts had been made by the Spaniards to salvage her. When some of the survivors were rescued eight years later by a Spanish ship they claimed that a witch in Cadiz, Spain, had put a curse on the vessel before they sailed.

As soon as the weather improved the following summer, Tucker and Canton returned to the *San Pedro*. In order to excavate the wreck faster they began using an air-lift, which works on the same principle as a vacuum cleaner. It was a long aluminum tube with a diameter of 6 inches (15 cm), into which air was pumped to the bottom through a hose connected to an air compressor on the boat. The diver held it vertically, and the suction created by the rising air drew sand up the tube. As the sand spilled out the top, the current carried it away.

Tucker and Canton soon discovered that it was more difficult to hold on to a treasure than to find one. They had wanted to keep the find a secret, but had been unable to resist telling friends about the wreck. Rumors were soon flying all over the island. One story, typical of inevitably exaggerated treasure tales, magnified the find to several tons of gold. A story soon appeared in a Bermuda newspaper, but the government, which they had feared might seize the treasure, remained silent. Having no idea of the intrinsic value of the find, Tucker contacted Mendel Peterson and invited him to Bermuda to appraise the treasure. Peterson's eyes almost popped out of his head when he saw their find. After several days of study, he evaluated the treasure and artifacts at $130,000, but subsequently raised the value to $250,000.

After *Life* magazine ran a feature article on the find, real trouble began. Every time the men went to sea they were followed by boats trying to pinpoint the wreck. A prowler attempted to break into Tucker's house, so he moved the treasure to a bank. Then he was notified that the government had decided the treasure was legally Bermuda's because it had been discovered in territorial waters. After an angry meeting with the colonial secretary, who told him that the government planned to confiscate the treasure, Tucker quickly retrieved it from the bank. That night he put it in a potato sack and hid it underwater in a cave several miles out to sea.

He learned later that the government planned to confiscate the treasure because they feared he would smuggle it from the island. Once officials knew he had hidden the treasure, they eased their demands. Tucker and Canton convinced them that they too wanted the treasure to remain on the island, and they cooperated with the government in establishing a museum. Tucker was not the curatorial type, so his wife and several friends managed the museum. Although experts assured him that he could sell the treasure for at least $250,000, Tucker didn't want to bother selling it piece by piece. In 1961 he sold the museum and all the treasure to the Bermuda government for only $100,000; today it would be worth far more. All of Tucker's finds were put on display in the Bermuda Maritime Museum. The witch's curse on the *San Pedro* seems to have been prophetic. In 1975 when museum officials opened the display case to transfer the cross to another case, prior to a visit by Queen Elizabeth II, they made a startling discovery. Someone had stolen the original and replaced it with a convincing fake. The original was never recovered and the thief never identified.

The gold cross with emeralds found by Teddy Tucker on the *San Pedro*.

In 1957 Mendel Peterson joined the team for the first of twenty-five summers of shipwreck exploration. They discovered more than thirty wreck sites that summer, ranging from early-seventeenth-century to late-nineteenth-century ships. Tucker has located more than 130 wrecks around Bermuda, using three methods of visual search. The waters are so clear around the island that he was able to find many simply by standing on the bow of a boat and looking down at the seafloor. When the seas were not completely calm he located wrecks by towing divers wearing face masks on a line behind a boat, or by flying in a light plane.

Tucker and Canton continued searching during the summer of 1958 and, toward the end of the season, made another significant discovery. While searching from the

bow of a boat Tucker sighted an iron cannon barely visible on the sandy bottom, and ordered the boat to stop. During the few remaining hours of daylight, the men dug a few holes on the site with an airlift. They discovered two dozen silver coins, several fragments of gold chain, a pair of brass navigational dividers, lead musket shot and many ceramic shards. The finds indicated that an old Spanish ship lay buried there, so Tucker decided to devote the remainder of the season to the wreck. Each day they uncovered more of the ship's timbers and made wonderful finds: a gold ring with a large emerald mounted on it, more silver coins, swords, pulley blocks, bits of rigging, leaf tobacco and many pieces of ceramic ware.

Research identified the wreck as the *San Antonio,* a Spanish merchant vessel of 300 tons that had been lost in 1621. Documents showed that colonists had rescued all of the crew and passengers and salvaged much of the cargo. Work continued intermittently on the *San Antonio* during the following three summers, when Tucker and his team were not engaged in locating and salvaging other wrecks. They found a large part of the ship's cargo of indigo and cochineal dyes and recovered several thousand cowrie shells, commonly used to purchase slaves in Africa.

In 1959 their outstanding discovery was the wreck of the *Vigo,* a small Spanish merchant vessel lost in 1639. During the two weeks remaining that season, Tucker and his team recovered a massive gold chain over 3 feet (1 m) long, two large gold nuggets and fifty silver coins. The following season's efforts were divided between excavating the *Vigo* and the *San Antonio.* At the end of the summer, Tucker gave Mendel Peterson several uninteresting-looking coral-encrusted conglomerates for preservation. One of Peterson's assistants at the Smithsonian Institution removed coral growth from one of them and found a gold ring set with three stones—emerald, almandite (a form of garnet) and crystal. On the inside of the band an inscription in Castilian read "Yours and Always Will Be." This lovely ring, the most important find made that year, had almost been overlooked.

During the summer of 1961, Tucker pioneered a method of locating shipwrecks using a helium-filled balloon that was towed behind a boat at an elevation of about 200 feet (60 m). The first wreck he found that way was the *Virginia Merchant,* an English merchant vessel sailing between Plymouth, England, and Jamestown, Virginia, which had been lost in 1660 with 179 persons aboard. Several weeks of excavation on the wreck produced clay pipes, tools, weapons, house bricks, writing utensils, pieces of silverware, pewter plates and many fragments of chinaware and pottery.

The next wreck sighted from the balloon turned out to be a sister ship of the *Virginia Merchant*—the merchant vessel *Eagle*. She also had sailed between Plymouth and Jamestown with trade goods and passengers in 1659. A tremendous number of trade-good artifacts were discovered on this wreck.

During the excavation, Tucker and Donald Canton, Bob's brother, almost lost their lives. They were using the airlift next to a massive coral ridge that rose almost to the surface of the water. Digging at the base of the coral formation they uncovered a large wooden chest filled with thousands of clay pipes. Digging deeper they found a copper teapot, then a slate and stylus, which were probably used by the ship's navigator in plotting the ship's position. Suddenly Tucker felt a strong tremor. Years of working underwater had taught him to act fast. He grabbed Donald Canton and they scrambled out of the hole seconds before a huge piece of coral, weighing at least a ton, toppled into it. After a large shark harassed them the following day, Tucker decided the wreck was jinxed and spent the rest of the season completing salvage of the *San Antonio*.

Spanish silver coins of different denominations recovered from the *San Pedro* shipwreck.

During the summer of 1962, he found that helium for the balloon was too expensive and resorted to visual search from a boat. The first wreck his team found and worked was the French frigate *L'Hermoine*, lost in 1838. Every wreck is different, furnishing a unique assortment of artifacts that illuminate the life and times of its sinking. The French vessel yielded large numbers of weapons, shot, uniform buttons, copper powder cans, porcelain objects and glass bottles—many with their original contents. Nearby the divers located the remains of an English merchant ship, the *Caesar*, lost in 1819, with hundreds of grindstones of various sizes, kegs of white lead used for caulking the ship's seams, and bottles of many different descriptions.

On the last diving day of the season, Tucker convinced everyone to "have a quick look" at the *San Pedro*, where they had already found so many valuable artifacts. It almost appeared that Tucker had planted treasure on the site, because he had been down only a few minutes when he discovered a small gold bar, later valued at $16,000.

Toward the close of that 1962 season, Tucker's sighting of a few ballast rocks on a sandy bottom led to discovery of the oldest ship ever found in Bermuda waters. While digging an exploratory hole on the site, he uncovered a vast amount of ballast rock buried not far under the sand, as well as a small clump of badly sulphated silver coins, some of which bore mid-sixteenth-century dates.

Historical research indicates that it was most likely the *Capitana* of the New Spain Fleet, commanded by Captain General Juan Menéndez, and lost in 1563. Tucker and his team devoted the summers of 1963 and 1964 to excavating the site. With the exception of the small clump of silver coins discovered in the exploratory hole, no other treasure was found on this wreck; in fact, it yielded very few significant artifacts, indicating that it was probably salvaged by the Spaniards. Nevertheless its early date, and the fact that a large section of the lower hull of the ship was intact and remarkably well preserved, convinced Peterson that the wreck should be excavated. A grant funded the project, which furnished valuable archaeological data regarding the ship's construction.

I was fortunate to spend most of the summer of 1963 working with Tucker on that site. Rarely have I seen a man so passionate about his work. Every day he would jump

Tucker with a seventeenth-century clay smoking pipe recovered from the *Virginia Merchant*.

over the side with his airlift tube and stay down on the wreck for hours. One day he was down for twelve hours before he finally surfaced. He came up then only because the rest of us were starving to death and had turned off his air compressor.

During the summers of 1965 and 1966, Tucker returned to some of the earlier wrecks he had discovered—*Virginia Merchant, Eagle, Caesar* and *L'Hermoine*—and recovered vast amounts of artifacts. In 1965 he also spent a few days on the *San Pedro* and discovered yet another gold bar, this one weighing 39 ounces (just over 1 kg). Peterson valued it at $50,000 and declared it to be "the most valuable numismatic item yet discovered in the western hemisphere."

After searching the waters around Bermuda for so many years, Tucker felt he had located all the wrecks that could be found by visual methods. Consequently, during the summer of 1967, with funding from the Explorers' Club of New York, Tucker's team conducted a magnetometer search in various areas around the island. The survey located a number of nineteenth-century wrecks and a new area of material associated with the *Virginia Merchant*. When excavated, it was found to contain a great deal of cannon shot and many personal objects, such as ivory combs, brass buttons and clay pipes.

The team's most important discovery was the English merchant brig *Warwick*, which arrived from England in Castle Harbour on October 20, 1619, with the fledgling colony's first governor and badly needed supplies. A month later the brig sank in the harbor during a storm. A preliminary survey of the wreck revealed extensive timber remains. The wooden hull was found to be more complete than any other yet discovered in the western hemisphere. The ship had settled quickly in the harbor silt, which preserved it from keel to gunwale. Tucker and Peterson devoted the next two summers to excavating the *Warwick*, which furnished a wealth of archaeological data.

In addition to working in Bermuda's waters Tucker has located and excavated shipwrecks all over the Caribbean and, although now in his eighties, he refuses to retire and live on his laurels. Most of his recoveries can be seen in the Bermuda Maritime Museum or his own Undersea Explorer's Museum.

"WRECK COUNTRY"

Another native Bermudan, prosperous businessman Harry Cox, has also been prowling the Bermuda reefs in a relatively relaxed manner. Over the years, Cox has spent weekends taking friends and sometimes tourists to an area of the reefs he calls "wreck country," where he has pinpointed more than fifteen old wrecks. It was on such an excursion in 1968 that he discovered a richly laden Portuguese treasure ship, lost in the second half of the sixteenth century.

Cox and friends were returning from a day spent recovering bottles from an eighteenth-century English merchant wreck. As they headed for port, one man was hanging on to a line from the rear of the boat, scanning the bottom through a face mask for signs of a wreck. He spotted a few scattered ballast stones and, despite the appearance of evening clouds on the horizon, Cox stopped to investigate.

While everyone donned diving gear, his friend surfaced with an elephant's tusk. After thoroughly combing the area and turning up nothing more than ballast stones and a few pottery shards, everyone but Cox returned to the boat. As he tells it, Cox "had a feeling that there was something great down there," so he continued searching in the rapidly darkening water. He fanned in a small sand hole on a nearby reef with his hand and uncovered a silver coin. Fanning faster he soon found two gold coins and a large, solid-gold bracelet. He surfaced shouting, "Gold, gold," and the others grabbed fins, masks and tanks and threw themselves overboard. In the next forty-five minutes, before it became pitch black and their air was consumed, they recovered treasure valued at more than $200,000. The find included a number of gold bars, pieces of gold jewelry, a massive 10-foot (3 m) double-linked gold chain, an elaborate gold manicure set, silver items and a brass mariner's astrolabe.

One of the many pieces of jewelry discovered that afternoon was a magnificently worked gold ring with a large empty socket. Cox vowed he would find the stone that had once graced the ring. Two years later, working on a million-to-one chance, he actually did find it—a breathtaking five-carat emerald that fit the empty socket to perfection. Cox has been back to the wreck site many times since and has found an assortment of additional artifacts but the bulk of treasure came up on that first thrilling dive. This seems to indicate that Cox has found the area where the vessel struck the reefs and dropped some of her contents, but not the main body of the wreck.

THE SEA VENTURE

Nineteen fifty-nine was the 350th anniversary of the sinking of the *Sea Venture*, the event that led to the settlement of Bermuda. That year the government asked Teddy Tucker to locate the site of this important shipwreck. Tucker found a shipwreck site that initially appeared to be that of the *Sea Venture*; however, when artifacts from it were analyzed at the British Museum in London they were identified as being from a later period and the project was abandoned.

Then in 1978 Allan "Smokey" Wingood, a retired professional diver and a keen student of Bermuda history, decided to locate the *Sea Venture*. After three painstaking years of research and search, he came to the conclusion that the wreck Tucker had found in 1959 was indeed the *Sea Venture*. He was right. Reexamination of the artifacts Tucker had submitted for identification proved that they had been mistakenly attributed to a later period.

Excavation of the *Sea Venture* differed from previous underwater projects in Bermuda, which had concentrated on salvaging valuable artifacts and treasure. This shipwreck, such an important part of Bermuda's cultural legacy, was surveyed, mapped and excavated over a period of six summers by a team led by underwater archaeologists from the United States and England. Today, thousands of fascinating artifacts found on the site are on display in Bermuda's Maritime Museum.

ACADEMICS AT WORK

In 1981 East Carolina University, in Greenville, North Carolina, created a Master of Arts program in Maritime History and Nautical Archaeology offering students an opportunity to combine maritime history and underwater archaeology. Field research sessions included remote sensing surveys, site testing, excavation and documentation of shipwrecks. During the first two summers students investigated several American Civil War shipwrecks along the coast of North Carolina. Too many days were lost due to inclement weather and poor underwater visibility on these sites, so program director Dr. Gordon Watts decided to find a better area to train his underwater archaeology students.

In 1983 Watts obtained permission from Dr. Edward Harris, the director of the Bermuda Maritime Museum, to work in the waters of Bermuda. Like Great Britain, Bermuda was a neutral port during the Civil War, and many Confederate blockade runners used Bermuda as a way station between Europe and the Southern ports. Although a neutral place, Bermudan hostility toward the United States was so pronounced that the American consul there wrote a letter to his wife in 1864 stating: "I have been attacked in my office and once knocked down in the street. The general sentiment among the locals is 'It's good for him; he's a damn Yankee.'"

An underwater metal detector being used in a sand pocket among Bermuda's reefs.

During all of the years that Tucker and others worked on dozens of shipwrecks around Bermuda, very little archaeological data had been obtained. The *Sea Venture* was one of the few exceptions as Dr. Margaret Rule and several other English archaeologists were called in soon after its discovery because of this ship's significance in British history. Spanish shipwrecks didn't get this kind of attention, and Tucker and the others were basically treasure hunters whose objective was to recover treasure and anything else of value. On the other hand, the treasure hunters, having located so many wrecks, saved Watts and his students the time involved in searching for them.

The first target Watts selected was the *Mary Celestia,* a 207-ton steamer built in Liverpool and launched in February 1864. Between May and September of 1864 the fast paddle-wheeled steamer made five successful runs between Nassau and Wilmington, North Carolina, bringing the South badly needed supplies and war materials. On September 6, 1864, the *Mary Celestia* set sail from Bermuda but struck upon a reef 7 miles (11 km) offshore and sank in only minutes in 60 feet (18 m) of water. The ship was considered a total loss, although local divers were able to recover some of her cargo, which was later auctioned on behalf of the owners.

During the summer of 1983 field research was conducted on this shipwreck with excellent results. Although the ship had broken up on the coral reef, more than three-quarters of her iron hull was still intact. Like many of Bermuda's shipwrecks, this hulk was protected from the ravages of the sea as it lay in a sand pocket surrounded by high reefs. The engine room area, which was flanked by two massive boilers, contained most of her propulsion machinery, her shaft and other equipment. On top of the machinery were part of her smoke stack and two of her large paddle wheels. Most of the students' time was devoted to mapping and photographing the site. Very little sand covered the remains of the wreck, so little excavation was required. However,

they did recover a nice assortment of artifacts, such as bottles, crockery and tools.

The following summer they had to conduct several surveys in home waters, but in 1985 and 1986 Watts and his students were back exploring in the waters of Bermuda. Their next target was the *Nola,* a 750-ton, 236-foot (71.9 m) by 25-foot (7.6 m) beam vessel built in Glasgow, Scotland, in 1863. Built specifically as a fast blockade runner, she never completed her first voyage. After an extremely rough Atlantic crossing in late 1863, she was forced to seek shelter in Bermuda. While attempting to enter port in heavy weather, the shallow-draft ship was wrecked on the off-lying coral reefs and sank in 30 feet (9 m) of water. Like the *Mary Celestia* the ship also settled in a sand pocket between coral reefs. Unfortunately, she was not as well preserved as the *Mary Celestia* as modern-day salvors had used explosives and ripped apart some sections of her iron hull. The paddle-wheels and bow section were her most dominant features. She was covered by several feet of sand, which the students removed with airlifts before they excavated.

In 1987, at the request of the Bermuda Maritime Museum, Watts shifted his focus to older Spanish shipwrecks that had been located and salvaged by Tucker. Some had large sections of their lower wooden hulls still intact, and these could provide a great deal of information on their construction. Watts's first objective was an unidentified Spanish merchant ship lost between 1560 and 1580 that Tucker had labeled the "New Old Spaniard."

The East Carolina team gleaned enough evidence to show that this vessel was not Spanish but a Dutch-built ship that the Spaniards had either captured or bought and put into use in the New World trade. Tucker had done a thorough salvage job on this wreck as the only finds were ceramic shards, part of a smoking pipe stem and a few small iron fittings.

Between 1988 and 1992 the East Carolina people studied the lower hull of another shipwreck that been excavated by a Bermudan named Brian Malpas in the sixties and again in the seventies by Tucker and Peterson. It must have been salvaged by contemporary divers as it produced only several iron cannon, a ship's bell, a few intact jars and several coins. This unidentified sixteenth-century wreck, which Tucker had dubbed the "Western Ledge Reef Wreck," was also a Spanish merchantman. Bottom sediment was removed to expose the wooden remains, and diagnostic similarities were found between the keels, keelsons, frames and deck planking of this ship and the "New Old Spaniard." On this wreck the mast step had also survived. In the area near the hull the divers found numerous metal fittings.

Shipwrecks have always been an important part of Bermuda's history; the government sponsors the Bermuda Shipwreck Festival every summer, which includes seminars with speakers attending from all over the world.

8 THE EAST INDIAMEN

Underwater archaeologist exploring the remains of a seventh-century Asiatic trading vessel off the Philippines. The large ceramic Dragon jars were made in Burma.

HE PORTUGUESE, INSPIRED BY MARCO POLO'S TALES of golden-roofed palaces and evidence of the marvelous treasures of the Orient, began to explore an ocean route to the Far East even earlier than Columbus and the Spaniards. In 1488, Bartolomeu Dias rounded the Cape of Good Hope. Ten years later Vasco da Gama reached India. In 1510, Afonso de Albuquerque conquered Goa in India, making it the center for further expansion in that part of the world. In 1511 the Portuguese captured Malacca and the Moluccas, and six years later most of Ceylon fell under their control. By 1557 they were right on the doorstep of China with a trading center in Macao, and they began trading directly with China and soon after with Japan.

The wealth brought back from the East Indies rivaled the treasures of Spanish America and propelled Portugal from an insignificant medieval backwater into a rich and powerful nation. Each year dozens of large vessels called carracks sailed from Lisbon down the west coast of Africa and around the dreaded Cape of Good Hope, then headed for various destinations in the Far East. The carracks were a combination of warship and merchantman. Like the Manila Galleons sailing from Acapulco, they carried a great deal of gold and silver specie and bullion to purchase the exotic goods of the Orient. On the homeward voyage, too, their cargoes were similar to those of the Manila Galleons: silks; porcelains; objects made of gold, silver, jade, ivory and sandalwood; large quantities of pearls and precious stones. But the most profitable commodity was spices, such as cloves, cinnamon, pepper and nutmeg.

Wanting to share in the wealth, first the Dutch, and then the British, French, Danes and Swedes founded their own East India companies, to challenge Portugal's monopoly of the Far East. Holland's economy had been greatly strengthened by the arrival of Jews from Spain, expelled by Queen Isabella in 1492. An infusion of capital brought by Jewish merchants made Holland a thriving mercantile nation. Prior to Portugal's takeover by Spain in 1580, the Dutch were content to act as middlemen in the Far East traffic. When the Spaniards closed this door to them, however, they had to go directly to the source for oriental goods. Once luxuries, such items had become necessities in prospering sixteenth-century Europe. At first, the Dutch sought a northeast passage around Russia. When this was unsuccessful, they attempted to establish a route via the Straits of Magellan, but found this too dangerous and expensive. Finally, they followed in the wake of the Portuguese via the Cape of Good Hope.

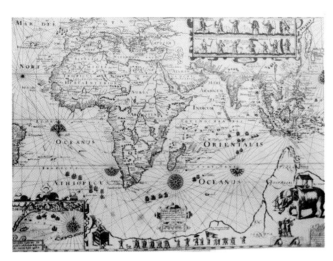

An early seventeenth-century chart showing the routes sailed by all of the East Indiamen.

When the first fleet of Dutch East Indiamen returned to Holland in 1599, an anonymous contemporary wrote: "For as long as Holland has been Holland, there have never arrived ships as richly laden as these." For days, church bells all over Amsterdam rang in jubilation. The Dutch made the Javanese city of Batavia, present-day Djakarta in Indonesia, their main base in the Far East and the capital of the Dutch East Indies. By the mid-seventeenth century, more than 200 large ships annually engaged in the Dutch East Indies trade.

The English, envious of the tremendous profits made by their Dutch rivals, soon formed their own East India Company, and before long the French, Danes and Swedes were also engaged in the East Indies trade. Competition among the rival European nations in the Far East was intense, with each company forever trying to cut into the trade of the others. Thus, throughout the colonial period they were perennially at war with one another; seizing trading bases and capturing and sinking each other's shipping. In the eighteenth century, tea became the greatest European import from China, eventually eclipsing all other products in profit-making.

The voyages made by the East Indiamen were long, arduous and very dangerous. It is not surprising that more than 2,000 of these ships were lost during three centuries of global navigation, sinking in the waters of the Far East, the Indian Ocean and the Atlantic. On their homeward voyages, almost all the East Indiamen stopped at the Azores or passed them as a checkpoint in navigation, and more than 150 were lost. More than 300 East Indiamen, many carrying immense riches, sank off South Africa, especially around the Cape of Good Hope.

The toll of East Indiamen in 1647 alone illustrates how treacherous this area is. In February, a fleet of seventeen Portuguese carracks was rounding the Cape when a sudden storm claimed sixteen of them; the only surviving ship made it to Madagascar, where it also sank soon after anchoring. In December 1646 a fleet of eight Portuguese carracks had set sail from Goa "very fully laden with the most beautiful goods which had come from the East over many years," according to contemporary documents. In early June 1647, as this fleet rounded the Cape of Good Hope, it too was overcome by a violent storm; six vessels went to the bottom during the first hour and the other two were wrecked on the coast.

The cost of bringing oriental luxuries to Europe was terrible. More than 4,000 people lost their lives in these two fleet disasters. The 1,200-ton *Sacramento*, one of the carracks wrecked on the coast, carried more than 800 souls. The Cape waters are frigid and infested with great white sharks; of the seventy-two men who reached shore alive, only four eventually reached Goa. The others were killed by native people or succumbed to thirst and starvation.

One of the first people in modern times to show any interest in searching for shipwrecks in the extremely rough South African waters was David Allen, a sport diver from Port Elizabeth. In 1973, he read a book about the *Sacramento*. He began spending weekends hunting for the wreck. On January 29, 1977, numb with cold, he was about to call it a day when he found what was left of her. Spread out on the bottom were forty-two great bronze cannon, exquisitely decorated with coats of arms and other markings. They proved to be the *Sacramento*'s most important artifacts. The wreck lies in shallow water, and centuries of high seas had ravaged the ship, carrying most of the vessel and her contents away. Allen did find several intact pieces of Ming Dynasty porcelain, a variety of gold and silver coins, and several ceramic jars of peppercorns and turmeric.

Soon after raising the *Sacramento*'s guns, Allen discovered the remains of a British East Indiaman. The *Dodington* had left London in 1755 with a large contingent of soldiers and a large amount of gold specie. It foundered within sight of Port Elizabeth, and only twenty-three of the more than 500 men aboard survived. Contemporary salvors recovered most of her treasure and cannon. Allen found only four bronze cannon, several thousand Spanish silver coins and some personal effects of the men who sailed aboard her.

Word leaked out, as it always does, about Allen's discoveries, stimulating the organization of dozens of shipwreck-hunting groups, most of them formed by sport divers. One commercial salvage company, Aqua-Exploration, formed in 1979 and led by Charles Shapiro, has found more than a dozen East Indiamen of different nations and dates in South African waters. The company's most significant discovery was the *Joanna*, a Dutch ship lost in 1682 while en route to Batavia. She struck a reef off Cape Agulhus and went down with more than 300,000 Spanish pieces of eight aboard and a great loss of life.

In 1684 Olaf Bergh, a Swedish salvor working for the Dutch East India Company, used a diving bell to recover about half of the *Joanna*'s coinage and some of the ship's artillery. In 1983 Shapiro and his divers discovered the wreck at a depth of a mere 15 feet (4.5 m). They recovered forty bronze and iron cannon and more than 100,000 Spanish silver coins that Bergh had missed.

Shapiro found another Dutch East Indiaman in 1991 after a five-year search. The *Brederode* sank in 1785 in 210 feet (65 m) of water, 6 miles (10 km) off the coast, about 150 miles (248 km) west of Cape Town. The ship was sailing back to Holland from the Orient with a cargo of tea, spices, satin and linen cloth; tons of tin, gold ingots and coin; and over 100,000 pieces of porcelain. Between 1991 and 1997 Shapiro tried to enlist the assistance of more qualified salvors for this high-tech deep-water excavation. All declined the opportunity since it was estimated that the project would cost over $3 million. Finally, in 1998 Sverker Hallstrom, a professional shipwreck salvor agreed to take on the project. Hallstrom had previous success locating and excavating other porcelain-carrying wrecks off South Vietnam and Thailand. The project was to commence in 2000, but lack of funding has delayed it. Hallstrom plans to use both mixed-gas divers and ROVs to recover the cargo of the wreck.

Mozambique, the country north of South Africa on the Indian Ocean facing Madagascar, was a Portuguese colony for centuries and is known to have hundreds of virgin shipwrecks that have been largely overlooked by shipwreck explorers because the country has been embroiled in civil strife for four decades. The nation has

Seventeenth-century Dutch East Indiaman.

A fine example of the elaborate care in producing cannon. Here, an East Indiamen galleon etched on a Dutch bronze cannon.

Diver taking great care, using his hand to fan away the sand covering a large Chinese jar from a Portuguese shipwreck.

produced copious amounts of gold since ancient times. The Egyptians sent ships to obtain gold, ivory and other products, and many scholars believe that the present-day city of Sofala was the fabled Ophir mentioned in the *Bible*. In the peaceful period before the arrival of the Portuguese, it is estimated that the area produced from 5 to 10 tons of gold a year. Of course Sofala was one of the first places the Portuguese visited after they rounded the Cape of Good Hope.

The first Portuguese reached there in 1490. They were frustrated at not finding the source of the gold and found the place very unhealthy. Seeking a better port for their ships on both the outward-bound and homeward-bound voyages, they selected an island several hundred miles to the north, which they named Mozambique. This heavily fortified island and the Portuguese ships that anchored there were attacked almost annually by the Dutch and British. Over the centuries at least a hundred richly laden Portuguese East Indiamen were sunk there; most by enemy action, but some were scuttled to keep their riches out of enemies' hands and others sank in storms.

In 1996 the government of Mozambique invited international salvage companies to work in their waters, but few accepted because the country had just ended a long civil war and was still unstable. Undeterred by this and the logistical challenges of working in such a distant place, Arquenautas, a company led by German Count Niki Sandizel, accepted the challenge and signed an agreement with the government in 1998. Sandizel's partners included: Dr. Margaret Rule, of *Mary Rose* fame; Dom Duarte, the pretender to the Crown of Portugal; and the Espiritu Santos Bank of Portugal. Starting in 2002 at Mozambique Island, Arquenautas found valuable wrecks during the first week and have found over thirty to date. By agreement with the government, the company hasn't revealed details about its finds but is known to have brought up millions of dollars in treasure and artifacts. The government has allowed the Arquenautas to sell some artifacts to raise operating funds.

By the end of the seventeenth century, the Portuguese were struggling to maintain their possessions in the Indian Ocean. The Portuguese were threatened by the Dutch, British and Arabs, who did their best to wrest the lucrative Indian Ocean trade monopolies from Portugal. In 1696 the local Omani Arabs rebelled against the Portuguese in Kenya. They laid siege to the port of Mombassa, a Portuguese stronghold in that area. In response, a small fleet of ships from Goa, India, the main Portuguese administrative center outside Lisbon, was dispatched to break the siege. One of this fleet, the *Santo Antonio de Tanna,* was lost right next to Fort Jesus where most of the Portuguese sought refuge. Eventually the fort capitulated, inflicting a serious blow to the Portuguese trade monopoly of this region.

Starting in 1977 Texas A and M University's Institute of Nautical Archaeology worked for three seasons on the *Santo Antonio de Tanna* site under the auspices of the National Museum of Kenya. An international team spent thousands of hours excavating the wreck in the shallow waters in the shadow of Fort Jesus. Once the excavation was completed, two years were dedicated to preserving, cataloguing and studying the abundance of objects recovered. The archaeological data obtained furnished valuable information about the ship's construction and what vessels of the period carried.

A ROMANTIC TALE

In many instances, East Indiamen damaged during storms while rounding the southern tip of Africa would either limp into nearby Madagascar for repairs or go farther east and stop at Mauritius Island in the Indian Ocean. The island's first visitors may have been shipwreck victims. The French, realizing the strategic importance of Mauritius, first settled there in 1721 and held it until 1810, when the British seized it. Over the years more than 600 ships of various nations have gone down along the island's miles of coast.

One of the most interesting of these was the *St. Géran,* a 600-ton ship of the French East India Company, lost in 1744. She was bringing the colony its first sugar-refining machinery and some desperately needed currency—more than 100,000 Spanish pieces of eight and more than 200,000 French copper coins. The *St. Géran's* captain overshot the main port on the western side of the island and was forced to anchor for the night off the northeast shore. Before dawn, a storm struck and drove the vessel up on a reef where she was battered by pounding surf. Jagged coral teeth quickly ripped the bottom out and within minutes the ship went to pieces. Only ten of the 267 people aboard reached shore alive.

The story of the *St. Géran* is familiar to almost every French person. The shipwreck inspired Bernardin de Saint-Pierre's *Paul et Virginie,* a classic novel published in 1788. The idyllic-tragic romance of two young lovers aboard the doomed ship has been published in more than 200 editions in numerous languages.

In 1977 a spear-fisherman discovered the wreck of the *St. Géran* by chance when he spotted twenty-two iron cannon and a large bronze bell scattered along the reef in very shallow, churning water. Inevitably, news of the find spread, and an underwater stampede ensued as salvors rushed to the site. Many salvors used dynamite on the reef. Silver coins began appearing by the hundreds, and underwater fights broke out as divers battled each other with spear-guns and knives. Once all visible artifacts had been plucked from the site, the wreck was abandoned to the buffeting surf, until Jean-Yves Blot, a young French underwater archaeologist, launched a project to excavate the wreck further.

As a child, Blot read *Paul et Virginie* and became fascinated by the *St. Géran.* He learned to dive at sixteen so that he could some day find the famous wreck. In August 1978, following six months working with me on a shipwreck in the Florida Keys, he went to Mauritius to fulfill his dream, unaware that the wreck had been found and plundered a year earlier. He dove on the site several times and was encouraged by what he saw: thick coral growth, which, he reasoned, probably concealed a considerable amount of *St. Géran* material.

It took Blot a year and a half to get a permit from the government of Mauritius and organize a three-month expedition, which he invited me to join. Our first task was by far the most challenging. The ship's remains lie tantalizingly close to the surface, in 3 to 10 feet (1 to 3 m) of water, but the area is subjected to relentless pounding surf. It was like working inside a heavy-duty washing machine. It took us almost a month, working from sunrise to sunset, to plot, measure, draw and photograph the site. Then we were ready to excavate.

Blot wanted to tackle the sand pockets first. In the shallowest areas the divers worked tied to a cannon, anchor or coral head to keep from being swept away. Turbulence prohibited the use of any equipment, so we moved the sand by hand, fanning to expose artifacts. The multitude of sand pockets yielded buttons, buckles, striking flints, tacks, nails, pins, beads, lead musket and pistol balls and a great number of coins. Once the sand pockets had been exhausted, we began the more difficult task of extracting artifacts embedded in the coral, using hammers and chisels. Crushed fingers were added to the numerous coral cuts and abrasions we suffered daily. In the deeper water, where we could use a suction pump to move sand off the reef, we found larger objects, including complete swords, pistols, ship's fittings, pewter and silverware cannonballs and other things. The pain and effort were forgotten as we brought to light more than 10,000 artifacts and an equal number of silver and copper coins that had

Diver recovering Spanish pieces of eight off the French East Indiaman *St. Géran*. The easiest ones to recover were in sand pockets; others, embedded in coral, were much more difficult to dig out.

spent almost 250 years underwater on the famed shipwreck. Everything we found is in the Mauritius Maritime Museum, displayed in a new wing dedicated to the *St. Géran*.

IN AUSTRALIAN WATERS

East Indiamen lie in watery graves around the globe, and the west coast of Australia has its fair share. One of these ill-fated Indiamen was the *Batavia*, lost in 1629. In the darkness of a June night, a lookout on the Dutch vessel mistook the breakers for the moon's reflection on turbulent water. Minutes later, the ship shuddered convulsively as the keel scraped along the bottom before grinding to a halt on the jagged edge of a reef.

Sleeping men were hurled from their bunks, waking in terror to the sound of rending timbers. Captain Pelsart ordered the heavy cannon thrown overboard in a vain attempt to lighten the ship, but she was already doomed and within two hours had broken up. Most of those aboard reached the safety of several nearby cays. Pelsart sailed for Java in a small boat to get assistance, leaving some 300 survivors stranded on the barren cays. Unable to find food or water, they managed to salvage some ship's stores that had floated free of the wreck.

The meager supplies couldn't sustain so many people, and a gang of crew members instituted a reign of terror. They seized men as they slept, dragged them to the water's edge and drowned them. Women and children were slaughtered, their throats cut. By the time the savage orgy was over, a week after the wreck, more than 125 people had been murdered and another forty had drowned trying to swim to neighboring inlets to escape the crazed crew. Some did reach safety and managed to repel the mutineers, but their numbers dwindled daily as starvation and thirst overtook them. By the time Pelsart returned five months later with a rescue ship, only forty-seven people remained alive. The mutineers among them were tried and hanged on the spot. In 2000 land archaeologists conducted excavations on the main cay where the survivors had lived and recovered the bones of dozens of the survivors and mutineers. Chop marks on human bones made it clear that some of the survivors had been butchered for food by the mutineers. A replica of the *Batavia*, which had been constructed in Holland, sailed to Australia in 2000 where it is on permanent display. Most of the artifacts and treasure recovered from the *Batavia* are in the Western Australian Museum in Fremantle, the port of Perth.

To modern salvors, the *Batavia*, in spite of her grisly history, was a dream wreck. Over 250,000 silver guilders and a casket of jewels went down with her. At an average price of $200 each, the coins alone were worth some $50 million in 1963 dollars. That was the year that a diver named Hugh Edwards discovered the site while spearing fish. Once his find was known, a scene reminiscent of Australia's nineteenth-century gold rush took place. Amateur scuba enthusiasts flocked to the site by the hundreds, scooping up handfuls of coins, filling buckets at a feverish pace. The total number salvaged is unknown, but there is general accord among local divers that the bulk of the Dutch treasure is still buried under the shifting sands and thick coral growth of the reef.

The best-known and most controversial wreck off Western Australia is the Dutch *Gilt Dragon,* which was destroyed on a shallow reef in 1656. The ship was wrecked at a point about an hour's drive up the coast from modern Perth while carrying a rich cargo and 193 passengers, only seventy-five of whom survived and reached Java. Numerous Dutch salvage expeditions failed to find the wreck. For three centuries it lay undisturbed, until Alan Robinson, a master pearl diver, chanced upon the site in 1957. He kept his discovery secret for seven years, working the site using his hands to fan away sand and rip apart treasure-concealing coral.

In 1964 the government learned of the find and took possession of the site, confiscating all the treasure and artifacts Robinson had recovered. He took the government to court and embarked on a thirteen-year campaign to regain "his" wreck. He eventually did, but it cost him his marriage. During the years of litigation he spent time in both a prison and a mental hospital. During a recent trip to Fremantle I learned that sport divers are still plundering the *Gilt Dragon* and finding large quantities of silver coins, which they have been selling in other countries.

In Australia there is an extraordinary East Indiaman wreck site that actually conforms to a Hollywood shipwreck fantasy: the seafloor is paved solidly with ancient coins and other treasures that are fastened to the bottom by a thin coating of coral and can be pried loose with a diving knife. This dream wreck's location has been widely known since 1927, when fragments of it were found on the nearby shore, but—incredibly—less than 1 percent of the treasure has been recovered. Nevertheless, there is a very good reason the *Zuytdorp* hasn't been excavated.

The site lies off one of Western Australia's most desolate stretches. Even today, it can be reached only with difficulty. Little lives in this waterless region but kangaroos, wild goats, emu and a few other animals. In 1712 the treasure-laden *Zuytdorp* was sailing between Holland and Batavia when it disappeared without a trace. The word "Zuytdorp" carved on a large rock near the wreck site indicated that some survivors made it to shore. What became of them remains a mystery.

In 1939 a Perth newspaper organized the first expedition to go after the *Zuytdorp*'s silver. Like the many who came after them, the expeditioners had to content themselves with imagining the sunken treasure, as they stared down from the 200-foot (60 m) cliff that overlooks the site. The treasure is guarded by the sea—by waves so enormous that they sometimes appear to be a continuing series of tidal waves thundering onto the shore in rapid succession. The waves originate off the east coast of Africa, and, as they travel across the Indian Ocean, they gain power until they break with unrestrained fury in the area where the *Zuytdorp* lies. The combers reach their peak more than one-half mile (about 1 km) out, and only a madman would try to swim through or under them to reach the wreck site.

Several years ago, a team of divers determined to overcome all obstacles set out to salvage the wreck. They flew in by helicopter, set up camp on the cliff and prepared to wait for a possible diving day. And wait they did. Day after day, tortured by voracious mosquitoes and stinging flies, they cursed the breakers as high as houses and the pounding surf ringing in their ears, as they endured the long wait. One morning, after almost six months at the site, they woke to diminished sound. Looking down, they were thrilled to see that the breakers were "only" about 15 feet (4.5 m) high. The men lowered their gear to the tiny beach at the base of the cliff and climbed down after it.

Two of the first four men to enter the water misjudged the timing of the breakers and were flung ashore with broken bones. The other two made it through the punishing waves by hugging the bottom, pulling themselves along. They were the first to gaze on the fabulous silver-strewn seabed. What they saw was well worth the wait. An area of about 130 by 200 feet (40 by 60 m) was so solidly paved with tens of thousands of Dutch and Spanish silver coins that it was difficult to see the coral they were embedded in. The two men pried loose coin after coin, filling their canvas bags to the top; then spilling out half of them because the bags were too heavy to carry. They also grabbed several gold snuffboxes, a gold bosun's pipe and about a dozen ornate gold uniform buttons before going ashore to see how their comrades were faring.

The safety of land was a mere 200 feet (60 m) from the inner edge of the wreck, but the surf turned that distance into what seemed like an interminable nightmare. One diver dropped his bag when he was dashed onto the rocks, his collarbone and leg broken. The other diver was luckier. He was flung ashore, exhausted, cut and scraped by the coral, but still holding his goody bag. Thus ended the expedition.

Successive attempts to harvest the great wealth of the *Zuytdorp* were even less successful, and a number of divers have been seriously injured. Several years ago the Australian government declared the *Zuytdorp* off limits to all divers, and so the bottom is still paved with treasure.

CLOSER TO HOME

The Dutch East Indiamen lost on the coast of Western Australia had voyaged for more than 10,000 nautical miles (over 18,000 km) before meeting their fate. Other East Indiamen didn't get far at all. Two sank before they were out of sight of Holland's coast—the *Anna Catharina* and the *Vliegenthart* (*Flying Hart*), which sailed for the Far East from the port of Rammekens on February 3, 1735. Both ships were loaded with a considerable amount of gold and silver specie, as well as other cargo. A pilot boat was assigned to escort them across the treacherous Schelder sandbank. As a result of pilot error, both ships struck upon the bank and quickly broke up and sank in rough seas. There was not one survivor among the 461 seamen, soldiers and merchants on both vessels.

The navigational bronze astrolabe—used for establishing latitude—recovered from the *Batavia*.

A few days later, the *Vliegenthart* was located by an English salvor, James Bushnell. Using a diving bell, he recovered a few pieces of artillery but little else. Almost 250 years later, Professor Gunter Schiler, a cartographic historian at the University of Utrecht, found a chart marking the shipwreck location. He contacted two well-known English treasure hunters, John Rose and Rex Cowan, to organize a search for the vessel. In 1979 they obtained a concession from the Dutch government. Despite having a chart with X marking the spot where the wreck lay, it took Rose and Cowan three summers to find the *Vliegenthart,* most of which was buried under deep mud, with a magnetometer.

In 1982 an Anglo-Dutch team, in collaboration with Amsterdam's Rijksmuseum, started surveying and excavating. Work proceeded slowly because of low visibility and poor diving conditions, but they eventually recovered a bronze cannon, several Chinese porcelain bowls, a nice collection of delicate Bavarian glassware, fine pewter tableware, a brass French horn, more than 200 bottles of German and French white and red wines, hundreds of Spanish silver coins and a few Dutch gold coins.

After they ended the season, the site was looted, and unknown quantities of artifacts and some treasure were removed. The next summer, before starting to excavate, they had to remove sand that winter storms had piled on the wreck and eliminate countless potentially entangling fish nets snagged on the bottom. Then they found what every treasure-hunter fantasizes about: a treasure chest. The pine chest still bore traces of the linen and rope once wrapped around it. They shook their heads in disbelief as they opened the lid. Inside were more than 2,000 Spanish pieces of eight and exactly 2,000 gold ducats, minted in Holland and all dated 1729. These coins had never been circulated, which greatly enhanced their value.

Several years later they found an identical chest containing an identical amount of silver and gold coins. According to the ship's manifest there should be several more such chests on the wreck. The *Vliegenthart* project continues each summer, with interesting and profitable finds. The Dutch government receives 25 percent of what is brought up for display in the Rijksmuseum. Initially it was thought five years would suffice to excavate the wreck. However, the shipwreck is spread over a much greater area than first believed, and at the end of the 2002 season the salvors estimate it will take another eight to ten years to complete the project. It will take an estimated five years before the entire site is excavated, and then Rose and Cowan plan to go after the sister ship, the *Anna Catharina,* which lies nearby.

The Dutch East Indiaman *Amsterdam,* commanded by Captain Willem Klump, set sail for Batavia from Holland in November 1748 with 385 passengers and crew. Strong headwinds made the passage through the English Channel very difficult and soon after, wallowing in brutal seas, the ship struck a sandbank close to England's southeast coast. The *Amsterdam's* rudder was lost, and the ship ran aground at Hastings. Most of those aboard reached shore safely, and the Dutch managed to get all twenty-eight large chests of silver ingots to the beach before the vessel began to break up. English villagers also managed to remove some of the ship's cargo before she was swallowed by shifting sands.

Over the centuries, the shoreline has moved about a one-quarter mile (400 m) seaward, and at certain times of the year when there are unusually low tides, the outline of the ship is visible. In 1969, during a spring tide, men working at a nearby sewage outfall used a backhoe to dig around the wreck and found hundreds of well-preserved artifacts. Peter Marsden, an archaeologist with the London Museum who specializes in Roman excavations around London, heard of this plundering and organized an excavation project under the auspices of the museum.

His survey of the site showed that the *Amsterdam's* entire hull was intact to the level of her second gun deck. She was the nearest thing to the *Vasa* in British waters. During periods when the exposed hull was out of the water, Marsden and his team recovered thousands of artifacts from the wreck. In 1975 the Dutch government laid claim to the wreck, announcing they wanted to raise the entire hull and tow it back to Amsterdam. The Dutch government built a cofferdam around the hull, removed all the mud inside and around the ship, attached pontoons to her and at high tide tried to pull her off the bottom and tow her back to Holland. This engineering feat was ambitious but not feasible as well as quite expensive. After numerous attempts they were unable to move the ship and finally gave up. Instead they built a full-size replica of the *Amsterdam,* which is berthed adjacent to the Dutch Maritime Museum in Amsterdam.

INGOTS AND DIAMONDS

After he excavated the Spanish Armada ship *Girona* (see Chapter 5), Robert Stenuit began researching East Indiamen in European archives. His studies led to his discovery of the Danish East India Company ship *Wendela,* lost in 1737 off Fetlar Island, and the Dutch East Indiaman *Lastdrager,* lost in 1653 on Yell Island—both in the Shetland Islands north of Scotland. He recovered an interesting collection of artifacts and treasure from both wrecks. His next target was the Dutch East Indiaman *Slot ter Hooge,* a ship of 850 tons commanded by Captain Steven Boghoute, which set sail from Holland for Batavia with a crew of 250 on November 19, 1724. The ship carried fifteen chests of silver bars, chests of Spanish pieces of eight and other valuables. She encountered a fierce Atlantic gale off the coast of Portugal and was driven off course toward Madeira Island, to be wrecked by night on the small island of Porto Santo. Only thirty-three men survived.

The Dutch East India Company hired John Lethbridge, an Englishman who was a technical genius and one of the best salvage divers of the time, to recover the treasure.

NEXT PAGE: After the French ship *St. Géran* wrecked on a reef off Mauritius Island, Virginia's body washed up on shore along with parts of the ship.

He used his "diving machine," which consisted of an irregular metal cylinder just tall enough to enclose a man. Armholes enabled the diver to work with his hands, and a glass window afforded visibility. The device had no air supply other than the air trapped inside before the chamber was closed, but it did have two valves on the top, which could be opened so that air could be pumped in with a bellows whenever the diver surfaced. The wreck was in 60 feet (18 m) of water, and Lethbridge was able to recover three tons of silver ingots and three large chests of silver coins. He was still at work on the wreck ten years after it sank, by which time the remaining treasure was so deeply buried under the sand that he had to give up.

Stenuit knew from the records that the ship lay somewhere around Porto Santo Island, but he wanted a more precise location before starting his search. He had a

Diver recovering gold and silver coins from a sand pocket on the *St. Géran*.

stroke of luck. When he was in London, *Vliegenthart* salvor Rex Cowan's wife, Zélide, showed him an article written in 1880 dealing with the life of John Lethbridge. There were two illustrations that had been copied from a silver tankard, since lost. One showed Lethbridge's salvage boat and his "diving machine" being lowered into the water. The other was a drawing of Porto Santo. Not only did it show the *Slot ter Hooge* sinking, but it gave the position of the disaster in latitude and longitude.

After Stenuit entered into an agreement with the Dutch government, which was to receive 25 percent of the recovery, the Portuguese disclaimed any rights to the wreck and gave Stenuit an exclusive license to recover and export any treasure he found. In May 1974 Stenuit arrived at Porto Santo with a salvage boat and dropped anchor where the illustrations had said the wreck lay. Going down for his first dive, Stenuit found that his anchor was right on top of one of the large anchors of the *Slot ter Hooge*.

Near the anchor were two half-buried iron cannon, hundreds of cannonballs, metal fittings from the ship's rudder and dozens of wine bottles, their corks still secured with twists of copper wire. A small brass cannon and a Dutch silver coin dated 1724 confirmed the wreck's identity. There was a lot of sand on the site that Stenuit and his divers first tried to blow away with a water jet. This method didn't work well, so they used an airlift to suck up tons of sand and expose thousands of artifacts. They found silver coins, a brass apothecary's mortar, a complete set of brass measuring weights and a beautiful little gold cuff link. By mid-August the wreck was almost entirely uncovered, but they had found none of the silver ingots. At first Stenuit thought Lethbridge must have salvaged all of them; but then a diver found one.

Almost daily for the next two weeks, as weather changes signaled the end of the season, they found one or two bars; then, next to a cannon, a treasure chest crammed with more than a hundred neatly stacked silver bars. Stenuit left the chest in place and called a friend in Belgium to bring an underwater movie camera. About this time a storm struck, and the divers took a few days' rest while awaiting the arrival of the photographer. When they went to the site with him they found that all but fifteen of the bars had been stolen. Stenuit suspected that some local sport divers were responsible. He convinced their leader to dig up the bars from his backyard and return them.

A more serious problem was increasing friction between the islanders and Stenuit's team. Local Portuguese authorities seized the silver bars and everything else Stenuit had recovered during the summer, claiming that everything belonged to the government. Stenuit produced documents showing clearly that the Portuguese government had relinquished all rights to the wreck, but local officials insisted that he and his team leave the island. Stenuit pursued his claim in the International Court in The Hague, and after seven years almost everything was returned to him and the Dutch government.

Two years later Stenuit pursued another Dutch East Indiaman, lost off the remote island of St. Helena in the South Atlantic. In June 1613 two Portuguese carracks sailing from the East Indies back to Lisbon anchored off this island to obtain fresh water. Four large Dutch East Indiamen also stopped for water, and a heated battle ensued. One of the Dutch ships, the 540-ton *Witte Leeuw* (White Lion) commanded by Captain Roelof Simonsz, blew up and sank in about 115 feet (35 m) of water with very few survivors. The other Dutch ships disengaged and sailed directly for Holland.

At low tide, the wreck of the Dutch East Indiamen *Amsterdam* is visible at certain times of the year on the beach at Hastings, England.

Stenuit was attracted to the *Witte Leeuw* because she carried not only the usual cargo of eastern spices, silks, porcelains and other luxury goods, but also 1,311 diamonds. On his third day of searching, in May 1976, Stenuit found the wreck with side-scan sonar. The bottom was littered with cannon, anchors, lead sheathing, timbers, bottles, ceramic jugs and thousands of pieces of broken porcelain. What the divers found next was as electrifying as it was unexpected. The airlift removed 10 feet (3 m) of sand to reveal large sections of the ship's wooden lower hull. Scattered over the timbers were thousands of intact blue-and-white porcelain plates, platters, bowls and cups from the Ming Dynasty. Diving conditions were ideal—the water was warm and clear—and day after day for seven months the airlift sucked up and spewed forth hundreds of tons of sand and mud, until it appeared that the excavation was completed. But where, Stenuit wondered, were the diamonds? He concluded that when the ship blew up, the stern castle, where valuable items such as the diamonds would have been stored, had detached itself from the main hull and drifted away in the current. He was quite content with having found the cache of porcelain and thousands of other artifacts, the most enchanting of which was a lovely silver chain with a silver bosun's pipe.

TREASURE IN THE SOUTH CHINA SEA

In 1983, on the other side of the world, the chance discovery of 22,000 pieces of intact Ming Dynasty porcelain from an old Asian trading ship in the China Sea netted Michael Hatcher $2 million. The auction house warned that Hatcher would flood the market trying to sell so many pieces at once; however, they underestimated the public's fascination with shipwreck artifacts, and every one of the pieces sold fetched a higher price then anticipated. Hatcher set up a commercial salvage company in Australia in 1970 to strip World War II merchantmen and warships of their cargoes of tin, rubber and scrap metals. In 1981 he discovered the Dutch submarine K-XVII, which sank in the South China Sea in 1941 after striking a Japanese mine. He recovered the steering wheel and other artifacts that the Dutch government were only too happy to receive for their maritime museum. He was a millionaire at forty. After his serendipitous Ming find he focused on old shipwrecks; picking porcelain off the bottom is a lot easier than spending months cutting into modern steel ships. He began collecting old charts and hired students to do research in the Dutch East India Company Archives in Holland. The best target they came up with was *Geldermalsen,* an East Indiaman that sailed from Nanking, China, with 343 tons of tea, 239,000 pieces of Chinese porcelain and more than 100 pounds (45 kg) of gold ingots. The ship was so overloaded that heavy porcelain replaced the normal ballast of rocks. Some time during the summer of 1752, the ship was en route to Batavia, before heading back to Holland, when she struck a reef in the South China Sea, taking all but thirty-two of those aboard down with her.

Gemstones found on an unidentified Portuguese East Indiaman wreck— c. 1640—off Malacca, Malaysia.

Research narrowed the search down to an area of about 100 square miles (260 km²), and in early March 1985 Hatcher began the search, aided by Max de Rham, a Swiss marine geophysicist who specialized in high-tech electronic search equipment. For two months they dragged side-scan sonar and magnetometer sensor heads around hundreds of reefs in the search zone. By the end of April they had spent more than $400,000, and Hatcher called a halt to the expedition. De Rham begged for just one more day—and on that day they found the *Geldermalsen.* Divers spotted two large cannon and thousands of porcelain shards at a depth of 130 feet (40 m). Probing into the mud with their hands, they could feel timbers. They extracted dozens of intact pieces of blue-and-white porcelain from several test holes. The expedition was just about out of food, water and fuel, so they returned to their home port of Singapore, where experts identified the porcelain as synchronous with the *Geldermalsen.*

Hatcher returned to his "secret reef" with a large salvage vessel, new diving and salvage equipment, and a team of fifteen commercial divers. Within minutes of starting work with an airlift, he knew he had a gold mine. Complete wooden crates and boxes took shape in the gloom of the deep water. As the divers pried open the lids, they saw row upon row of tea cups, plates, bowls, butter tubs, teapots, gravy bowls, jugs and cuspidors. They were all hand-painted in blue and white, with the familiar Chinese vistas of arched bridges, river landscapes, lattice fences, peonies and fishermen on every piece.

Tea leaves covered every inch of the bottom, and as the airlift sucked up the bottom silt, the leaves showered down on the divers like raindrops. As Hatcher described it, the excavation was like "working in a gigantic teapot." The most challenging part of the operation was sending the porcelain to the surface. The crane aboard the salvage boat operated hour after hour pulling up tens of thousands of pieces of porcelain, but no matter how fast the crew worked on the surface, there was always a backlog waiting on the bottom. As they dug into the wreck they discovered that the whole lower hull was intact and it was there that they made the best finds. During the third week, they found 17 gold ingots, and by the end of the expedition they had recovered a total of 125 ingots. Eighteen were in the shape of the famous Nanking shoe, stamped with the symbols of longevity and wealth.

It took four tiring months to recover the greatest collection of Ching Dynasty porcelain ever found—more than 170,000 pieces in pristine condition. Hatcher sold about half of it at a 1986 auction at Christie's in Amsterdam. The sale netted in excess of $15 million, of which more than $3 million went to Hatcher, with the rest going to his investors and crew. The porcelain became known worldwide as the "Hatcher Collection," and today many of these porcelain pieces are being resold for as much as ten times the auction prices.

Not surprisingly, there was more porcelain on the ship than the cargo manifest stated and two years after Hatcher abandoned the wreck a salvage group from Singapore recovered another 24,000 pieces of intact porcelain from the wreck. Most of it was sold at auction in Switzerland, cloudily identified as coming from "a shipwreck on the high seas." This spurred on a group of Americans who visited the wreck in hopes of finding the chests of diamonds that eluded Hatcher—or so it is believed. The wreck actually lies in Indonesian waters, and this time the authorities were ready. The boat was confiscated, and the Americans languished in jail for over a month until the United States government intervened and obtained their release.

Hatcher also ran afoul of the law. When he heard that fishermen in the Gulf of Thailand had brought up a number of Chinese celadon ceramics, he quickly mounted an expedition. The wreck was 60 miles (100 km) off the coast of Thailand so he assumed the site was not in Thailand's territorial waters and he didn't need to obtain a permit. However, within hours of arriving at the site he was surrounded by four Thai naval vessels. Hatcher refused permission to board his vessel and a standoff ensued. After four days he gave up. His boat was confiscated, and he and his crew were arrested and taken ashore. It took a month of diplomatic haggling and an undisclosed sum of money paid as a "fine" before the boat and crew were released.

Undeterred, Hatcher returned to Thai waters the following year and, again without a permit, recovered a large quantity of large ceramic storage jars from a tenth-century A.D. Asiatic junk. He auctioned them in London and gave all the proceeds to Barnardo House, the orphanage where he had spent several years of his youth.

Once the Indonesians learned the location of the *Geldermalsen* recovery, they wanted Hatcher for questioning and demanded that all the ship's cargo be turned over, but this didn't deter him. In 1999 he was back in Indonesian waters, where he discovered the *Tek Sing (True Star)*, a Chinese vessel that sank in 1822 with 350,000 pieces of Chinese porcelain aboard. He brought up some 20,000 pieces of porcelain that he sent to Singapore for auction. However, there was no real market for such late Chinese porcelain, so he stopped the excavation and went after other shipwrecks in the area. Hatcher is now 65 and quite wealthy but he has no intention of retiring and continues to chase after shipwrecks, spending less than two months a year on his 10,000-acre (4046 ha) cattle ranch in Australia.

Early Chinese porcelain is amazingly popular worldwide; no matter how much turns up on the market, it always finds eager buyers. Ceramic ware from the Ming Dynasty, which ended in 1644, and earlier pieces bring higher prices than later porcelain. One salvor learned this the hard way. Singaporean Dorian Ball, who cut his teeth working with Hatcher, struck out on his own after the British East Indiaman *Diana*, which was lost in 1817 near Malacca, Malaysia. He got a Malaysian permit, raised money and then spent six years searching before he found the wreck. Most of the thousands of pieces of relatively new porcelain he recovered are stored in a warehouse and might never be sold for lack of a market.

9 PRIVATEERS, PIRATES AND MUTINEERS

I N THE CENTURIES FOLLOWING COLUMBUS, the maritime nations of Protestant Europe—England, France and The Netherlands—contested Spain and Portugal's New World monopoly, covetous of the river of gold, silver, pearls, emeralds, sugar, dyewoods and other treasures unloaded from the great galleons at Seville and Cadíz. Privateers and pirates took a leading role in the geopolitical drama played out among the European powers, prowling the seas and preying on treasure galleons, merchantmen and slavers. They nibbled at Iberian claims and ravaged coastal settlements.

PRIVATEERS

For centuries, Portugal's most important New World seaport was Brazil's Bahia de Todos os Santos, familiarly called Bahia. The city, also known as Salvador, was founded in 1549 and remained the colony's capital until 1763. Bahia, with its great sweeping bay, was a major entrepôt for commerce, a port of call for homeward-bound East Indiamen and an irresistible lure to pirates and privateers. During the sixteenth and seventeenth centuries, Bahia suffered repeated attacks by marauders of many nations.

Some 300 shipwrecks of the colonial period lie in the broad, egg-shaped bay of Bahia de Todos os Santos. One, the *Hollandia,* is particularly significant. It was the flagship of Admiral Piet Heyn, a privateer whose daring exploits are commemorated in a Dutch national song. Heyn, a brilliant tactician and an implacable adversary of Catholicism, particularly loathed Spaniards, having survived three terms as a galley slave aboard Spanish

Cannon being raised off the *HMS Bounty.*

vessels. He harassed Portuguese shipping and possessions and later turned his attention to Spanish ships. His most notable accomplishment was the capture, against overwhelming odds, of the 1628 Mexican treasure fleet. The vast amount of plunder he took was a principal factor leading to Dutch independence and the decline of the Spanish Empire.

In 1624, Heyn descended on Bahia with a fleet of thirty-four warships. He sacked the city and seized fifteen richly laden Portuguese ships that were in port. The Dutch East India Company craved control of Brazil's northeast coast. Most of Europe's sugar was cultivated there on Portuguese plantations, using slave labor. The booty Heyn shipped back to company warehouses in Holland included 200 tons of sugar. But the following year, before reinforcements for the Dutch could arrive from Holland, a combined Spanish-Portuguese armada retook Bahia.

Heyn returned to Bahia in March 1627, sweeping boldly into the harbor, where twenty-six large merchant ships lay at anchor near several forts. Surprise was out of the question, so the dauntless Heyn took his flagship, the *Hollandia,* into the midst of the enemy, dropping anchor between the ships *Capitana* and *Almiranta*—the two largest and best-armed of the Portuguese vessels. While half his men returned the enemy's fire, Heyn and the rest of the Dutch scrambled into small boats and boarded the two ships. In less than ten minutes, both massive galleons struck their colors and surrendered. Heyn spurred his men on to take another twenty-two ships right under the noses of the Portuguese shore batteries. His flagship was left within range of the main fort to draw fire while the Dutch ships and the captured Portuguese vessels were moved farther from shore. The *Hollandia's* guns slammed cannonballs into the fort without a break but took such return fire that by sunset the flagship was battered almost beyond recognition, riddled with more than 500 holes. At midnight, Heyn set the remains of his ship ablaze and escaped in a sloop with the surviving members of his crew. Thirty-seven of his men had died and seventy-seven had been wounded. The other Dutch ships combined lost some one hundred men. This was the most rewarding Dutch privateering enterprise to date. The booty amounted to more than two million guilders in gold and silver specie and bullion, worked silver, hides, tobacco, valuable dyewoods, cotton and 2,500 tons of sugar. A company administrator rejoiced: "The Company begins to breathe again…thanks to that courageous sea beggar Piet Heyn."

In 1628 the Mexican treasure fleet was sailing between Veracruz and Havana en route to Spain with a year's supply of gold and silver from the Mexican mines and all of the exotic products from the Orient brought to Mexico on the Manila galleons. Blockading the entrance to Havana Harbor, Heyn forced the Spaniards to seek refuge to the east in Matanzas Bay. With the Dutch at their heels, the Spaniards entered the bay and ran their ships aground. The Dutch were so close that the Spaniards fled ashore without following the standard protocols of throwing treasure overboard or setting the ships afire. When Heyn's men boarded the galleons they could scarcely believe their eyes. It seemed impossible that so much treasure existed in the entire world. After loading as much treasure as they could on their own ships they had to refloat four of the largest galleons to carry the rest. A day after setting sail the Dutch fleet ran into a fierce storm; two of the galleons were wrecked on Grand Bahama Island and totally lost. In 1965 amateur divers accidentally found a part of one of these wrecks and recovered over 25,000 pieces of eight. Since then many divers have found unknown amounts on this site, which is now called Treasure Reef. The rest of the galleons are much sought after but remain elusive.

During the thirty-five years that Heyn prowled the seas he captured more treasure from the Spaniards and Portuguese than all other pirates and privateers of the sixteenth and seventeenth centuries combined. I had long been fascinated by Heyn and

A portrait of the Dutch Admiral Piet Heyn, one of the greatest sea dogs who ever sailed the high seas.

wrote a book about him, *The Capture of the Treasure Fleet.* In May 1979 I set out to locate and excavate the *Hollandia,* with the permission of the Brazilian navy. I had documents showing the wreck's approximate position and hoped we'd find it quickly. But we were hampered by near-opaque water and daunting tidal currents running between two and four knots. In addition, we faced the hazards of working in the center of the main shipping channel. Nine hundred hours of diving and one month turned up nineteen other wrecks, but failed to disclose any sign of the admiral's flagship. I began to think that the contemporary divers who removed the *Hollandia'*s bronze cannon might have salvaged her so thoroughly that nothing remained.

In January 1981 we returned to Bahia to resume the search. Underwater visibility was better, averaging 10 feet (3 m), and our hopes began to soar. After a month, however, when we still hadn't found the ship, we were ready to abandon the project. Then luck prevailed. At the request of the Naval Museum in Rio de Janeiro, we retrieved a sampling of artifacts from each site we found. One day while I was digging a ceramic jar out of the mud on the site of a nineteenth-century shipwreck, I felt a mass of solid metal below it and dug deeper. To my astonishment, it was a large iron cannon that predated the wreck I was exploring by two centuries. At first I thought it might just have been one used as ballast on the later wreck, but when I found a Dutch Bellarmine jar next to the cannon my heart skipped. (These ceramic vessels bear the likeness of Spanish Cardinal Bellarmine, the much-hated governor-general of The Netherlands during Spain's domination of that region.) A

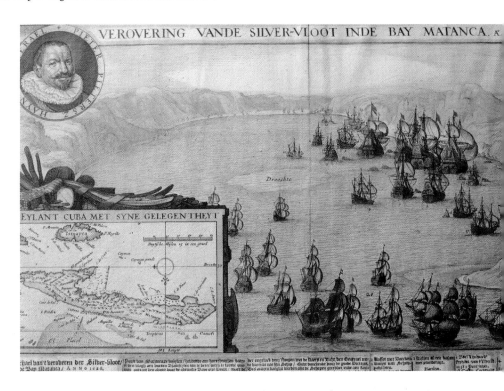

Heyn's fleet of privateers attacking the Spanish treasure fleet in 1628 at Matanzas Bay, Cuba.

series of test holes revealed artifacts that proved the elusive *Hollandia* lay under the nineteenth-century wreck. It took three weeks to remove the later wreck from the site so we could excavate the flagship.

For four months, with the propellers of ships churning dangerously close overhead, we worked the site with an airlift for an average of twelve hours a day. Seventeenth-century divers had removed the *Hollandia'*s bronze guns, but we found six more iron cannon. In all, we recovered more than 5,000 artifacts, and some treasure as well. We brought up cannon, cannonballs, pistols, muskets, swords, lead musket and pistol balls, glass hand grenades, cutlery, a fine collection of pewter and silverware, ceramic objects of all types—including more Bellarmine jars—and many personal items, such as buttons, buckles and leather boots.

In the area of the stern castle we found several brass dividers, sounding leads, fragments of an hourglass and a lead compass rose from the ship's binnacle. Hundreds of gold and silver coins, several gold buttons and 7 pounds (over 3 kg) of gold nuggets were all that remained of the *Hollandia'*s treasure. By far the most significant find was a collection of 200 pounds (90 kg) of human bones, including a number of skulls. I took these remains of Heyn's brave privateers back to Holland, where they were laid to rest with great ceremony. The most important artifacts recovered from the *Hollandia* are on permanent display in the maritime museum in Rio de Janeiro. The remainder were sold at an auction in Amsterdam and ended up in various museums throughout the Netherlands.

PIRATES

The line between piracy and privateering was often blurred. Privateers, who operated under the rule "no prey, no pay," were in effect legally sanctioned pirates. By law they were restricted to attacking enemy shipping and installations. In reality, they were often uncontrollable, their actions indistinguishable from piracy. Depending on the political climate, seaborne raiders sailed as outright pirates or as privateers with letters of marque that might be genuine, forged or bought from corrupt officials.

One of the greatest of these pirates-cum-privateers was Henry Morgan, who in 1670 set off on his most ambitious undertaking—the capture of Panama, one of the richest cities in Spanish America. It was too well protected to capture by seaborne assault, so Morgan planned to land on the Caribbean side of the isthmus and march his 1,400 men overland to approach the city from the rear. Arriving at the mouth of the Chagres River with his pirate fleet, Morgan was leading the way in his flagship, the *Oxford,* when it struck a hidden reef and sank. Four more pirate vessels were also wrecked on the reef.

Morgan's band captured Fort San Lorenzo and then trekked across the jungled mountains of the isthmus and attacked the unsuspecting city. Panama fell after a series of battles and was so badly destroyed that it was abandoned and a new settlement built a short distance to the west. Although Morgan missed the biggest treasure of all—a solid gold altar in the cathedral that Spanish friars disguised with paint—the pirates' plunder was so great that it took 175 mules to carry the enormous treasure back to the ships. The taking of Panama was a big step toward breaking the back of Spain's power. A grateful King Charles II of England later knighted Morgan and sent him to Jamaica as lieutenant governor, where he became a wealthy plantation owner.

In 1954, when I was a diver and salvage expert in the U.S. Marine Corps, I was in Panama for a short time and looked for the *Oxford*. I had, as a guide, a copy of an old manuscript with a chart showing the position where all five of Morgan's ships were wrecked in 1670. The reef, with waves breaking over it, was easy to find and so were vestiges of the pirate wrecks embedded in it. In quite shallow water I found 128 iron and 16 bronze cannon, 22 large anchors, thousands of cannonballs and tons of lead and iron ingots—most likely used as ballast. Also in evidence were hundreds of rum and wine bottles, some still full. I spent an exciting five days digging in the reef and discovered many artifacts from Morgan's ships—from small pewter buckles to muskets as long as a man's body. The only piece of treasure I found was a gold pocket watch inscribed "James Moore, 1657."

Eighteen years passed before I was able to return to Panama with a salvage vessel to explore Morgan's wrecks further. Anticipation turned to disillusionment when I found nothing but deep holes in the coral reef where salvors had used explosives to dislodge the cannon and anchors. I learned from fishermen that, two years earlier, divers from California had salvaged all five of the ships. I wonder if they even realized that they were on Henry Morgan's shipwrecks!

One of the best-known pirate shipwrecks, the *Whydah,* which was lost off Cape Cod, Massachusetts, in 1717, was salvaged in 1984 by a salvor who was very much aware of the history behind it. Barry Clifford, who grew up in nearby Hyannis, first learned the story of the *Whydah* when he was eight years old. Four years later he started diving and searching for the wreck.

Sir Henry Morgan, one of the most famous and successful pirates of the seventeenth century.

The pirate captain Samuel Bellamy, who preyed on Caribbean shipping routes during the first two decades of the eighteenth century, was as notorious as Blackbeard and Captain Kidd. He was based on New Providence Island in the Bahamas and had "fished" treasure from the wrecks of the 1715 Spanish treasure fleet off the Florida coast. In February 1717 "Black Sam" captured the *Whydah,* a slave ship that had just unloaded human cargo at Port Royal, Jamaica, and made it his flagship. In the next two months, he and his crew captured five or six other ships, netting a gratifying amount of plunder. Bellamy, an Englishman whose wife and children lived near Canterbury, then headed for England.

On April 26, 1717, the *Whydah* ran into a storm near Wellfleet, Cape Cod. The crew, drunk on plundered rum, failed to keep the ship from running aground on a sandbar a short distance off the town of Wellfleet. Most of the men drowned, and parts of the ship and its plunder were flung up on nearby beaches. The governor of the Massachusetts colony sent a Boston mapmaker, Captain Southack, to see what could be salvaged. Southack drew a chart of the wreck's position and wrote to the governor: "there have been two hundred men from twenty miles [32 km] distance plundering the wreck," the implication being that whatever treasure was aboard her had been carried off by the scavengers.

Nevertheless, Barry Clifford thought it unlikely that eighteenth-century salvors had extracted all the *Whydah's* treasure from the frigid April waters. Year after year he combed the seafloor off Wellfleet. He found many shipwrecks, but no sign of the *Whydah.* He spent winters pursuing a paper trail in New England's libraries and archives, and his big break came when he found Southack's report and chart showing where the ship had been wrecked.

In 1984 Clifford mounted a full-scale expedition and found the *Whydah* within an hour, using a magnetometer. She was exactly where Southack had reported—in 25 feet (7.5 m) of water. A further 18 feet (5.5 m) of sand were piled on her, however. Several of the *Whydah's* cannon and a Spanish silver coin dated 1684 were recovered in the first hole, dug by two prop-washes mounted on the stern of Clifford's salvage vessel. He soon discovered that the pirate wreck was scattered over an area of several square miles; salvaging it would be difficult and costly.

Three pistols and pistol balls after conservation, recovered from one of Henry Morgan's wrecks lost off Panama in 1670.

The first summer, divers found loot galore: more than 1,000 silver and gold coins, several small gold ingots, dozens of pieces of gold jewelry and hundreds of artifacts whose origins reflected the pirate's varied prey. The wreck was painstakingly excavated over six summers, and the total amount of treasure and artifacts recovered was valued at US$5 million. For Clifford, the most valuable find was the *Whydah's* bronze bell with the ship's name on it. Scholars were particularly interested in 200 unusual gold beads from Africa made by the lost-wax process. They were probably taken from a slaver who had acquired them on the Ivory Coast from the Akan people in what is now Ghana. Bellamy and his pirates seemed more real to the divers when they found a pair of pistols tied at the ends of a silk sash so they could be slung around a pirate's neck, allowing him to continue firing when one pistol was spent.

The divers had to work in cold, dirty water and remove hundreds of tons of sand to find the treasures of the *Whydah,* but the biggest problem Clifford faced wasn't under water. Soon after he found the wreck, the state of Massachusetts demanded the rights to the wreck and its cargo. Clifford challenged the state and, after a three-year court battle, won exclusive rights to the shipwreck.

The following year investors poured $6 million into the *Whydah* project; when that money ran out, Clifford sold his house to keep going. Unsubstantiated reports state that the ship had over 5 tons of gold and silver when lost, and Clifford is still determined to find it. For the last two decades he has spent a month or two searching each year, thus far finding artifacts rather than precious bullion or coins. He thought the missing treasure would be on or close to the main hull of the wreck; however, when he reached the lower deck of the hull in 1998 there was none. Many historians believe that when the ship first wrecked the local residents were able to plunder the bulk of her treasures.

When the 1998 season ended Clifford headed south to a barren reef off the coast of Venezuela in quest of a whole fleet of pirate vessels. In 1678 a fleet of thirty-five French warships and pirate vessels commanded by Vice Admiral Count D'Estrees set out to capture the Dutch stronghold of Curacao Island. Many believe that the pirate vessels were loaded with plunder from previous voyages. During a moonless night the entire fleet wrecked on the uncharted reefs of Aves Island. Documents are scarce about this event, but it is known that eighteen of the ships and over 500 men were lost. Some of the 1,200 survivors reached Martinique, a French island several hundred miles away, in small longboats. The majority made it ashore onto insect-infested, waterless Aves Island, and over half died from hunger and thirst. As word of the disaster spread, bedlam ensued as Spaniards from nearby Venezuela, Dutch from Curacao and French from Martinique fought over the fleet's cannon—more than 1,000, many of them bronze.

But not all of the cannon were raised. A conch fisherman had recently found the site of several of these wrecks, one believed to be *Le Terrible,* the flagship of the fleet. Clifford learned of this accidental find and quickly mounted an expedition. Among his crew of volunteer divers were Maxwell Kennedy, son of the late Robert F. Kennedy, and the sons of the famous authors Norman Mailer and Stanley Karnow, both named Michael.

When the expedition arrived on the site they found a shipwreck graveyard with cannon all over the place. They first worked on *Le Terrible,* which yielded bronze cannon but only a small number of artifacts such as jars. After only a week a Venezuelan patrol boat arrived and chased them away because another American treasure-hunting group had obtained a permit from the Venezuelan government while Clifford and team had been hard at work chopping into the coral reefs in search of treasure and artifacts. Nothing has been done on these wrecks since Clifford returned home vowing to never go after any shipwreck until permission had been obtained from a government, as the rival group failed to raise the necessary funding to undertake the project.

It wasn't long before Clifford made the news again with another pirate discovery. In 2000 he announced the discovery of a pirate ship in Madagascar's Sainte-Marie Harbor, a popular hangout for eighteenth-century pirates. His archaeologist, John De Bry, was able to identify the ship as the *Fiery Dragon,* captained by a pirate named Billy-One-Hand, and lost in 1721. It was laden with treasure worth over $300 million in today's value looted from a Bombay-bound ship carrying religious pilgrims and merchants. Billy-One-Hand was able to buy a pardon from the French governor of Mauritius Island and retired a respectable and wealthy gentleman in France. Clifford and his team found some gold coins and other interesting artifacts on this wreck.

Sainte-Marie Harbor was frequented by pirates of many nationalities. There they replenished stores, obtained water, repaired vessels and refreshed their spirits in the town's many grog shops and brothels. One such pirate was Scottish-born Captain

William Kidd who lived well on New York's Wall Street with Turkish carpets on his floor, a cellar full of casks of Madeira wine and a pew at Trinity Church. He is one of history's most ill-fated pirates. He actually started out as a privateer; charged with hunting down pirates, he had a letter-of-marque from the governor of New York, but this document was lost (until 1911 when a researcher found it in a British archive). Pressured by a mutinous crew, he turned to piracy in the Indian Ocean. Eventually he was captured, tried and hung in London in 1701, his body displayed in an iron cage as a warning to kindred souls.

Kidd's vessel was the *Adventure Gally,* so named because it could be rowed when necessary. Shortly after finding the *Fiery Dragon,* Clifford and De Bry found the *Adventure Gally* nearby. They made three expeditions to the *Adventure Gally* sponsored by the Discovery Television Network. They didn't expect to find much since Kidd had scuttled the ship because the hull was rotten and leaking badly. He burned the part of the ship sticking out of water to recover structural iron and fittings that could be sold.

THE QUEEN ANNE'S REVENGE

Blackbeard the pirate was a giant of a man who cultivated a fearsome aspect that included slow-burning hemp fuses woven into his great wild beard. His real name was Edward Teach, and he gained a reputation as one of the most bloodthirsty of all pirates, terrorizing shipping in the Caribbean and along the Carolina and Virginia coasts. Even his own crew feared him. In spite of this he seems to have had a way with the ladies; he is reputed to have married no fewer than fourteen times. On November 22, 1718, he met his doom when two Royal Navy sloops, under command of Lieutenant Robert Maynard, surprised him at Ocracoke Inlet, on the Outer Banks of North Carolina. A terrific battle ensued, and Blackbeard and Maynard engaged in a fierce duel. Blackbeard was wounded several times before he finally fell. The victorious Maynard had Blackbeard's massive head cut off to hang from the bowsprit of his ship as he sailed back to Virginia. It is said that Blackbeard's headless body swam around the ship several times before sinking, and that his skull was eventually plated with silver and used as a drinking cup. Today three people claim to own his skull.

In 1996 the North Carolina Underwater Archaeology Unit hired Intersal Inc., a Florida firm devoted to locating and excavating historical shipwrecks, to find the wreck of the *Queen Anne's Revenge,* which had been Blackbeard's flagship for six months until it ran aground off the Outer Banks.

The British-built ship began life in 1710 as the *Concord* but was seized by French privateers a year later, rechristened the *Concorde* and used as a slaver carrying slaves, gold dust, silver and jewelry from Africa to the Caribbean until Blackbeard got his hands on her. He renamed her and added twenty additional cannon, making her unusually well armed even for a pirate vessel. However, within six months she ran aground, and he had her stripped and burned after removing valuables.

The site was narrowed down through research in historical documents to near Fort Macon at the entrance to Beaufort Inlet. Intersal divers located the wreck using

CAPTAIN TEACH, GENERALLY KNOWN AS BLACKBEARD

The pirate Edward Teach, also known as Blackbeard.

Pewter urethral syringe used to cure various types of venereal disease, recovered from the *Queen Anne's Revenge* in October 1988. Analysis of the sediment inside showed a high concentration of mercury.

magnetometers, and a limited excavation project took place yielding cannon, two large anchors, grappling hooks, clusters of cannonballs, rigging parts, barrel hoops, and a host of bricks, bottles and other artifacts. Work ceased when North Carolina legislators cut off funding. However, a team led by underwater archaeologist David Moore has done some excavation, finding pewter plates, ceramics and cannonballs. Moore anticipates continuing and says, "What we hope to find is a multitude of material and a wealth of everyday artifacts connected with the seafaring activities of the most notorious figure ever associated with the Golden Age of Piracy and a man who, over the past 200 years, has become synonymous with the term 'piracy.' We should be afforded an unparalleled glimpse into a little understood society, which, until now, has been shrouded in myth, legend and folklore."

THE CONFEDERATE RAIDER CSS ALABAMA

During the American Civil War the CSS *Alabama* was the Confederacy's deadliest raider, yet she never once berthed in a Confederate port. During a 22-month campaign she circled the world and captured or sank sixty-five Union merchant vessels at a cost to the North of over $6 million. Her epic and deadly maritime exploits greatly boosted Southern moral.

Built in Liverpool, England, as a sloop-of-war, she was commissioned in August 1862 as CSS *Alabama*. Under the command of Captain Raphael Semmes the ship spent the next two months seizing and burning ships in the North Atlantic and intercepting American grain ships bound for Europe. The *Alabama* then wreaked havoc throughout the West Indies and sank USS *Hatteras* along the Texas coast, capturing her crew. She sailed as far as the Indian Ocean and East Indies, destroying seven more ships before heading to Europe.

On June 11, 1864, she arrived in Cherbourg, France, to overhaul and secure supplies. Three days later the American sloop-of-war USS *Kearsarge* arrived and lay in wait outside the harbor. Captain Semmes ordered his ship to sea a few days later to give battle. The *Alabama* was the first to fire, and both ships kept circling one another, firing away. The battle soon turned against the *Alabama* as her powder was old and the *Kearsarge* was protected by chain cables along its sides that deflected Confederate fire. Less than an hour after the first shot was fired the *Alabama* was close to sinking, and Captain Semmes struck his colors and surrendered. The ship went down and most of the survivors were picked up by the *Kearsarge*, although 42 men—including Captain Semmes—were pulled aboard a British yacht and escaped to England.

In 1985 a French navy mine hunter conducting sonar training came upon the *Alabama* in 185 feet (55 m) of water 7 miles off Cherbourg. France notified the U.S. government of the find, and in 1989 the Joint French-American Scientific Committee for Archaeological Exploration was formed to conduct archaeological exploration of the wreck. This Franco-American agreement set a precedent for international cooperation in archaeological research and in the protection of a unique historic shipwreck, recognizing the wreck site as an important heritage resource of both nations.

Naval Commander Max Guerout of the French Ministry of Culture had the task of verifying the vessel's identity. Starting in 1986 he and volunteers, many of them Americans, worked for eight summers on the site. It was not an easy job; the divers had to deal with tidal currents that ran as high as 5 knots (9 km/hr), generally very rough seas and underwater visibility that was often very poor, but they recovered a number of interesting artifacts including weapons, tools, cutlery, bottles, clay smoking pipes, coinage and a smattering of personal effects.

In 1988 the U.S.-based nonprofit CSS *Alabama* Association was founded to conduct scientific exploration on the wreck. In March 1995 the French government and the association signed an agreement making the association the principal investigator of the wreck site. Commander Guerout is co-director of the project with Dr. Gordon Watts, who had retired from East Carolina University and was working for various cultural organizations and governments as an underwater archaeologist. During three seasons the joint Franco-American team completed all of the archaeological data, collecting and recovered hundreds of artifacts that included several of the ship's guns and anchors. After a year's hiatus they worked the site again in 1999 and 2000 and brought up many more artifacts including cannon, bowls, plates, a gravy boat, a spice or condiment bottle with the unidentified contents intact, an ironstone condiment or salve jar, an ornate brass escutcheon for an oil lamp and a lead scupper that channeled water overboard from the weather deck.

MUTINEERS

Centuries ago, life at sea was harsh, mirroring the inequities and brutalities of the age. Only on a pirate ship, where there was relative equality, was a seaman free of the tyranny that oppressed him. An ordinary seaman aboard a naval ship or a merchant vessel had little to look forward to but a lifetime of grueling, repetitive work, low wages, scant benefits, stinking accommodations, foul food and the cut of the lash. He had little hope of advancement and was subject to the whims of despotic and sometimes sadistic officers. It is hardly surprising, then, that mutinies were not uncommon aboard ship.

History's most famous mutiny occurred on April 28, 1789, aboard HMS *Bounty*. The *Bounty*, under British captain William Bligh, was on its way from England to Tahiti to take on a cargo of breadfruit. The starchy fruit was to be introduced to the West Indies as a staple in slaves' diets. Near Tahiti, mutineers, led by Fletcher Christian, seized control of the vessel. Captain Bligh and eighteen men loyal to him were cast away in a small open boat. Their involuntary voyage from Tahiti to Timor covered 3,618 nautical miles (5822 km) in forty-one days. Not a man was lost.

Sixteen of the mutineers elected to remain in Tahiti. Eight others joined Fletcher Christian and, with six Tahitian men and thirteen women, sailed away on the *Bounty* and vanished. The mystery of their fate was solved eighteen years later when a Boston whaling ship found them living on otherwise uninhabited Pitcairn Island, 1,300 miles (2080 km) southeast of Tahiti. After they reached Pitcairn, Christian and his followers had stripped the *Bounty*, run her in close to shore and set her afire. Descendants of the mutineers still live on the island.

Luis Marden, a well-known underwater explorer and a staff writer for *National Geographic* magazine, had always been fascinated by the story of Bligh and the *Bounty*. When he was on assignment in the Fiji Islands he visited the museum in Suva and saw worm-eaten planking, held together with copper fastenings, from the rudder of the *Bounty*. The curator told him it had been fished up from 40 feet (12 m) of water at

Pitcairn in 1933. Marden convinced his editors at *National Geographic* to send him to Pitcairn Island to find the remains of the *Bounty*.

When Marden arrived on the island in 1957, about 150 people lived there; fifty-five were surnamed Christian. They spoke of the arrival of the mutineers and the destruction of the *Bounty* as if these events had happened only recently. The shipwreck, which lay in Bounty Bay, was easily found. Marden hoped to locate the fourteen small cannon she had carried and also expected to find some of the wood from her hull, which had been completely sheathed in copper as protection against shipworms. The two men who had found the rudder in 1933 showed him where it had lain. Donning his scuba tank, Marden went down. He immediately spotted a large copper ingot wedged in a crevice and, soon after, many of the pig-iron bars that had been used as ballast on the

Burial of Sir Francis Drake in a lead casket cast into the sea off Porto Bello, Panama.

Bounty. Nearby he found large bronze pintles, the fastenings on the ship's stern where the rudder was attached. A six-week "famine" followed, during which he saw no trace of the wreck. Then he found the first conclusive evidence of the *Bounty*, a brass oarlock bearing the British Broad Arrow, indicating Royal Navy property.

Soon after, Marden located a large pile of the iron-ingot ballast and beneath it many copper-sheathed planks from the ship's hull and hundreds of copper tacks. HMS *Bounty* had been found. Her guns and almost everything else she carried had been removed. Two years after Marden's discovery, divers from an American yacht found one of her anchors near the entrance to Bounty Bay.

In 1998 a team of archaeologists and divers from James Cook University in Townsville, Australia, arrived to continue exploring the *Bounty*. The expedition's primary task was to locate, define and map all remaining artifacts on the site. The first find was a cannon. For years after Marden's discovery local divers had been picking over the site, chiefly bringing up copper tacks and brass nails that they sold to tourists from the occasional cruise ship to Pitcairn. The Australians found a lead scupper, cannonballs, grapeshot, ceramic shards, copper sheathing and some wood from the hull. The near total absence of personal items suggests that the *Bounty* was stripped before being burned.

There was a second casualty in the *Bounty* drama. When Bligh returned to England with his tale, the Admiralty sent Captain Edward Edwards in pursuit of the mutineers. Edwards sailed from Portsmouth in November 1790 with HMS *Pandora*, a twenty-four-gun frigate. Five months later he reached Tahiti and arrested fourteen of the mutineers who had stayed there; the other two had died. He had a cell built on the *Pandora*'s quarterdeck, which became known as Pandora's Box. It was exposed to the elements and a true hell for the prisoners crammed into it. For five weeks he cruised in search of Christian and the others and then the *Pandora* started the slow voyage home. She never got there.

The *Pandora* met her end on the Great Barrier Reef while trying to pass around the northeast corner of Australia. One afternoon, the lookout high on the mast shouted that the ship was dangerously close to the reef. As they readied to bring her about, she struck the reef with a sickening crash. The crew threw some of the cannon overboard to lighten the ship and vainly attempted to pull her off with stern anchors. Throughout a terrifying night she bounced along the reef, suffering great damage to her hull and the loss of her rudder. Daybreak found her inside the reef, so wounded that not even both bilge pumps could stem the rising water. Captain Edwards ordered his crew to abandon ship.

Little attention was paid to the frantic cries of the prisoners in Pandora's Box, and they would have died if not for one man's compassion. The bosun's mate, one of the last to jump overboard, pulled the bolt on the box and ten prisoners were able to get to safety; the other four, two still in irons, along with thirty-one of the crew, went down with the ship. The survivors spent nineteen days on a deserted cay before setting out in four of the ship's boats on a difficult voyage to Timor, ironically the same landfall Bligh had made two years earlier. They returned to England, where three of the mutineers were hanged from the yardarm, two were pardoned and the others given long prison sentences.

In 1977 Ben Cropp and Steve Domm, both professional underwater photographers, located the Pandora, which they had sought for five years. The Royal Australian Air Force assisted in the search, contributing a Neptune submarine-hunting plane, which carries a magnetometer to detect submerged submarines. Flying close patterns in an area Cropp had defined, the plane found a target and dropped a buoy on the spot. When Cropp and Domm went down the following morning to check the anomaly, they landed right on top of the Pandora. She lay in almost 110 feet (33 m) of water.

Cropp and Domm were in the process of organizing an expedition to salvage the wreck when the Australian government declared the site a protected monument and announced its intention to supervise an excavation. After six years' delay, government funding was found, and Australian archaeologist Ron Coleman was appointed to direct the archaeological survey and excavation. Cropp and Domm joined the twenty-five-member team as photographers.

The lower part of the ship's hull was buried under the sand, but its outline could be discerned on the sandy bottom. Coral growth covered the cannon, anchors and other artifacts. A series of frames about 6 1/2 feet (2 m) square were positioned over the site in order to plot the finds as they were uncovered with an airlift. The work was slow and tedious. Because of the depth, divers were limited to two dives a day of fifteen and twenty-five minutes each. At times, the current was so strong that work stopped for hours.

It took five summers to complete the excavation, which yielded more than 10,000 artifacts. Among them were hundreds of bottles and ceramic objects, weapons, tools, leg irons—most likely the ones used on the Bounty's mutineers—and a surgeon's chest. In the chest they found a urethral syringe of ivory and ebony containing crystals of mercury, as well as ointment jars, pots and bottles. There was also a silver pocket watch, found in 1985, inscribed "J. & J. Jackson, London," with hallmarks showing that it had been made between May 1786 and May 1787.

That same summer of 1985, Luis Marden, the discoverer of the Bounty, joined the expedition and dove on the Pandora. Nearly thirty years after finding the first ship, he became the first person to dive on both wrecks.

In 1996 Townsville's business community formed The Pandora Foundation and raised over $500,000 to complete the Pandora's excavation. For five seasons the divers and archaeologists concentrated on the wreck's stern section where the officers' cabins and storerooms were located. More than 3,000 artifacts were brought to light, many illustrating how the officers lived on board the ship and others offering clues as to the crew's personal life. An additional five years will be required to complete the excavation of the wreck.

10 SHIPWRECKS-IN-WAITING

OME WRECKS ARE LUCKY FINDS; others are located only after painstaking archival research and laborious underwater exploration. And locating a wreck is just the beginning of a long-drawn-out process of exploration and salvage. Sometimes this process is successfully completed, but often it is not. There are many reasons for delay, including physical conditions too daunting to be overcome with the technology currently available and lack of funds.

A FORTUITOUS FIND

In the latter category is the wreck of a ship dating from the thirteenth century A.D. that was found in South Korean waters. One day in 1975, when Korean fisherman Choi Hyunggun pulled up his nets, he was surprised to find six ceramic jars mixed in with the catch. It wasn't the first time that fishermen off Sinan, a district on the southwestern coast of South Korea, had snagged ceramics and ceramic shards heavily encrusted with marine growth. They generally threw them back into the sea. Choi took his finds home, however, and showed them to his wife, who told him to put the "dirty pots" outside. He forgot them until months later when his brother, a teacher, spotted them. Choi removed the encrustations to reveal the translucent green glaze characteristic of celadon, a type of antique Chinese stoneware. He was sure they were ancient and took them to a local museum for identification. To his chagrin, he was told they were imitations.

In January 1976 another fisherman from the same area reported to the government

Treasure from the *Chameau* included gold coins, a silver pocket watch, two large sounding leads, ceramic shards and parts of a sword.

that he had found two intact celadon vessels. Korea's Cultural Properties Preservation Bureau, having heard of Choi's find, decided to investigate. Experts examined the two vessels and Choi's six jars and identified them as authentic pieces from China's Yuan Dynasty (A.D. 1279–1368). The government gave each of the fishermen a $2,000 reward to encourage other fishermen to report similar finds. Officials were aware that the ceramics came from a shipwreck and debated placing the site under naval protection. Meanwhile, news of the discoveries leaked out, and dozens of fishing boats began dragging nets in the area. A considerable quantity of ceramics was fished up and sold to antique dealers. One enterprising fisherman hired a commercial diver, who managed to bring up more than 200 intact celadon vases before the local police learned of his activities, arrested him and confiscated his finds.

A squadron of naval vessels from Seoul was dispatched to the wreck site to prevent further looting and to investigate the wreck with navy divers. The squadron was commanded by Captain Choi Insang, who had an interest in marine archaeology. He was assisted by a history professor, Jho Sung-ho, who had worked on an underwater archaeological project in the Mediterranean several years earlier. The expedition found the Sinan wreck site far from idyllic. The men were challenged by strong bottom currents, high seas and daily storms. The water was black, and the divers, with zero visibility, worked by touch. They were elated to find that most of the vessel's wooden hull was preserved in the mud.

The wreck, a Chinese merchant ship headed for Japan with trade goods, had sunk in about 60 feet (18 m) of water while attempting to cross the Yellow Sea, most likely overcome by a storm. We may never know the name of the ship, her captain or her crew, but we do know that this is one of the oldest Asian trading ships ever found, and it has yielded the largest collection of Yuan Dynasty ceramics found outside China. Although other ancient Asian trading vessels have been found, they were coastal traders. The Sinan wreck is larger: the first ancient ocean-going ship discovered in East Asian waters.

The whole cargo lay exposed on the bottom, and at first the team didn't even have to dig. As winter approached, however, the weather deteriorated even further. By mid-December the divers were so cold that they were biting the rubber mouthpieces of their scuba regulators in two while shivering, and Captain Choi halted the operation.

After three months of steady work on the wreck, divers had recovered more than 6,000 copper coins and 2,000 other artifacts—an incredible number, but a mere fraction of what remained. They brought up many types of ceramic objects: celadon, porcelain, stoneware and painted objects; inkstones; grinding stones; a silver ingot; a wooden bucket; a bamboo basket and art objects cast in various metals. There were some wooden artifacts and even items as small as peppercorns, peach pits, beans and cinnamon bark. After more than seven centuries on the seafloor, several remarkably well-preserved wooden packing crates with their contents saw the light of day. The top of one of the crates was clearly marked with the playing-board grid pattern of the Chinese game of Go, which is still played today.

Prior to the 1977 season on the wreck, the Korean government approached the National Geographic Society for help, since Korea had no diving archaeologists. The society hired Donald Keith—who is now working on the *Gallega* (see Chapter 3), but was then a graduate student at Texas A & M University—to help the Koreans survey and map the site. The navy divers then began bringing up coins and artifacts in such incredible quantities that by the end of the season they had recovered more than 200,000 copper coins and 12,000 intact pieces of pottery of many types. The following year's work was just as productive, but by this time most of the objects exposed on the surface had been recovered. When the 1979 season began, the team utilized an airlift and concentrated on the inside of the hull. Inside one compartment they found more than 200 good-sized red mahogany logs and more than three tons of copper coins, too many even to count.

At the end of the 1979 season, however, the government decided that it could not afford to continue, for a while at least, and called a halt to the operation. Should funds become available, there are plans to bring the wooden hull to the surface so it can be preserved and exhibited along with the ship's fabulous cargo. The site was guarded by naval vessels for several years to prevent looting. What started off as a chance discovery led to one of underwater archaeology's most important finds. To date no further work has been done on this intriguing wreck.

THE ROYAL NANHAI

Swedish engineer Sten Sjostrand was president of a firm in Singapore that constructed large offshore oil platforms but his first love was the sea, and he spent his free time searching for old shipwrecks off Indonesia and Malaysia. After making a number of interesting discoveries he decided to leave the confines of an office and the business and devote his full attention to shipwrecks. I worked with him on several occasions in 1993 and never saw a more obsessed man in my life. To him meals were a waste of time that could be better spent looking for wrecks. Together we found two very valuable Portuguese East Indiamen near Tioman Island off the east coast of Malaysia and made plans to excavate both, but politics came into play. Although I had received a permit from the federal government in Kuala Lumpur, the wrecks were in the waters of Pahang State, and the local sultan refused to acknowledge our rights. We knew better than try to fight with a sultan!

Divers examining several seventh-century Chinese Tang Dynasty dragon jars.

Sjostrand continued on his own, usually alone except for the occasional acquaintance looking for thrills. He had a new boat fully equipped with sonar, a magnetometer and all necessary diving equipment and relied on information from fishermen who had pulled up objects in their nets. In October 1998 Sjostrand made news around the world when he and five others—two Swedes, two Germans and a Thai—were arrested for plundering a wreck site. Apparently the sultan had them under observation and waited for the right moment to nab them. Aboard Sten's boat the authorities found over 500 late–Ming Dynasty bowls, cups and dishes. A search of his home in Mersing turned up more than 17,000 intact Chinese porcelain objects, most of them eleventh-century celadon.

Vikings never take matters lying down; Sjostrand was released and, while he awaited trial, he approached the director of the Maritime Museum in Malacca on the other coast of Malaysia. He knew the museum had sponsored shipwreck groups working off that area. The director realized that Sjostrand was very knowledgeable and knew the locations of many shipwrecks in Malaysia waters and they forged an agreement; henceforth Sjostrand agreed to work only under his direction and to turn over all finds to the museum. Sjostrand was already wealthy and his real passion was to find and excavate old shipwrecks, so he jumped at this opportunity.

The western and eastern Nanhai trade routes were established by the Chinese in 1340 and used for centuries. One route led from China to Malacca and the other to the

Two sixteenth-century blue and white Chinese porcelain figurines found on a junk wreck off Singapore.

Blue and white Chinese Ming Dynasty jarlet found on a junk wreck in the South China Sea off Malaysia.

island of Java in Indonesia. In 1993 Sjostrand found one of the junks from this trade and dubbed it the *Royal Nanhai.* Study of materials recovered from the wreck established that most of the cargo had originated in Siam (Thailand). The wreck most likely sank in a storm around 1460 and went down in 150 feet (46 m) of water. Most of her cargo consisted of iron ore, iron ingots, a large consignment of ceramic storage jars and thousands of Chinese celadon ceramic ware.

The *Royal Nanhai,* so named because of a large elephant-shaped ceramic royal seal that came off the wreck, was the first target of the joint collaboration between the Malacca Museum and Sjostrand. Criminal charges against him were dropped when he agreed to work with the government. He was delighted to no longer be working alone or with a couple of volunteers but with a full team of archaeologists, conservators and divers. Once all visible objects exposed on the seafloor had been picked up, an airlift and other tools were used to excavate the site. Once the remaining cargo and the coral growth covering the wreck had been removed a large section of the wooden bottom and keel of the ship was found. This was raised and taken to the museum for preservation. Over 23,000 artifacts, mainly celadon ware, were recovered. After completion of this excavation, Sjostrand disclosed the locations of four other shipwrecks he had found on his own; these have been surveyed by archaeologists and will be excavated. Discovery of the *Royal Nanhai* shows that one does not have to spend a fortune and have a large team to find important wrecks; Sjostrand the Viking did most of this alone.

THE MARY ROSE

On the other side of the world is a marvelous example of a ship that was finally raised, though for centuries the task seemed impossible. On July 19, 1545, England's King Henry VIII reviewed his fleet from Southsea Castle in Portsmouth as it set sail to repel a French invasion. The most prominent vessel was the *Mary Rose,* a warship that carried ninety-one guns. That day there were 700 men aboard, far exceeding her normal complement of 415. The *Mary Rose* was so heavy that there was barely 20 inches (50 cm) of freeboard between her lower gun ports and the water. Four French galleys converged on her, but before any shots could be fired, the ship heeled sharply to one side, the sea ran into her open gun ports and she sank. There were fewer than three dozen survivors. Ironically, the sea battle never materialized. When the *Mary Rose* went to the bottom, the French ships, for some unknown reason, turned about and headed for France.

King Henry ordered salvage efforts to commence immediately. The *Mary Rose* had sunk in water so shallow that her great masts showed above the surface. Salvors planned to harness the power of the tides to raise the ship. They made a sling of cables underneath the hull, attaching the ends to a surface vessel on either side of the wreck. At low tide the cables would be tightened and, as the tide rose, the warship would be lifted off the bottom and dragged closer to shore. This procedure was to be repeated over and over until the ship was afloat. Unfortunately, she was too heavy and unwieldy, and the plan failed. Several other schemes were equally ineffective, and the pride of King Henry's fleet was abandoned. The mast tops, ravaged by the elements, disappeared after a few decades, and eventually the wreck was forgotten altogether.

Then in 1836, two brothers, John and Charles Deane, who had invented the first practical diving helmets, happened upon the *Mary Rose* while clearing obstructions in the area for local fishermen. Over the next four years they recovered many of the ship's bronze cannon and hundreds of other artifacts, carefully recording the results of their work in drawings. Soon after, the shifting seabed covered the site with mud.

More than a century later, in 1965, Alexander McKee, an English student of history and a diver, resolved to find the *Mary Rose*. He enlisted the help of Dr. Margaret Rule, initially a land archaeologist. The two were confident that the mud would have preserved the wreck. They started searching for it with members of a local sport diving club, but that year found nothing. The following year, McKee discovered an 1841 chart with a red cross marking the spot where the Deane brothers had found the *Mary Rose*. In 1968, realizing that the wreck was probably completely buried, McKee and Rule asked MIT's Dr. Harold Edgerton to help them. Edgerton had recently developed a new type of sonar called a mud-penetrator, which could find large objects buried under the seafloor. During the summer of 1968, he used it to locate the *Mary Rose*.

Over the next ten years, working on a very limited budget, McKee and Rule dug numerous test holes and found convincing evidence that they had indeed located the *Mary Rose*. They also discovered that a substantial portion of the wooden structure remained under the mud. After countless meetings of archaeologists, historians and government officials, a nonprofit organization, the *Mary Rose* Trust, was created, with Prince Charles, the Prince of Wales, who had made numerous dives on the wreck in the past, as its president. Funds began pouring in from various sources, and excavation began in the summer of 1979.

Dr. Rule, the director of the project, had a team of six diving archaeologists working under her. During this first season, most of the work was done by 180 volunteer divers from seven different countries. They made more than 7,000 dives between May and August. Using airlifts, they dug seven trenches across the wreck and recovered thousands of interesting Tudor relics—among them longbows, ceramics, coins, ship's fittings, tools and intact leather shoes. Several skeletons were also recovered, enabling scientists to learn much about Tudor man. The season ended with the raising of a beautiful bronze cannon still mounted on its wooden carriage. The most important discovery was that a large starboard section of the hull was intact and in an exceptional state of preservation.

A photograph of the *Mary Rose* today, taken from the bow. Water is sprayed on the wooden hull to prevent it from drying out.

The 1980 summer season was even more exciting. Volunteers working under the archaeologists' guidance recovered in excess of 3,000 artifacts from inside the *Mary Rose*. Two intact chests were brought up, one containing more than a thousand arrows and the other a barber surgeon's chest, filled with razors, syringes, glass flasks and pots of salves. Among other remarkable finds were two pocket sundials and a shawm, a double-reed wind instrument resembling an oboe.

Most of the following summer season was dedicated to recording and dismantling all the internal structure and cannon in preparation for raising the wooden structure in 1982. The team also brought up 2,958 timbers and 11,362 artifacts. Those of special interest were 140 longbows—the celebrated man-high bows that won so many battles for the English over the centuries—the two oldest compasses found to date, a backgammon table complete with counters, two bosun's pipes, leather jerkins and a manicure set made of bone.

A conservation laboratory was constructed ashore to clean and preserve the 17,000 artifacts recovered, and also to preserve the hull after it was raised. It took several months to build a specially designed 217-ton frame and cradle and position it under the wooden hull. On October 11, 1982, Prince Charles, Dr. Rule and Alexander McKee presided over the climax of one of the greatest marine archaeological projects in history. Thousands of cheering spectators, on the shore and in boats, watched as a floating crane slowly hoisted the hull. As the *Mary Rose* surfaced after 437 years on the seafloor, Dr. Rule exclaimed: "That's a damn strong ship." The project had cost more than $8 million, and since the hull was raised another $3 million have been spent on preserving the hull and artifacts. The *Mary Rose* is now on permanent display in Portsmouth, admired by millions of visitors.

The project had a dramatic impact on Dr. Rule's career. She had learned to dive during its course, and, soon after the *Mary Rose,* she began excavating a Roman galley in the Channel Islands; she has since dedicated her professional life to underwater archaeology. The raising of the *Mary Rose* turned the dream of Alexander McKee into a truly wonderful reality and was a personal triumph for him. One of the most important results of this fantastic expedition was the lesson that under guidance from professional archaeologists volunteer divers can make an outstanding contribution to underwater archaeology.

A TREASURE SHIP IN CANADIAN WATERS

The saga of Canada's most famous treasure shipwreck has yet to have its happy ending. The story began early in July 1725, when *Le Chameau,* a 600-ton transport, sailed from France for the fortress of Louisbourg, at the eastern end of Cape Breton Island, Nova Scotia. Aboard her were 310 crew and passengers. In addition to livestock, munitions and gunpowder, she carried about 300,000 livres in gold and silver coins with which to pay French troops in Canada. (A livre was a French monetary unit and coin, originally equivalent to a pound of silver.) Disaster struck on the night of August 26, when the ship's pilot decided to enter the Louisbourg harbor instead of waiting for the light of day. A gale was blowing and at about 4:00 a.m. the ship struck a submerged rock—known ever since as Chameau Rock. The ship rapidly broke up, and every soul aboard her perished. As the sun came up, it showed the beach littered with bodies and debris from the wreck.

The commandant of the fortress engaged the services of an ex-privateer named Pierre Morpain to salvage the wreck, which was scattered over a wide area of the seafloor. For some reason, it took Morpain more than a year to begin the salvage, by which time a great deal of the wreck had been covered by shifting sands. His methods were primitive: he would drag a grapnel until it snagged something and then send a diver down to investigate. It was excruciating work for the divers, who had to wear a thick coating of grease to protect their bodies in the 40° Fahrenheit (4°C) waters. They found cannon and anchors, but none of the treasure.

The wreck was forgotten for two centuries, until in 1914 a steamship, the SS *Ragna,* sank after striking on Chameau Rock. A diver working for an insurance company surfaced after his first dive shouting that he had seen a great number of gold and silver coins. He vowed to salvage the coins after surveying the *Ragna,* but never got the chance because he drowned several days later. Two other salvage firms went after the *Chameau* treasure soon afterward. One found nothing and the other recovered only several iron cannon. A few years later, a fisherman snagged a chest so heavy that he could barely pull it to the surface. Just as he was lifting the chest into his boat, it split apart

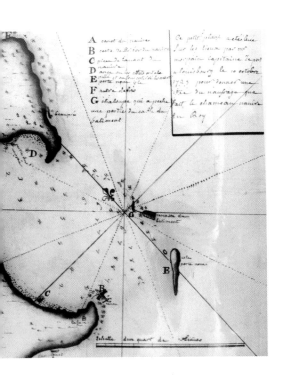

Chart from the French National Archives showing the exact position where the *Chameau* was lost off Louisbourg, Cape Breton.

and he watched forlornly as a cascade of gold and silver coins fell back into the sea. At least he had the chest to substantiate his story.

In 1965 the *Chameau* surrendered her treasure—or at least some of it—to Alex Storm, David MacEachern and Harvey MacLeod, three sport divers who had grown up listening to tales of the *Chameau*. Within minutes after they entered the water near Chameau Rock, they spotted dozens of cannon and several large anchors in about 20 feet (6 m) of water. Their first dive ended abruptly when a 40-foot (12 m) basking shark appeared overhead, but they came up with the first signs of treasure—a silver fork and small silver coin. The second day they found a well-preserved pocket watch with "Hanet, London" inscribed on its silver face, two large sounding leads and more silver coins. Several more days around the rock convinced the men that the treasure was somewhere else, since the wreck had broken up over a large area. For two months they contended with frigid water, strong currents and limited visibility as they followed a trail of cannonballs, ballast, ceramic shards and occasional silver coins.

Finally, on September 22, they found the treasure. Under a shallow layer of sand they encountered gray-green mounds, which originally had been chests and sacks containing coins. When they struck the mounds with hammers, hundreds of gold and silver coins spilled out. They scooped them up in buckets, retrieving eleven silver and 2,000 gold French coins in less than a week. They also found dozens of silver spoons and forks, ceramics, pewterware and numerous ornate sword hilts of brass and silver. Experts estimated the find's value at over $1 million; predictably, rival claimants materialized.

A handful of the thousands of French gold coins recovered from the *Chameau*.

Canada had no laws regarding the recovery of sunken treasure when the three Cape Breton divers found the *Chameau*. Soon after, however, the government ordered the men to surrender everything to customs officials until the matter could be studied. They were unable to dive or to raise money to finance future work on the site. It took the Canadian courts three years to rule that the government was entitled to 10 percent of the find, with the remainder going to the salvors. The government filed an appeal with the Supreme Court; a judgment rendered in June 1971 gave 25 percent to the government and 75 percent to the salvors.

During the six years of litigation, the divers were forbidden to dive on the *Chameau*. When the matter was finally settled, they spent three summers recovering several hundred gold and about a thousand silver coins. Then, it seemed, the treasure petered out. Five additional summers produced a mere handful of silver coins and a few artifacts, so they abandoned the project. The bulk of the treasure is still hidden somewhere between the rock and the beach, where the *Chameau's* debris and the bodies were cast ashore.

During the summer of 1979 my company, Phoenician Explorations, with a permit from Parks Canada and the assistance of Alex Storm, worked on the *Chameau* for almost a month while waiting for better weather to go after our primary target. We did no excavation but using metal detectors we found hundreds of silver coins wedged in narrow cracks in the rocky bottom, which had been missed by Storm and his divers in prior salvage efforts. In 1997 a group of sport divers spent several weeks on the wreck and recovered over a thousand gold and silver coins. Not surprisingly, they prefer to remain anonymous because they were working without authorization from the Canadian government. This just goes to show that no matter how many people work on a wreck and no matter how much is recovered, there is always something more to be found.

THE IRONCLAD MONITOR

The Civil War–era *Monitor,* dubbed the "Yankee cheese box on a raft," was, like the *Mary Rose,* a wreck of considerable historical interest. Unlike the *Mary Rose,* however, she may never see the light of day. A federal ironclad, she defeated the Confederate ironclad *Merrimack* at Hampton Roads, Virginia, on March 9, 1862. This battle probably had little effect on the outcome of the Civil War, but it did mark a new era in naval warfare, since it was the first time that two ironclads fought.

Later that same year, on December 29, 1862, the *Rhode Island,* a paddle-wheel steamer, towed the *Monitor* out of Fort Monroe, Virginia. They headed south toward Charleston, South Carolina, where the *Monitor* was to participate in a blockade. The *Monitor* rode so low in the water that her decks were usually awash, and only her circular gun turret amidships was visible. Definitely not a seaworthy ship, she was designed for giving battle in calm, protected waters. The first night after leaving port, the two ships were off Cape Hatteras, North Carolina, when a sudden squall came up, and the *Monitor* began taking on water at an alarming rate. The tow line parted, and the captain gave orders to abandon ship. After sighting a flare, the *Rhode Island*'s crew lowered lifeboats and rescued all but sixteen of the sinking ironclad's crew. Soon after, the *Monitor* went to a watery grave.

There was no salvage attempt at the time, although reports by both ships' officers gave a vague location. For more than a century, she was just another carcass in the "graveyard of the Atlantic," which has claimed hundreds of ships over the years. Then in 1973, a multidisciplinary team was organized to find her. The National Science Foundation and the National Geographic Society gave financial support to the project, which was headed by underwater archaeologist Gordon Watts from East Carolina University, oceanographer John Newton of Duke University, geologist Robert Sheridan of the University of Delaware and the ubiquitous Dr. Harold Edgerton.

Duke University provided its research vessel, *Eastwind,* and the search got under way in August. The search focused on a 100-square-mile (2.5 ha) area with a center about 17 miles (27 km) southeast of Cape Hatteras. Using magnetometers and side-scan sonar, the team worked in shifts around the clock. During the first week they located twenty-two targets. In each instance a closed-circuit television camera was lowered to inspect the anomaly, but none of these was their objective. The twenty-third target, lying in 230 feet (70 m) of water, proved to be the *Monitor*. Edgerton's super-sensitive sonar revealed the outline of a ship conforming to the shape and length of the ironclad. Excitement mounted aboard the research vessel when the television screen showed a circular structure in the center of the ship that appeared to be the rotating gun turret.

The *Eastwind* anchored over the site, and the television camera was lowered to survey and photograph the hulk from stem to stern. Ashore the searchers matched the photographic data they had collected with the original plans of the famous ship and confirmed the find in every detail. On January 30, 1975, President Richard Nixon signed a law designating the *Monitor* a National Marine Sanctuary to protect the site from plunderers.

The *Monitor* lies beyond safe depths for scuba divers. Compressed air cannot be used at such depths because of impractical decompression times and the increased risk of nitrogen bubbles forming in a diver's blood or body tissues. Instead, divers can reach depths of as much as 2,000 feet (610 m) using a mixture of oxygen and helium. So in May 1974 the team returned to the site with the *Alcoa Seaprobe,* a specially designed oceanographic vessel capable of working on shipwrecks at depths of almost 4 miles (6000 m). A tall derrick aboard the *Seaprobe* lowers lengths of drilling pipe into the sea through an opening in the center of the ship. A pod containing an array of electronic detection equipment and still and video cameras is attached to the bottom of the pipe. The operation is controlled in the ship's search control room. The week spent on the *Monitor* produced hours of video film and more than 2,000 still photographs. From these a partial photo-mosaic of the wreck was made to determine if it was complete enough to raise.

Two years later, Gordon Watts returned to the wreck with a research vessel from Harbor Branch Oceanographic Foundation in Fort Pierce, Florida. On the deck was the manned submersible *Johnson Sea-Link I*, a vessel capable of operating in depths of up to 3,000 feet (900 m). The forward transparent sphere, made of 4-inch (10 cm) acrylic, accommodates the pilot and an observer. The aft section of the submersible holds a second observer and a diver. In depths of 1,000 feet (300 m) or less, a diver can "lock out" or exit the *Sea-Link* using special mixed-gas breathing apparatus, and can dive and work on the bottom.

Watts and his team each made one four-hour dive per day for a month using the submersible. The submersible divers were monitored on closed-circuit television by the observer in the forward sphere as they used a hydraulic dredge to remove the sediment covering the wreck. They learned that the hull had been damaged during World War II when the *Monitor* was apparently mistaken for an enemy submarine and depth-charged. They collected a small number of artifacts, including a brass marine navigation lantern, and took samples of the ship's metal plating. Analysis of the plating proved that the hull is too weak to raise without danger of it breaking apart. During another mission to the *Monitor* in 1983, Gordon Watts led a successful expedition to recover the anchor. Not surprisingly, at a cost of $100,000 for the expedition, there was some furor in the media over the amount spent to recover a single anchor; the public is generally unaware of the extreme cost of working in deep water.

The *Monitor* was designated the nation's first marine sanctuary in 1975 by the National Oceanographic and Atmospheric Administration (NOAA) and placed under the protection of several government departments. A committee was formed comprising historians, archaeologists, salvage experts, engineers and navy divers, led by NOAA's Dr. John Broadwater. In 1998 navy divers employing the use of saturation diving returned to the wreck and successfully recovered the ship's 9-foot (3 m) propeller and other artifacts. In 1999 they concentrated on smaller artifacts concealed among the wreckage and brought up some 400 objects that were turned over to the Mariners' Museum in Newport News, Virginia, for preservation. The following year their most noteworthy recovery was a 10-foot (3 m) length of the propeller shaft; in 2000 they performed the incredible feat of bringing up the ironclad's 40-ton engine.

The committee continued to study the feasibility of raising the entire wreck. Ultimately they determined it was too expensive an undertaking considering that the fragile decayed hull might break up while being raised. Although the experts agreed that the famous 160-ton gun turret could be recovered, there was some concern that two heavy Dahlgren cannon inside the upside-down turret might break through the turret. Divers first had to cut away a 30-ton section of the hull attached to the turret and, while doing so, found two long human bones. In the same area they found a pile of nails, soldering irons, thermometers and glass lantern chimneys.

New technology was brought into play with the building of an eight-legged pneumatic cage named the "Spider." After all of the debris was removed from the turret this lifting structure was attached to the 21-foot (6 m) wide turret and, using a deck crane on a barge, the turret broke through the surface on August 5, 2002. Four feet (1 m) of silt was found inside the turret, and a vast hoard of interesting and poignant artifacts were soon uncovered including three silver spoons, a silver fork, ivory knife handles, fragments of a wool overcoat, a key, coins, uniform buttons, fragments of a wooden cabinet and many implements for loading the cannon. The Mariners' Museum in Newport News, Virginia, is constructing a $30 million *Monitor* display to house the turret and the other artifacts after they are preserved, a process that will take many years.

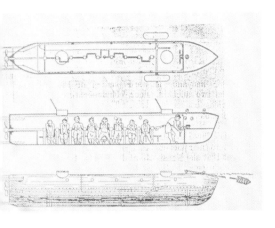

Drawings of the Confederate submarine *H.L. Hunley* show how it was propelled and where her torpedo was mounted on the bow of the vessel. There was a crew of nine in the 39-foot (12 m) ship.

The *Hunley* being placed ashore shortly after being raised from the seafloor.

THE H.L. HUNLEY

The *H.L. Hunley* was the first submarine in naval history to sink an enemy ship. By early 1864 the Civil War was going badly for the Confederacy, and the end was seen looming. The Union Navy's blockade of Charleston, South Carolina, was a major blow, preventing direly needed war materials from arriving and ships leaving there with cotton to finance the war. If desperate action were not taken, all would be lost.

The *Hunley*'s story is one of technological innovation, bravery and sacrifice. Construction of the vessel was financed by New Orleans lawyer Horace Lawson. An ordinary steam engine boiler was transformed into a sleek and dangerous war machine, which became the template for submarine design for decades to come. Initially the *Hunley* was a disaster as a naval weapon. During trial runs she sank twice, killing 13 members of two crews and was raised each time. Many Confederate officers considered this "secret weapon" a foolhardy dream. How could a 39-foot (12 m) craft weighing 7 1/2 tons sink a 207-foot (63 m) ship of 1,240 tons?

A veteran of the Battle of Shiloh, Lieutenant George Dixon was given command of the *Hunley* and entrusted with the critical mission of sinking the flagship of the Yankee blockade fleet, USS *Housatonic*.

On the moonless night of February 17, 1864, eight audacious Confederate seamen led by Dixon set off in the *Hunley* on their quixotic mission. Wedged shoulder to shoulder in the claustrophobic iron vessel, seven men furiously hand-cranked the propeller as Dixon steered for the target. A torpedo with 235 pounds (106 kg) of powder in it had been attached to a spar mounted on the bow, and the plan was to run submerged until the *Housatonic* was close by. Then they would surface just enough so Dixon could observe through the sub's tiny forward-view port. As they neared the massive Yankee ship, lookouts spotted something strange in the water and began firing small arms. Undeterred, Dixon rammed the spar into the ship's hull below the waterline and as he backed off, a trigger cord detonated the torpedo, blowing off the entire aft quarter of the ship. Within minutes the ship sank as the *Hunley* headed for the safety of the shore. But she never reached it and what happened to her remains one of the Civil War's great mysteries.

Efforts to locate the *Hunley* date back to the nineteenth century when showman P.T. Barnum offered a $100,000 reward for her recovery. Numerous modern-day salvors conducted fruitless searches as well. In 1980 author Clive Cussler founded the National Underwater Marine Agency (NUMA) for the specific purpose of finding the *Hunley*. On May 4, 1995, NUMA divers finally located the submarine under 3 feet (1 m) of mud in 30 feet (9 m) of water near Sullivan's Island. Local authorities created the Hunley Commission and teamed up with the Navy Historical Center, led by archaeologist Robert Neyland. They hired Oceaneering International of Houston to undertake the recovery of the *Hunley*.

In May 2001 Oceaneering divers began removing 25,000 cubic feet of sediment surrounding the hulk so cables could be slung beneath it prior to recovery. She was raised on August 8, 2000, as thousands of spectators cheered, placed on a barge and taken to a massive fresh-water tank as the first stage of her preservation. Eventually she will be put on display in the Charleston Museum, which existed at the time the *Hunley* disappeared.

The bones of all eight of the brave men lost on the *Hunley* were recovered and will be given military burials after forensic studies have been completed. Forensic studies are lengthy. The Smithsonian Institution spent more than fifteen years studying the human bones I recovered at Port Royal. Other finds included a great wealth of other artifacts, including a gold coin believed to be a good luck piece of Dixon. The cost of locating and raising the *Hunley* was $2.7 million; preserving the sub and the artifacts she contained may well exceed an additional $7 million.

The *Hunley* is not the only small submarine found in recent years. On August 28, 2002, two submersibles, the *Pisces* IV and V, operated by the Hawaii Underseas Research Laboratory, found a Japanese midget submarine used in the attack on Pearl Harbor on December 7, 1941. It was the first Japanese casualty of the war; spotted entering the port by the destroyer USS *Ward,* it was destroyed by gunfire and rammed before sinking in 1250 feet (400 m) of water. The sub was found sitting upright and totally intact with its two torpedoes ready to be fired. It is protected as a war grave and the location is a secret.

THE SLAVE SHIP HENRIETTA MARIE

In July 1700 the 120-ton English slaver *Henrietta Marie* was sailing back to England having sold 190 African slaves in Jamaica when she was lost under unknown circumstances 35 miles (56 km) west of Key West. Divers working for Mel Fisher discovered her in 1972 while searching for the Spanish treasure galleon *Atocha*. They only partially excavated her remains as their main objective was to locate the elusive *Atocha*. Although he had already determined that this wreck, which they dubbed the *English Wreck*, was not a treasure ship, Fisher sent his archaeologist David Moore to further explore the wreck in 1983.

Moore found hundreds of shackles and soon realized he was looking at an unusually significant wreck: the first slaver found in the western hemisphere. Although Fisher was already strapped for money in his long-drawn-out search for the *Atocha,* he managed to find some to further excavate the wreck. One of the first of many important finds was the ship's bronze bell bearing the inscription "The *Henrietta Marie* 1699." Once the ship's identity was known, researchers were able to find a great deal of historical information about her in various archives.

Over a period of five years Moore, aided by volunteers when funds ran low, recovered over 7,000 artifacts including pewter ware, bottles, elephant tusks, glass trading beads, cannonballs and more shackles. Apparently someone had recovered the cannon before the wreck was found in 1972, for they found not even one. An exhibition called "A Slave Ship Speaks," sponsored by General Motors, has been touring the United States since 1997, and it is hoped that a museum will eventually house the artifacts and a large section of the ship's lower hull that is being preserved at the Mel Fisher Maritime Heritage Society in Key West. The recovery is believed to be the world's largest source of tangible objects from the early slave trade

THE BATTLE OF THE NILE

This famous battle is actually misnamed. It should be "The Battle of Aboukir Bay" since that is where it took place during the night of August 1–2, 1798. This event destroyed Napoleon's dream of conquering Egypt and crushing the British Empire. It pitted Britain's finest, under command of Admiral Horatio Nelson, against a French fleet led by Admiral François Paul Brueys d'Aigaillier. The English had been pursuing the French fleet for nearly four months when they spotted the fleet of thirteen battleships and four frigates in Aboukir Bay, 15 miles (24 km) east of Alexandria. Disregarding Napoleon's orders to anchor in Alexandria, Brueys decided to use Aboukir Bay instead, claiming it would be more difficult for the British to enter or blockade.

Nelson and his "band of brothers," as he called his men, took the initiative, and before the French could even raise anchor to fight, the British fleet of thirteen warships sailed down the line in which the French ships were anchored, picking off one after another with devastating cannon fire on both sides. The French had expected a battle of one ship against another, but catching them by surprise was a brilliant move on Nelson's part. In a matter of a few hours all but two of the French ships had been sunk

The special cradle used to raise and hold the *Hunley* before the conservation treatment began.

or captured. The British lost only two ships and 218 men. Some 3,000 Frenchmen were taken prisoner and 1,700 lost their lives, 800 of whom died instantly in the explosion of *L'Orient,* the 120-gun flagship of Admiral Brueys. "Victory is not a name strong enough for such a scene," Nelson would later write in a letter to the English monarch. This disaster was a decisive turning point in French history

Over the years numerous expeditions sought *L'Orient,* but it wasn't until 1983 that the late French underwater explorer Jacques Dumas found her. During a survey he discovered that the debris of a wreck was spread over ½ square mile (3.5 km²) and mixed in with that of two other French warships, *Artémise* and *Sérieuse.* Dumas didn't understand that he had found *L'Orient* because he found a bronze nameplate of a ship called "Royal Dauphin"—the name of *L'Orient* before the French Revolution. Dumas was unable to raise funding to continue his work in Egypt, and the wreck was forgotten until Franck Goddio went after it in 1996, by which time Dumas had already died.

Over the next four years Goddio's team recovered thousands of objects from both *L'Orient* and *Sérieuse.* Cannon and anchors, firearms and ammunition, as well as thousands of other artifacts and some treasure, came up from the site. Numerous bones and several complete skeletons were also exhumed and buried back in France. In an effort to focus on archaeology rather than treasure, the amount of gold, silver and copper coins wasn't made public; but it is thought there are thousands. Some of the French coins date as far back as the reign of Louis XIV. Many were from the Ottoman Empire, Spain, Portugal, Venice and Malta—part of the Maltese Treasure the French had captured on the way to Egypt. Among the most interesting artifacts were thousands of lead typefaces that were part of a printing press aboard *L'Orient.* All of the recoveries were turned over to the Egyptian government, and negotiations are under way to have them shown in international exhibitions.

TREASURE SHIP S.S. BROTHER JONATHAN

On July 28, 1865, S.S. *Brother Jonathan* set sail from San Francisco. The 221-foot (67 m) side-wheel steamer had been making the San Francisco–Portland–Victoria run for four years carrying businessmen, government employees, entertainers and miners. She was primarily a passenger ship, but that day was so dangerously overloaded with as much as 700 tons of freight that the captain himself expressed misgivings. From shore onlookers noted how low the ship rode in the water as she sailed out of the harbor.

General George Wright, California's foremost Civil War hero, his wife and the rest of the more than 240 passengers could scarcely move about the decks, which were crammed with railroad ties and rails, an ore crusher, wool mill machinery, 346 barrels of whiskey, two circus camels, some horses, a Newfoundland dog and a wide assortment of other merchandise destined for the growing northwest. The *Brother Jonathan* also was reported to be carrying $200,000 in gold coins to pay U.S. Army garrisons in Oregon and Washington, an unknown amount of passengers' money, as much as $100,000 in gold coin treaty payment and a Wells Fargo bank shipment—possibly $250,000 in gold bullion.

The following morning the ship reached Crescent City, where she offloaded some cargo. Although a gale had sprung up, the captain foolishly decided to leave port. Several hours later the storm worsened, and he ordered the ship to turn back for Crescent City. They almost made it, but the *Brother Jonathan* struck an uncharted rock pinnacle (now Jonathan Rock) and in less than forty-five minutes sank 250 feet (76 m) to the bottom as horrified onlookers watched from Crescent City's high bluffs. Six lifeboats were launched. Five were crushed or capsized. All but nineteen of the 244

Nelson's fleet destroyed nearly all of the French ships before they could raise anchor, ending the decisive Battle of the Nile before it even began.

poor souls aboard drowned. A moving letter penned by passenger James Nisbet, editor and part owner of the *San Francisco Bulletin,* survived. In the time it took the ship to sink, Nisbet calmly wrote out his will and a note to Almira Hopkins, the wife of San Francisco insurance agent Caspar Hopkins. His body, with two life preservers wrapped around it, was washed ashore two days later, and the penciled will and letter were found in his coat pocket. The letter read:

> *My dear Almira, A thousand affectionate adieus. You spoke of my sailing on Friday— Hangman's Day—and the unlucky Jonathan. Well here I am with death before me. My love to you all—to Caspar, to Dita, to Belle, to Mellie and little Myra—kiss her for me. Never forget Grandpa.*

The ship's original manifest was destroyed in the 1906 San Francisco fire and earthquake; so no one knew for sure if there really was a fabulous golden treasure on the wreck. The lure of treasure and the aura of tragedy made the *Brother Jonathan* wreck unforgettable, and there were many fruitless searches for the wreck. In May 1991 treasure hunters Harvey Hamilton, James Wadsley and Donald G. Knight joined forces determined to find her. They formed Deep Sea Research (DSR) and devoted two years to intensive magnetometer and side-scan sonar surveys, inspecting possible sites using an ROV. On October 1, 1993, they discovered the sought-after ship and then investigated the wreck with two small mini-subs to shoot hours of video to show potential investors.

The State of California claimed ownership of the wreck and started a long and costly legal tussle. DSR continued surveying the wreck using the mini-subs during this five-year period. As long as the company maintained control, as evidenced by continuous marking of the site by an identifying buoy and by working on the site as weather permitted, no third parties could come in and claim the find. On August 30, 1996, during a mini-sub dive they saw the first gold coins, and great excitement ensued amongst the salvors aboard the mother vessel. During the next week, before foul weather halted the exploration, DSR brought up 875 gold coins, mostly freshly minted $20 Liberty gold coins known as double eagles.

The State of California took its fight for ownership of the *Brother Jonathan* to the United States Supreme Court twice and twice the justices unanimously ruled that DSR owned the wreck and its treasure. Many archaeologists deplored the Court's decision, claiming Uncle Sam was giving away treasures belonging to all Americans.

DSR carried on excavating using mixed-gas divers, who have more freedom of movement on the bottom than an ROV or submersible. In August 1997 an additional 332 gold coins were recovered, bringing the total to 1,207. The project had cost almost $3 million by then, and the investors were clamoring for their share of the profits, so salvage was discontinued and DSR concentrated on selling the gold coins, which had been restored to almost mint condition.

The numismatic world was electrified. There are an estimated 20 million coin collectors in the United States alone—a huge market for Civil War–era coins. The 1865 "California Gold Rush" date was so rare that only eight were known to exist in mint condition in 1995. The wreck also yielded a valuable variety of pre–Civil War coins carried by the passengers. In the first-ever sale of U.S. gold coins reclaimed from a sunken ship, the cache of gold coins from the S.S. *Brother Jonathan* was sold at auction in Los Angeles in 1999. They fetched a landmark total of more than $5.3 million. The average price of a coin was $30,000, and one double eagle with inverted dates sold for an impressive $115,000.

11 DEEP-WATER SHIPWRECKS

TENS OF THOUSANDS OF SHIPWRECKS rest in the silent darkness of the oceans' depths. The numbers seem staggering, but mankind has been plying the seas and losing ships since the dawn of time. The remains of a Mediterranean trading ship sunk 4,000 years ago may lie next to the twisted hulk of a German submarine, or a modern Cuban fishing boat may rest on the site of a Spanish galleon. Until recently 98 percent of this vast nautical storehouse lay beyond conventional diving limits. Today, revolutionary developments in deep diving and robot technology bring deep-water wrecks within our reach.

NEW TECHNOLOGIES OPEN NEW FRONTIERS

Since archaeologists began underwater exploration in the early fifties, they have known that wooden wrecks in deep water are much better preserved than those in shallower sites because they lie beyond the reach of shipworm and other marine borers. Less than 2 percent of the ocean's depths have been explored, and very few deep-water wrecks have been located. As deep-ocean technology evolves, however, techniques developed for industry are being applied to underwater archaeology. In fact, the earliest discoveries of deep wrecks were byproducts of other applications. In 1952, a closed-circuit television search for the wreckage of a commercial airliner off the island of Elba in the Mediterranean discovered an ancient amphora-carrier at a depth of 2,500 feet (760 m), or almost one-half mile. Two years later, a firm studying

An ominous artist's rendering of an ROV surveying the German battleship *Bismarck* at the bottom of the sea.

the feasibility of laying a pipeline from France to Africa reported sightings of more than two dozen intact ancient shipwrecks. Then in 1966, while searching for a hydrogen bomb lost when two planes collided off the Spanish coast near Palomares, the crew of the submersible *Aluminaut* reported a remarkable sight. Sitting on the ocean floor, down 2,000 feet (610 m)—close to one-third of a mile—were two intact ships, their masts still standing and the cannon projecting from the gun ports, just like Hollywood's fantasy wrecks.

On January 23, 1960, the bathyscaphe *Trieste II*, piloted by its inventor, Jacques Picard, and with U.S. Navy lieutenant Don Walsh on board, made history by descending 35,797 feet (10,911 m) in the Pacific Ocean to the bottom of the Marianas Trench, the deepest known point on the globe. A bathyscaphe is a free-diving deep-sea vessel consisting of a large flotation hull with a crewed observation capsule attached to its underside. It is capable of reaching full ocean depths.

Picard's descent was a breakthrough in deep-water technology and inaugurated the era of safe deep-sea exploration. In the same year, Cousteau launched his "diving saucer," the first of the many manned submersibles that are in wide use today. Cousteau was also a pioneer in mixed-gas diving.

In 1974 British scientist Graham Hawkes invented the Atmospheric Diving Suit (ADS), which permits divers to reach depths of almost 3,000 feet (900 m) while remaining in a surface-pressure atmosphere. A diver who tries to work at the pressure of, say, 1,000 feet (300 m) soon has "saturated" blood—blood with a very high level of dissolved nitrogen that must be released very gradually to avoid "the bends." Such a diver would need about twelve days to compress to bottom pressure, carry out the work assignment, and decompress to surface pressure. With the ADS system the same dive can be safely completed in a matter of hours.

Nevertheless, sophisticated unmanned, remotely operated vehicles (ROVs) are now the undersea tool of choice. They eliminate all danger by keeping workers on the surface, and they are less costly to operate than other deep-diving systems. The oper-

Technicians preparing to launch an ROV to inspect a deep-water shipwreck.

ator of an ROV, safe and dry on a surface vessel, "flies" the robot by controlling it with joysticks and monitoring a television screen. The operator can activate the ROV's lights and cameras and operate its manipulator arms to recover objects at any depth.

Oceaneering International has a facility in Morgan City, Louisiana, where divers receive 40 hours of training in diving in the WASP suit—an improved version of Hawkes's ADS dive system. In 2000 the firm, which works primarily in the offshore petroleum industry, used a WASP suit to reveal one of Hitler's last secrets. Oceaneering divers plumbed Austria's Lake Toplitz to recover millions in counterfeit United States currency and British pounds that the Nazis had printed with the intention of undermining the economy of both nations.

Graham Hawkes designed and built a one-man submersible, the *Deep Flight,* and has been testing it in relatively shallow water; ultimately, he hopes it will reach the deepest ocean floor. Several Japanese firms have designed and are testing similar submersibles. Unlike a bathyscaphe that only moves vertically, these newer submersibles can move in any direction.

SOME EARLY DEEP-WATER SUCCESSES

In the nineteenth century, divers in helmet suits could go no deeper than 150 feet (46 m). Hand-operated air pumps couldn't provide sufficient air for greater depths and little was known about how to avoid decompression sickness, known as the bends, which is often fatal. Later, the armored diving suit, similar to Hawkes's ADS system, was constructed of steel to withstand the great pressure. The diver encased in it breathed air at normal surface pressure. The suits allowed divers to go deeper, but were impractical because their weight and bulk greatly restricted mobility.

An armored diving suit was used in the renowned salvage of the Pacific & Orient liner *Egypt*. On a foggy day in 1921 she collided with another ship in the Bay of Biscay and sank in 425 feet (130 m) with more than $6 million in gold bullion aboard. Because of the depth, salvage experts said it would be impossible to recover the treasure, and Lloyd's of London paid the insurance claim. But there are always people willing to tackle the impossible, particularly when a lot of gold is at stake. The challenger this time was an Italian, Giovanni Quaglia, director of the Sorima Salvage Company of Genoa. He had already used his armored diving suit successfully to salvage several other deep-water wrecks. In 1930 Quaglia located the *Egypt*, and in 1931 returned to salvage her. The steel-clad diver didn't try to move around on the bottom in the bulky suit. Rather, he served as an observer, using a telephone in his helmet to direct such equipment as grab buckets and electromagnets lowered from the surface. It took more than a month of blasting to reach the strong room. Explosives were lowered and placed where the hull was to be opened. The diver then surfaced and the charges were detonated. The armor-suited observer reported that the "floor was paved with gold bars." The venture was a complete success, with the recovery of all the *Egypt*'s gold.

Within a few years, Quaglia's deep-water recovery record was broken. In 1940 the Australian mail steamer *Niagara*, carrying more than $12 million in gold, hit a mine 30 miles (48 km) from the entrance to Whangarei Harbour, New Zealand, and went down in 448 feet (136 m) of water. The Australian firm that salvaged the *Niagara*'s gold used Quaglia's methods to recover all but a few bars of the gold.

THE ANDREA DORIA

One of the most celebrated shipwrecks of the twentieth century was the *Andrea Doria*. On July 26, 1956, with 1,134 passengers and 572 crew, the Italian liner (en route from Genoa to New York) collided with the Swedish passenger liner *Stockholm* about 50 miles (80 km) south of Nantucket. The *Stockholm* managed to limp back to New York, but the *Andrea Doria* sank in 240 feet (73 m) of water. Fifty-one people died and more than 1,650 were rescued. It was one of the most bizarre sea disasters since the *Titanic* forty-four years earlier.

Within twenty-four hours, Peter Gimbel, an avid sport diver, who for years had spent vacations shipwreck-diving in the Caribbean, was diving on the *Andrea Doria*. Gimbel was a New York–based documentary filmmaker and took the first photographs of the ill-fated liner. "She seems almost alive," he told reporters. He returned again and again on dozens of photographic expeditions, initially using standard compressed-air scuba equipment. He changed to mixed-gas breathing apparatus after several scuba divers, on expeditions separate from his, died from the bends.

The sinking of the *Andrea Doria* gave birth to two persistent rumors: that her two safes held a fortune in cash and precious stones, and that the liner could have survived the collision if a crucial watertight door had been closed. In 1981 Gimbel and his wife, Swedish movie actress Elga Andersen, set out both to investigate the rumors, and to

Divers preparing their specialized equipment prior to making a deep dive.

Similar to passenger liners like the *Andrea Doria* and *Titanic*, the *Laurentic* carried thousands of passengers across the Atlantic.

make a major documentary movie. They contracted with Oceaneering International, a world leader in deep diving, to use the salvage vessel *Sea Level II*, with what was then the world's most sophisticated mixed-gas saturation diving system on deck. Gimbel and Andersen remained on the site for thirty-three days, despite raging storms.

They found that seams had opened on both sides of the *Andrea Doria*'s watertight door, so that closing the door would not have saved the ship. They also discovered that the safes were located deep inside the ship under tons of debris. Removing the debris was a lengthy process, but eventually one of the safes was found and brought to the surface. Before Gimbel and Andersen could find the other safe, they were driven back to port by the approach of Hurricane Dennis, and the expedition ended. When the recovered safe was opened during a live, nationwide television broadcast, thousands of viewers saw that it contained not the rumored treasure of cash and precious stones, but treasure of another sort: stacks of U.S. silver certificates, which could be redeemed for full value, and thousands of Italian lira bills, which had lost most of their value as a result of inflation. The safe had not remained watertight, and all its contents were soggy.

Every year *Andrea Doria* expeditions are organized for sport divers, who brave the deep, chilly waters for a glimpse of the once-majestic ship. Diving below 100 feet (30 m) for nonprofessional scuba divers is a risky business, and over the years more than 25 sightseers have perished. The first was the son of the late Dr. Harold Edgerton, who died just two months after the ship went down. Most casualties occur when a diver is trapped inside the ship and runs out of air.

WARTIME TREASURES

The most lucrative deep-water treasure recovery was 5 1/2 tons of gold ingots from HMS *Edinburgh*, a British cruiser that sank in 1942. The gold, valued at $91 million in the early 1980s when it was salvaged, was a consignment from the Soviets to the United States in payment for military supplies for Stalin's forces in World War II. The *Edinburgh* was north of Murmansk in the Barents Sea and steaming toward New York when she was attacked by German U-boats and destroyers and sunk in 820 feet (250 m) of water. Sixty lives were lost, and the British designated the wreck a war grave and for a time prohibited salvage. In 1957, after the government ban was lifted, several attempts were made to locate the ship, which had gone down far from sight of land. The attempts failed primarily because the location had been incorrectly reported by the British Navy vessel that had rescued the survivors.

Keith Jessop, an English diver in the North Sea petroleum industry, decided to find and salvage the *Edinburgh*. What he lacked in financial resources he made up in deter-mination. He found backers and embarked on a two-year, $4 million search, combing vast areas of the Arctic. Side-scan sonar located the 10,000-ton warship in 1981, and an ROV confirmed the find with excellent video footage. Before he salvaged the gold, Jessop negotiated an agreement with the British and the Soviets that gave the two gov-ernments 55 percent of the gold and awarded the remainder to Jessop's group.

The project was meticulously planned and executed. At that depth there is a crush-ing pressure of 350 pounds per square inch (25 kg per cm²), and before the divers went down to the *Edinburgh* they spent two days acclimating in a pressure chamber. They descended in diving bells and worked in shifts on the bottom, breathing a mix of oxygen and helium. Diving suits with circulating hot water protected them from the frigid waters. The divers spent several days at a time on the bottom, sleeping and eating in a specially designed chamber. Upon surfacing, they spent seven days aboard the salvage vessel in a decompression chamber that was gradually adjusted back to sea-level pressure.

Their courage and doggedness paid off. In the first week they cut into the side of the ship where the strong room was located. Then they spent two weeks removing all sorts of debris that blocked their way. The obstructions included 250-pound (115 kg) bombs and other live munitions. Finally, on September 16, 1981, cheers went up on the salvage vessel when John Rossier, a twenty-eight-year-old diver from Zimbabwe, issued the victory cry: "I found the gold!" Rossier, working in near darkness, had been lifting debris near the entrance to the strong room when he grabbed something heavy and found the first of 431 gold bars. Even the Soviet treasury officials, who were along as observers and who had been very aloof, joined in a jig when the first shiny bar reached the surface. It took three weeks of working around the clock to find the remaining gold. Thirty-four bars were still missing when a fierce gale ended the expedition. However, the salvors had certainly found enough to satisfy them. Each diver was sud-denly a rich man, and Jessop's personal share was $3.5 million.

Late in the summer of 1943 the U.S. Joint Chiefs of Staff took stock of the world situa-tion and, fearing that the Allies might run out of oil before the war ended, recommended constructing a massive oil refinery in Saudi Arabia. The Saudi king demanded payment in silver coinage for his cooperation. So, in a most unusual operation, Saudi riyals were pro-duced at the Philadelphia Mint. Some three million coins and 2,000 tons of silver ingots were secretly loaded, and in July 1944 the S.S. *John Barry* steamed toward the port of Ras Tanurah in Saudi Arabia to deliver the king's payment. She never made it.

On August 28, 1944, as the ship was passing the coast of Oman, it was struck by three torpedoes fired from the German submarine *U-859*. The *John Barry* went down with her vast treasure, sinking quickly in 8,500 feet of water (2,580 m). Sixty-six of the crew were rescued by other ships in the convoy, and only two were lost. The level of technology at the time precluded such a deep-water salvage effort.

In 1989 Keith Jessop formed the John Barry Group to take advantage of innovations in deep recovery and go after this wreck. He acquired the rights from the U.S. Maritime Administration; but when he failed to raise capital for such a costly undertaking they were transferred to the Ocean Group, a deep-water salvage company based in Houston, Texas.

A consortium of British and American salvors and Sheikh Ahmed Farid of Oman hired Oceaneering International, the largest commercial dive company in the world, which is also Houston-based, to locate the wreck. In 1990 Jim Whitaker of Jupiter, Florida, found it using sonar. The consortium obtained salvage rights from the U.S. Maritime Commission and contracted the French Government Marine Research Institute, IFREMER, to survey the site. Using the manned submersible *Cyana* they found that the ship had broken in two, and the sections had settled upright 1,200 feet (364 m) apart. The decks and holds were covered with all sorts of debris, especially heavy machinery that had been stored as deck cargo.

The salvors attempted to reach the cargo using dynamite; since the *John Barry* is a modern wreck they were not concerned with preserving her remains. However, this didn't work, and in 1994 new technology was introduced, using a drill ship with 90-foot (27 m) sections of pipe reaching to the bottom, where a huge grab bucket capable of lifting 50 tons was used to remove the debris. When they reached the area where the silver was stored the salvors found their way blocked by 500 tons of timber and other cargo. Thirteen days after the grab bucket operation began they found the first of the Philadelphia riyals that had been minted 50 years earlier. In two weeks the grab bucket brought up over 2,000 boxes of coin-filled canvas bags. The project was terminated after 1,300,000 silver riyals had been salvaged. The partners agreed that the remaining coins and silver bars were, for the time being, unrecoverable because they lay in a section of the wreck that could not be reached without the expenditure of a great amount of more money.

JAPANESE GOLD

The largest World War II Japanese submarine was the *I-52*. She was 365 feet (110 m) long, had a tonnage of 2,564 tons, a cruising range of 21,000 nautical miles (33,600 km) and a crew of ninety-four. In March 1944 she left her base in Kure, Japan, destined for *L'Orient* in occupied France, carrying two tons of gold and raw materials urgently needed in Nazi Germany. In return the Japanese were seeking German technology, including radar and bomb sights. Allied code breakers intercepted and read all of the traffic between Tokyo and Berlin, and a decision was made to intercept the submarine and deprive Germany of this valuable cargo.

On June 23, 1944, the German submarine *U-530* rendez-voused with the *I-52* in the mid-Atlantic about 870 nautical miles (1,392 km) west of the Cape Verde Islands to transfer two technicians and radar detection equipment to be installed before the *I-52* reached the dangerous European waters. As the two submarines cruised tied to one another on the surface they were unaware that an American task force with an escort carrier, the USS *Bouge,* carrying fourteen aircraft, was close by. After the German submarine left the Japanese felt safe enough on a moonless night so they stayed on the surface to recharge their batteries. Suddenly an *Avenger* bomber appeared, dropping two flares that illuminated the *I-52,* and then dropping a torpedo that hit the submarine, sinking it in 17,000 feet (5,156 m) of water with the gold, ninety-five seamen and fourteen Mitsubishi technicians. For fifty years the precise location of the *I-52* remained unknown because relevant documents in the National Archives in Washington, D.C., were off-limits to researchers.

In 1991 Texan Paul Tidwell, who won the Purple Heart fighting in Vietnam, began scouring recently declassified documents in the National Archives after deciding he wanted to find the *I-52* and her gold. He was able to narrow the search area down to a formidable 100-square-mile (258 m²) area. After an investor put up $1 million dollars for the venture he hired Meridian Services Inc. of Colombia, Maryland, a navy contractor that analyzes secret navigational data for nuclear submarines. Meridian was able to recalculate the positions of the *Bouge* and determine where the *I-52* lay. The submarine was found only one-half mile (866 m) from the position they gave to Tidwell.

In 1995 Tidwell and his investor aboard the Russian research vessel *Yuzhmorgeologiya* reached the spot and initiated an intensive side-scan sonar search. On the third day they located the *I-52*. After identifying the submarine Tidwell went home to raise more funds for a salvage operation. It took three years to find the money, and in 1998 Tidwell returned to the *I-52* with big hopes. This time he used the Russian oceanographic vessel *Keldysh* with her two submersibles *MIR I* and *MIR II*.

Tidwell went down in one of the submersibles while the other was used to lay transponders to facilitate the salvage. Tidwell's submersible brought up a metal box that he believed contained the gold, but, upon opening it, they found opium, which was flung back overboard. Unfortunately the *I-52* is intact, and it is impossible to get inside her to grab the gold. On another dive Tidwell planted a Japanese Naval Ensign on the tower of the *I-52*. It was estimated that it would take an additional $8 million to cut into the submarine—a sum that his investors were unwilling to invest, so the gold is still down there.

ROBERT BALLARD: THE TITANIC AND THE BISMARCK

In 1985 the discovery of the legendary *Titanic* in the North Atlantic captured the world's attention and inaugurated space-age shipwreck exploration. Most people know the tragic story of the British luxury liner, considered unsinkable, which collided with an iceberg on its maiden voyage in April 1912 and sank with 1,513 of the 2,224 people aboard. In the early 1980s, a team of scientists and marine explorers financed by Texas oil baron Jack Grimm spent $2 million in a vain three-year quest to locate the liner. Then during the summer of 1985, Dr. Robert Ballard of Woods Hole Oceanographic Institution led the joint American-French expedition that found the shipwreck after searching an area of 150 square miles (almost 40,000 ha) with high-resolution side-scan sonar and a towed sled, the *Angus*, mounted with cameras and lights. Finally, on September 1 the world's most famous shipwreck appeared on film.

A dinner plate recovered from the *Titanic*.

The *Titanic* lies at a depth of 2½ miles (4000 m), deeper than any previous shipwreck project. The following summer, Ballard returned to the site, which is 95 miles (150 km) off the coast of Newfoundland, with the *Alvin*, a manned submersible capable of reaching the *Titanic*. The *Alvin* has an impressive record of accomplishments, including the recovery of the American hydrogen bomb lost in more than a ½ mile (866 m) of water off Palomares, Spain, in 1966. It was launched in 1964 with an operational depth of 6,000 feet (over 1800 m) and carrying a crew of three, and was later modified to reach 2 ½ miles. It took the *Alvin* two hours to travel to the bottom of the sea to the *Titanic*. Once there, the crew took excellent photographs and recovered objects by using the *Alvin*'s two manipulator arms. A small, tethered robot called *Jason, Jr.*, was used to get inside the *Titanic*. Controlled by the *Alvin*'s pilot, the 250-pound (115 kg), *Jason, Jr.*, which is only 28 inches (71 cm) long, was also invaluable in obtaining data from areas outside the immense wreck, where twisted metal made other methods too dangerous. The explorers made sixty hours of video film and took 60,000 still photographs during a twelve-day period. The previous summer, using the less advanced *Angus*, they had made only two minutes of video and taken nine still photographs.

Ballard, who believes the *Titanic* site should not be disturbed further, ended his explorations when bad weather set in at the end of the summer. In the summer of 1987, a well-financed French expedition used a submersible similar to the *Alvin* and several sophisticated ROVs to obtain additional video and still photographs of the *Titanic*, and to recover an assortment of artifacts. They proved that even shipwrecks at that immense depth can be successfully salvaged. Many people regarded the removal of artifacts as plundering, however, and there was an international outcry.

For the past decade a company named Zegrahm Deep Sea Voyage has been taking ordinary people out to dive on the Titanic, using the *MIR I* and *MIR II* to take passengers down to the wreck. They enjoy exciting views of the entire wreck and sections of the mile-long (1.6 km) debris field. For many this is the adventure of a lifetime, but it doesn't come cheap; each person pays $35,000. The submersibles take two hours to descend, spend an hour on the bottom and another two hours ascending. No artifacts are recovered on these dives.

In June 1989 Ballard scored another deep-sea coup with the discovery of the deepest shipwreck ever found, the German battleship *Bismarck,* which lies about one-half mile (866 m) deeper than the *Titanic.* The sinking of the *Bismarck* in almost 2 miles of water (4760 m) was the culmination of one of the most dramatic sea hunts in naval history. In May 1941 Britain was in desperate straits, as the Germans had firm control of the North Atlantic sea lanes. The *Bismarck* had been wreaking havoc on Allied shipping, and Churchill sent an armada of British warships after her. Day and night, they chased their quarry across the high seas. The battle that ensued when they found her lasted three hours, as salvo after salvo was fired by both sides. Finally, the *Bismarck* blew up and sank 600 miles (960 km) west of Brest, France, with more than 2,000 German seamen aboard.

The location of the *Bismarck* was only vaguely known, and Ballard and his team combed hundreds of square miles of the seafloor using sonar before the wreck was located. Although there are no plans to salvage the ship, the wreck was extensively filmed and photographed, using an improved ROV, the *Argo.* The *Argo* was developed by the U.S. Navy at a cost in excess of $3 million. Designed to hover 120 feet (36 m) off the bottom, it is tethered to a surface vessel by coaxial cable.

Soon after this discovery Ballard designed a more sophisticated version of the ROV *Jason.* The new ROV, which carries three high-resolution video cameras, a 35mm still camera and high-intensity lights, is more economical to operate, but limited to a depth of 6,000 feet (1830 m). Ballard then initiated Project *Jason,* to find ancient shipwrecks in the Mediterranean. His team

An ROV examining the interior of the *Bismarck*.

of archaeologists, following an ancient sea-trade route between North Africa and Rome, surveyed an area of 50 square miles (129 km²) at a depth of 2,500 feet (760 m). They found numerous shipwrecks, the most interesting of which was a fourth-century A.D. Roman galley. They were able to use *Jason's* manipulator arms to recover amphorae and other artifacts from this wreck. But Project *Jason's* most significant accomplishment was the involvement of many thousands of American schoolchildren, who watched the operation via satellite on television screens in their classrooms.

Ballard, like Franck Goddio, is regularly in the news with remarkable finds. Many of his discoveries, such as the carrier *Yorktown,* were made for the specific purpose of making documentary films for the National Geographic Society. Another such discovery took place in July 2002 when Ballard announced finding John F. Kennedy's famed torpedo boat *PT-109* in 1,300 feet (394 m) of water in the Solomon Islands. It had been rammed by the Japanese destroyer *Amagiri* in 1943 and sunk. Two of the crew were lost, and the others swam to shore with Kennedy.

SOME STATE-OF-THE-ART RECOVERIES

The sinking of the side-wheel steamer *Central America* was the worst American maritime disaster of the nineteenth century. It claimed 425 people and more than three tons of gold. The *Central America* was a luxurious packet plying between New York and Panama, where she took on Californian gold and miners returning from the goldfields. In four years she made forty-three of these round-trip voyages, and more than one-third of all the precious metal found in the goldfields reached the east coast on this ship. On September 9, 1857, one day out of Havana en route to New York, she was overwhelmed in a hurricane. She began taking on huge amounts of water, lost power and then sank. Only fifty-three souls survived. The loss of her cargo of gold touched off a wave of bank failures across the United States and contributed to the panic of 1857, one of the country's most severe economic depressions.

In the early 1980s, Tommy G. Thompson, an oceanographic engineer specializing in deep-sea mining, developed a consuming interest in deep-water shipwrecks. He and Bob Evans, a geologist, spent several years researching various deep-water wrecks before selecting the *Central America* as their target. In 1985 journalist Barry Schatz joined them, and they formed the Columbus-America Discovery Group. They spent a year raising $1.5 million to finance the project, much of it from friends and neighbors in Columbus, Ohio. Even before they raised the first dollar, the three were also designing the *Nemo,* a revolutionary ROV. Unlike previous ROVs, which were designed and constructed for survey and sampling rather than heavy salvage work on the bottom, the *Nemo* was built to perform every function necessary to recover the *Central America*'s treasure.

Thompson, the project director, assembled a multitalented team of high-tech treasure hunters, and the venture got under way during the summer of 1986. Research in nineteenth-century records and newspapers led them to focus on an area encompassing 1,400 square miles (over 3636 km²)—ten times the search area for the *Titanic.* Using sonar they completed their survey in a mere forty days. One promising target, 160 miles (250 km) off Charleston, South Carolina, was found at 8,000 feet (almost 2500 m). The *Nemo* was still under construction, however, so a year went by before the men had

An artist's depiction of the *Central America*.

proof they had found the *Central America*. On July 8, 1987, the first item, a lump of anthracite coal, was recovered.

They rushed to the U.S. District Court in Norfolk, Virginia, where they presented the coal as evidence that they had found the *Central America*. A judge granted them exclusive rights to the wreck and its treasure. While they surveyed and mapped the wreck that summer several rival salvage groups appeared on the scene, claiming that the wreck lay outside government jurisdiction. At the same time, Thompson and his team realized that the *Nemo* needed major modifications to ensure a successful recovery. They decided not to attempt to salvage the gold until the *Nemo* was ready and their legal problems were resolved. When the next summer season began, their lawyers were still battling it out. To keep possession of the wreck they spent the summer using an upgraded *Nemo* to further survey the site and to salvage the ship's bronze bell, recovery of which confirmed the *Central America*'s identity. It wasn't until July 1989 that the challenging salvors lost their appeal in the U.S. Court of Appeals, and the Columbus-America Discovery Group got the green light to go after the sunken treasure.

Divers decompress on their way to the surface after searching a deep-sea wreck off the Azores.

On July 20, 1989, their salvage vessel RV *Arctic Discoverer* arrived on the wreck site. By the next day, the *Nemo* was on the bottom searching for signs of gold. There were setbacks, however, such as bad weather that held up the operation for days at a time. After probing a large part of the twisted remains of the wreck, they were beginning to wonder if there really was any gold on her. Then, on August 27, they were using the *Nemo*'s water jets to blow silt from a section of the wreck they hadn't yet explored, when suddenly the men monitoring the color television screens in the control center saw what they described as "the yellow brick road." The high-intensity lights revealed a dazzling array of hundreds of gold coins and gold bars. The largest bar recovered the first day weighed 62 pounds (over 28 kg). A dazed Thompson said: "It's like a storybook treasure in a kid's book. I never dreamed it would be like this."

For the next two months they worked twenty-four hours a day—whenever the capricious weather permitted. The key to their success was the 6-ton *Nemo*, which was capable of picking up a half-ton anchor or retrieving coins as small as a dime. By the end of the summer, when the weather turned foul and supplies were low, they had recovered more than three tons of gold bars and coins. The gold coins were especially valuable because of their extreme rarity. Many had been made by private mints in San Francisco that had been hastily set up to meet the needs of the gold miners as they traded in their gold dust and nuggets. Others came from the San Francisco U.S. Mint. All the coins were in beautiful condition, many still in their original rolls or storage boxes. Not bad for a group of guys who had never found a single piece of treasure in the past!

Within weeks of the team's arrival in port with the treasure, new legal problems flared up. Thirty-eight insurance companies had paid claims on the gold soon after the ship went down. Now they joined forces, claiming that all the recovered gold belonged to them. In June 1991 the U.S. Circuit Court of Appeals in Richmond, Virginia, ruled in favor of the Columbus-America Discovery Group, but the insurance companies further appealed the decision.

Finally in February 2002 the gold of the *Central America* was free of legal entanglements and could be put on the market by the Columbus-America Discovery Group. In a series of auctions they began selling the treasure. The prices realized for some pieces were fantastic; one gold ingot was sold for $8 million to a *"Forbes* 400" business executive. In November 2002 a spokesman for the company announced that almost 90 percent of the gold recovered had been sold. Soon after the first gold came up rumors spread that the U.S. Army also had a secret consignment of gold on the wreck. The numismatic world is hopeful that this is true and that Thompson will go after the gold in the near future.

In 1965, not far off the Dry Tortugas to the west of Key West, Florida, the shrimp boat *Trade Winds* was dragging her nets in 1,500 feet (over 450 m) of water when she snagged an obstruction that brought the vessel to a shuddering halt. When the badly

damaged nets were brought to the surface, they contained three complete Spanish olive jars (similar in appearance to Mediterranean amphorae), various metal artifacts, some bits of a ship's rigging and a considerable amount of wood, including a section of ornately carved railing. Captain Lewis described the wood as being "as good as the day the ship was made." Lewis, a veteran shrimper who was not himself interested in old wrecks, contacted me and gave me the location.

In 1972 I teamed up with a group of oceanographers from California, and we chartered the oceanographic research vessel *Alcoa Seaprobe* to search for the Dry Tortugas wreck. Deep-water technology at the time was less advanced than it is now, and we failed to locate it. Several months later, we resorted to methods that had been used by salvors for thousands of years. By dragging a steel cable between two shrimp boats, we were able to snag a huge anchor and bring it to the surface. ROVs were not in use in those days, so we couldn't survey the wreck, and we had no idea exactly what was hidden in the deep, although I knew from the artifacts the *Trade Winds* had recovered that the shipwreck was Spanish and had sunk some time between 1590 and 1630.

Seahawk's ROV *Merlin* being lowered into the sea while co-author Jenifer Marx watches the action.

By 1988, when I teamed up with Seahawk Deep Ocean Technology, a Tampa-based company, deep-water archaeology had made giant strides. Seahawk, which had been involved in deep-water oceanography for the previous three years and was committed to deep-water historical wrecks, easily located the wreck in April 1989. A sonar silhouette showed the site to be about 118 feet by 50 feet (36 m by 15 m). Seahawk's ROV, *Phantom,* was flown to the bottom. As it glided gracefully over the seabed, a video camera transmitted pictures of the ghostly remains of the Spanish ship, unseen for almost 400 years, to a television monitor aboard the research vessel. A jubilant crew watching the screen exclaimed over the images of ship timbers; an extensive mound of ballast;

heaps of earthenware Spanish olive jars; ceramic objects, including a Chinese porcelain plate; and bits of rope.

Since this ship lies in international waters there are no governmental agencies to protect the site or dictate the manner in which it is excavated. If John Morris and Greg Stemm, the two principals of Seahawk, had been motivated by profit alone, there would have been nothing to stop them from using a grab bucket to tear the wreck apart and salvage her treasure. Instead, within days of the find, they formed a committee of underwater archaeologists and conservation experts to advise them how best to excavate this remarkable wreck.

In June 1989 Seahawk used the ROV *Phantom* to recover the bronze ship's bell to establish ownership of the wreck. Their commitment to archaeological procedure led them to the conclusion that an even more sophisticated ROV than the *Nemo* was needed, so they commissioned the ROV *Merlin,* designed by Gordon Richardson, a top ROV expert, and built by Ametek Offshore in Aberdeen, Scotland. In April 1990 the new ROV was completed at a cost of more than $2 million. The *Merlin* was a technological marvel. It contained three video cameras capable of providing 180-degree underwater vision, and three 70mm still cameras for taking pictures of artifacts *in situ* to be digitized into a computer for later mapping of the site. The *Merlin* was also equipped with two manipulator arms, suction pumps, water jets to remove bottom sediment and a number of other revolutionary devices.

The control room where the *Merlin* is operated from the surface.

The *Seahawk Retriever,* a recovery vessel outfitted with the *Merlin,* and a crew of thirty scientists and archaeologists, reached the Dry Tortugas site in mid-May 1990. It was an international project with members from twelve countries, including China, whose government lent three young oceanographic scientists. The team spent two months mapping the site. At a cost of $18,000 a day, this was an expensive undertaking. By the end of the summer the divers had recovered more than 10,000 artifacts, including three bronze navigation astrolabes, twenty-seven gold bars, over 1,000 silver coins, jewelry, ceramics, cannon and musket balls, and several dozen intact olive jars. Efforts at identification narrowed the field of possibles to three galleons lost in 1622 in deep water in the general area—making the wreck a sister ship of the famed *Atocha* (see Chapter 4).

The 1991 season was as exciting as the previous one. The ROV recovered additional gold bars and hundreds of gold and silver coins. The richest single find was a gold chain almost 33 feet (10 m) long—one of the longest ever recovered from a shipwreck. The *Merlin*'s fine-tuned hand also brought up more than 5,000 small but beautiful pearls. Among many pieces of ceramics found on the site was a plate bearing the Pope's coat-of-arms, which most likely indicates that a papal nuncio, a Vatican official, was aboard the doomed ship. Among the strangest items recovered were fourteen very small bird beaks; it appears that someone was shipping a cage full of exotic birds back to Spain.

In 1965, the same year that Captain Lewis discovered the Dry Tortugas shipwreck, another shrimper dragging his nets at a depth of 1,200 feet (365 m) snagged a wreck about 60 miles (96 km) east of St. Augustine, Florida. He pulled up six large copper cooking kettles, some ballast rock and three cannonballs. Using sonar, Seahawk found this shipwreck again in early 1990. Because the *Merlin* was committed to the Dry Tortugas site, Seahawk signed a research agreement with the Harbor Branch Oceanographic Foundation in Fort Pierce, Florida, which had earlier worked on the *Monitor*.

In October 1990 a ten-day survey of the wreck was conducted with the submersible *Johnson Sea-Link I*. I served as chief scientist/archaeologist and had one of the greatest thrills of my life working on the bottom at this depth. This is, to date, the deepest that anyone has used a submersible to recover historical artifacts from the Spanish colonial period. Each day we made two dives of three to four hours' duration, and in the sixty-six hours I spent on the wreck site, we were able to make as comprehensive an archaeological survey of the site as if we had been in shallow water. Using the *Sea-Link*'s manipulator arm, we first laid out a grid pattern of buoys. Then, using both a video camera and a 70mm still camera mounted on the bow of the submersible, we made a photo-mosaic of the wreck. It shows thirteen cannon and two anchors lying on or close to a large ballast pile, as well as copper cooking kettles, ceramics, cannonballs, ship's fittings, tools and other artifacts, which were all measured, plotted and photographed *in situ*.

The next phase entailed obtaining samples of the artifacts and digging test holes using a small suction pump. Overall we retrieved a variety of artifacts, including a glass rum bottle, two small iron cannon, hundreds of cannonballs, a brass telescope, a stone grinding wheel, ceramics and hundreds of lead musket balls. The most interesting item was a piece of wood with cotton fishing line still wrapped around it.

I found that the small suction pump was unable to dig very deep, so when we returned to the site in April 1991 we brought a better excavation tool—a thruster, which was mounted on the bow of the submersible and worked in the same manner as the prop-washes used on shallow-water sites. We were able to remove a great deal of sand from the ballast pile and were delighted to discover that most of the ship's lower hull was well preserved. We could see that the ship was of typical Spanish construction, with pine planking, and oak used for the structural members such as the keel and ribs. Another cannon and

Co-author Robert Marx examining some of the many gold bars recovered by the *Merlin*. The 1622 Spanish Galleon was found in 1500 feet (450 m) of water off the Dry Tortugas.

an anchor were recovered, as well as hundreds of other things, such as wooden pulley blocks, fragments of rope and anchor cable, tools, brass buttons and buckles, sheets of lead and copper, a pewter spoon, animal bones, ceramic shards, leather, tools and six Spanish silver coins from the early eighteenth century. One of the missing ships from the convoy of 1715 (see Chapter 4) was lost in this area, and comparison of the artifacts recovered to date supports the likelihood that it may well be one of these wrecks.

In 1993 John Morris and Greg Stemm left Seahawk and formed Tampa-based Odyssey Marine International. Their first target was a rich Portuguese warship, *Santa*

Rosa, which sank en route from Brazil to Portugal in 1726 carrying over 30 tons of gold coins and ingots. It was the single largest loss of gold in colonial times. She caught fire off Cape San Augustine, Brazil, blew up and sank in deep water with all of her gold and most of the people aboard. This same year Odyssey obtained a search permit from the Brazilian Navy and hired Oceaneering International to locate the wreck. Several weeks of sonar search produced several likely targets. Unfortunately, terrible weather prevented further investigation of the targets and the research vessel returned to the United States.

Stemm and Morris had broken a basic rule of shipwreck salvage; they had obtained a search permit without any assurance that they would be granted a salvage permit after locating their target. Consequently, despite expending vast amounts of money and effort, they are still seeking a permit for the *Santa Rosa.* It may be that the Brazilian government plans to go after this enormous treasure itself after the Odyssey group throws in the towel.

Less than a month after he returned to Tampa, Stemm was approached by a historical researcher with original documentation on a shipwreck named the HMS *Sussex,* which the *New York Times* recently, albeit erroneously, stated had over $4 billion in treasure on board when she sank! It took several years before Odyssey had the funds available to go after the *Sussex* and to get a permit from the British government.

In December 1693 a mighty fleet of 166 merchantmen and 40 warships gathered off Portsmouth with the 80-gun HMS *Sussex* as flagship under the command of Admiral Sir Francis Wheeler. Loaded into the hold of the *Sussex* was a secret cargo of 9 tons of gold coins that the British monarch had ordered to be paid as a bribe to the Duke of Savoy to buy his goodwill. He was the ruler of the small state of Savoy flanking the southeast corner of France, which controlled the key invasion routes to Paris. Britain wanted to keep Savoy on its side in the Nine Years' War against France.

But the gold never reached the duke. A day out of Gibraltar the *Sussex* was caught in a gale that sprang up and soon grew to unprecedented ferocity. In current terms it was "the perfect storm," of the type seen only once in 100 years. The *Sussex* went to the bottom after capsizing, and only two of her crew were rescued. The Admiral's body and other bodies drifted ashore near the Rock of Gibraltar. When he didn't receive his anticipated shipment of gold, the Duke of Savoy defected and joined the French in their war with England. This created a stalemate in which the French–English Wars also took place in North America, forcing the beleaguered colonists to look to their own defenses and culminating in the American Revolutionary War.

Among the documents the researcher sold to Odyssey were logbooks of other ships in the convoy that had survived the disaster with the approximate location of the *Sussex*'s sinking. Despite having this information, Odyssey still had to cover 400 square miles (1036 km^2) in a three-year search using sonar to locate and ROVs to identify targets. The team encountered more than 400 "hits" ranging from modern debris to ancient wrecks. One find was that of a 2,500-year-old Phoenician amphora-laden wreck 3,000 feet (910 m) deep, which they plan to excavate in the future. The *New York Times* also exaggerated the importance of this find, declaring it to be the oldest known Phoenician shipwreck ever found. In fact, more than a dozen even older Phoenician shipwrecks have been found in Turkey, Greece, Israel, Lebanon, Italy, France and Spain. During the summer of 2001 Odyssey searched around the clock for seventy-five days before pinpointing the *Sussex.* One of her iron cannon was raised as proof of the find. Videos taken by an ROV show the wreck site is confined in a relatively small area, which will facilitate recoveries.

Stemm and Morris had to seek permission from the British government to work on the *Sussex*. Not only did the Crown own it, but also there is an international law that all warships belong to the nation of origin no matter where they are lost. Odyssey is now gearing up to go after the wreck during the summer of 2003.

In 1994, to the envy of others in the deep-water shipwreck exploration business, Robert Ballard managed to secure the use of the U.S. Navy's nuclear-powered research submarine *NR-1*. The once-secret vessel carried a crew of eleven and two visiting scientists. The sub has viewing ports, sonar sensors, lights, cameras and manipulators to recover objects. Its strangest feature are wheels that let it crawl along the seafloor.

Ballard wanted to search the route between Carthage on the coast of Tunisia and the ancient Roman port of Ostia, which was one of the most used sea lanes during the Classical Period. His expedition disproved the long-held contention that the ships of antiquity always sailed in sight of land and never ventured far on the open seas.

During a month-long search in 1994 he located a Roman wreck at a depth of one-half mile (866 m), and when the *NR-1* was withdrawn for a secret navy project he used his ROV *Jason* to survey the wreck after enlisting the services of archaeologist Dr. Anna Marguerite McCann, who was then with the Archaeological Institute of America. Using *Jason* they recovered forty-eight artifacts including amphorae, iron anchors and a grindstone. A cooking pot and a copper coin dated the wreck to the reign of Constantius II (A.D. 355 to 361).

While searching for a lost Israeli submarine in 1997 off the coast of Israel the *NR-1* accidentally found two wrecks in 1,300 feet (395 m) of water. From videos made by the *NR-1* archaeologists were able to determine they were of Phoenician origin, and Ballard was off and running again. After raising $1.2 million he mounted an expedition in 1999 using his submersible *Medea* and ROV *Jason*. He named the wrecks *Tanit*, for a Phoenician goddess and *Elissa* for the legendary Phoenician princess, also called Dido, who founded Carthage. Marine worms had devoured all of the ships' wooden hulls, but 385 visible amphorae were stacked in the neat rows they had been placed in by Phoenician sailors over 2,500 years ago. Ballard brought up a limited number of artifacts because he is committed to leaving most of what he finds on the bottom for scientists to find and study in the future. Among the artifacts were amphorae, cooking pots, other pottery and a cooking stand. These objects were used to establish that the ships most likely sailed from Tyre in Lebanon around 750 B.C. to carry cargoes of wine to North African ports including Carthage. Both of these wrecks were found 33 miles (53 km) offshore, once again proving that ancient vessels did sail on the open seas far from land.

The discovery of the deepest historical shipwreck ever found was announced in 2001. Underwater explorer Curt Newport, well known for locating and recovering Gus Grissom's Mercury space craft the *Liberty Bell 7*, found the wreck in 1999 in the heart of the legendary Bermuda Triangle at a depth of 16,000 feet (4,854 m). In 2001 Newport returned to the site with archaeologist Jim Sinclair, a protégé of the late Mel Fisher. Using the *MIR I* and *MIR II* submersibles they first mapped the site and then began retrieving artifacts. The most interesting were an intact hourglass (an item never found on shallow-water shipwrecks); a sextant; an octant made of ebony, ivory and brass; a spyglass; a man's boot; two flintlock pistols; many bottles and ceramic objects; as well as coins from various countries that place the date of the wreck around 1810. She was a merchant ship most likely in trans-Atlantic trade. Research indicates that there were four hurricanes in the Caribbean in 1810, and she probably sank during one of them.

12 PORT ROYAL: THE SUNKEN CITY

*t*UESDAY JUNE 7, 1692, DAWNED MUGGY AND STILL. The sun rose in a cloudless sky, and the sea was a mirror. The sultry weather, which had set in two weeks earlier, bred uneasiness among the inhabitants of Port Royal on the Caribbean island of Jamaica. Almost every year since Cromwellian troops founded the prosperous town in 1655, earth tremors had shaken the island. Every one had been preceded by a spell of stiflingly, hot, windless weather. Shortly before, a visiting astrologer had predicted that a cataclysmic earthquake was imminent, and people remembered that only four years before a similar prognostication had been followed by a quake that knocked down three houses, damaged many others and dislodged cannon from their gun ports on ships in the harbor.

However, the citizens of the bustling town went about their normal business on the day that, for many, would be their last. As the morning wore on and the heat became more oppressive, people anticipated the noon hour when all activity would cease for dinner and the siesta, usually taken in a swinging hammock. Shortly before noon, at approximately 11:40 a.m., Port Royal was rocked by three strong earthquakes in a matter of minutes. The third and most severe was followed by a massive tidal wave that broke the cables of ships anchored in the harbor, wrecked the vessels near the wharves, and caused 90 percent of the town to sink or slide into the harbor.

In a London broadside published shortly after the disaster a merchant who lived through the cataclysm described what happened:

A gold pocket watch and all its inner workings, recovered from Port Royal, an entire city sunk by an earthquake in 1692.

Betwixt eleven and twelve at noon, I being at a tavern, we felt the house shake and saw the bricks begin to rise in the floor, and at the same instant heard one in the street cry, "An earthquake!" Immediately we ran out of the house, where we saw all people with lifted up hands begging God's assistance. We continued running up the street whilst on either side of us we saw the houses, some swallowed up, others thrown on heaps; the sand in the streets rise like waves of the sea, lifting up all persons that stood upon it and immediately dropping down into pits; and at the same instant a flood of water breaking in and rolling those poor souls over and over; some catching hold of beams and rafters of houses, others were found in the sand that appeared when the water was drained away, with their arms and legs out. The small piece of ground whereon sixteen or eighteen of us stood (praised be to God) did not sink. As soon as the violent shake was over, every man was desirous to know if any part of his family were left alive. I endeavored to go to my house upon the ruins of the houses that were floating upon the water, but could not. At length I got a canoe and rowed upon the great sea towards my house, where I found several men and women floating upon a wreck out to sea; and as many of them as I could I took into the boat and still rowed on till I came to where I thought my house stood, but could not hear of either my wife nor family; so returning again to that little part of land remaining above water.

By the time the sun set on Port Royal over 1,800 buildings had disappeared. All that remained above water was a mere 10 acres (4 ha) of land in the shape of a small cay. The toll of property taken by the upheaval was incalculable, but not the toll of lives. More than 2,000 people perished, and an additional thousand survivors, who moved across the harbor and founded the town of Kingston, died from epidemics that followed the disaster.

Old Port Royal was no ordinary town. A legend from its beginning to its end, a period that spanned less than half a century, it was a Mecca for pirates and privateers. In the closing years of the seventeenth century it was known as the wickedest city in the New World, and tales of its wealth and debauchery circulated around the globe. It was said that in Port Royal there was "more plenty of running cash proportionately to the number of inhabitants than in London." Rumors abounded that in Port Royal fortunes were made in a day and spent in a night. How they were spent is not hard to guess, since it was also said that there was one tavern for every ten men and countless brothels.

The town was established in 1655 when the English wrested Jamaica from Spain. They recognized that the island's position in the center of the Caribbean made it an ideal spot from which to attack Spanish fleets carrying the gold, silver and precious stones of the New World home to the mother country. The English also appreciated the strategic importance of the barren, sandy cay where Port Royal was established. Separated by a shallow marsh from a long, low sandpit (known today as the Palisadoes) curving south and west away from the mainland and almost enclosing a body of water (Kingston Harbor), this cay could accommodate more than five hundred ships with ease. Ships entering the harbor had to round the cay or risk running aground on the reefs blocking the southern and western approaches. The English built their main stronghold on the cay, named it Port Royal, and the boom began.

It was ushered in by the men who were the major contributors to Port Royal's reputation for boozing, wenching and brawling—the buccaneers—who were invited to make Port Royal their base. The English Crown, fearing a Spanish attempt to recapture Jamaica, granted them letters of marque authorizing their attacks on Spanish ports and shipping, thus making them lawful privateers. Some of the buccaneers, accepting the privateering commissions, served the English Crown as zealously as did the navy they aided. Among them was pirate-turned-privateer Henry Morgan, whose expeditions against Panama City and sister ports on the Spanish Main earned him a knighthood. Others, such as the infamous and erratic Roche Brasiliano, served only themselves; his fondness for shooting up the town made him feared by friend as well as foe. Privateers and pirates alike were welcome in Port Royal. Their raids, aside from keeping the Spaniards too busy to think about offense, amassed fortunes in plunder, which filled waterfront warehouses and made many of the town's merchants very rich indeed.

Port Royal's advantageous location assured its success as a seaport, and it continued to flourish even after the departure of the buccaneers in 1675, when the English Crown, at peace with Spain, rescinded all letters of marque and made determined efforts to suppress piracy in the Caribbean. The greatest source of wealth was contraband trade with the Spanish colonies, but the town had other irons in the fire. There was commerce with England and the English colonies in North America, traffic in slaves and the fledgling industry of treasure hunting, or the "wrecking trade." In "wrecking's" most outstanding incident, William Phips stopped at Port Royal to pick up divers for his hugely lucrative 1682 treasure hunt for the *Nuestra Señora de la Concepción* on Silver Shoals, north of Hispaniola. He was later knighted by the king and made the first governor of the Massachusetts Colony.

Contemporary woodcut showing Port Royal being destroyed by the earthquake.

So many people flocked to where the money was that Port Royal expanded into the marshy area separating the cay from the Palisadoes. When the seventeenth century entered its closing decade, the town had more than 8,000 inhabitants and 2,000 buildings, some of the structures three or four stories high. These were crowded together in what appeared to be a solid mass, its edge reaching out into the harbor. Houses even stood on pilings driven into the sand. Many of the houses were as fine as any in London and were stocked with gold, silver, pewter, jewels, porcelain, silks, laces and brocades from all over the world. Small wonder the town was referred to as "the Storehouse" or "Treasury of the West Indies." Everyone, except God-fearing souls who predicted that the town would be punished for its wickedness, expected the boom to last forever.

A few years after the 1692 calamity, part of the town was rebuilt, but it suffered from one natural disaster after another, and few wished to live there. Except for some prominence as a naval base during the eighteenth and nineteenth centuries (several illustrious English naval figures did duty there, including Horatio Nelson, who served two tours), Port Royal never regained even a hint of its former glory. Only the legend survived, and a new legend grew up around it—of a city filled with gold, silver and precious stones that waited intact under the sea for some brave adventurer. Through the centuries currents and hurricanes deposited a mantle of sediment over half of the sunken city and formed a new land mass, connecting once again to the Palisadoes.

Mention of Port Royal generates as much excitement in a marine archaeologist as Pompeii does in his land counterpart. Both cities met sudden destruction, one vanishing into the sea, the other inundated by molten lava, and both have tantalized students of history. Since 1763 excavations at Pompeii have yielded a wealth of information about the Roman city's past, but Port Royal remained hidden for as long as the world beneath the sea was unfathomable territory.

In 1959 American Edwin Link, inventor of the flight simulator, who had a great interest in underwater archaeology, led a brief expedition to Port Royal that recovered a number of interesting artifacts, including a small cannon and a brass pocket watch. In 1965 the government of Jamaica selected me to direct the first large-scale archaeological excavation of the sunken seventeenth-century site. There was a certain urgency about the project, because of a plan to turn modern Port Royal into a tourist haven. The proposed project entailed dredging a deep-water port that would have destroyed more than half of the town.

When I undertook the excavation of Port Royal, it was not with the expectation of finding any treasure. Salvors were on the scene immediately after the earthquake, recovering valuables from submerged buildings with nets or grappling hooks. No part of the sunken town lay more than 60 feet (17 m) below the water's surface, a depth seventeenth-century divers could easily reach with diving bells or by simply holding their breath. Valuables overlooked by contemporary salvors would have been recovered during the salvage efforts that continued for years after the disaster.

For centuries fictitious accounts were published in England and the United States about divers who claimed not only to have recovered gold from Port Royal but to have entered taverns in the submerged city where skeletons sat eternally at the tables. Some told of hearing the cathedral's bells tolling beneath the waves. The cathedral, however, happens to be buried under land, and there is only one recovery of treasure that is a matter of historical record—three leopard's teeth covered with gold that were found in the belly of a shark in 1788. All other claims are romantic fiction.

I was not interested in fiction nor in treasure. I was excited by the unique opportunity to investigate a late seventeenth-century town; one I had read so much about in crumbling archival documents. Although the Port Royal site is less than 300 years old it has been significantly disturbed by both man and nature. Consequently, I didn't expect the kind of spectacular historical time capsule archaeologists unearthed at Pompeii, where the town had been covered quickly with volcanic ash and had remained virtually untouched for almost 2,000 years. I discovered how far we were from Pompeii in the first week of exploring the site in December 1965. I was underwater when a large freighter dropped its anchor nearby, which dragged on the bottom, gouging a trench a yard (1 m) wide and 1 1/2 yards (1.5 m) deep across some 200 feet (60 m) of the site. Scattered on the seafloor lay hundreds of artifacts dating from the time of the earthquake, while in the trench lay Coca Cola bottles, tin cans, automobile hubcaps and other modern debris. Obviously, how far beneath the seafloor an object was found wouldn't be a certain indication of its age. Nevertheless, we intended to excavate layer by layer, plotting the locations of the major finds as precisely as we could.

Mapping the site, the first step, presented two problems. The murky waters of Kingston Harbor, where Port Royal lies, ruled out any procedures requiring visibility such as aerial photography. To locate concentrations of metal, I relied on a metal detector; to find walls and other nonmetallic objects, I used a long metal rod as a probe. The Jamaican government erected permanent markers ashore and supplied a chart of the site marked with a grid, so I was able to plot locations with great accuracy.

The second problem was the sheer magnitude of the task. We operated with government funds on a shoestring budget. There was no money for hiring assistants so that even though I mapped only a relatively small portion of the site, an area roughly 200 feet (63 m) by 100 yards (91 m) in the section of old Port Royal where the jails, fish and meat markets, craftsmen's shops and private houses stood, the job took months because I had to work alone. Thanks to good weather I was able to spend ten or twelve hours underwater every day, and the job was done by the time I was able to assemble a team. I had good luck in the two chief assistants I found: Kenute Kelly, an amateur swimming champion and a professional salvage diver, and Wayne Roosevelt, both natives of Kingston.

We didn't use scuba equipment but instead a recent invention consisting of a small air compressor set inside a floating tube with hoses carrying air to the divers. This Aquanaut device freed us from cumbersome air tanks and having to come to the surface periodically for more air. An attendant in a skiff put fuel in the Aquanaut every hour, so we could stay submerged all day.

In selecting excavating equipment I avoided any device that might endanger fragile objects such as glassware. Digging by hand would have assured the safety of the artifacts, but while I anticipated that the Port Royal project would take years (it was the largest marine excavation project in terms of scale and duration ever attempted anywhere in the world), I had hopes of finishing the job before the age of ninety-two. I decided on an airlift with a tube 4 inches (10 cm) in diameter, smaller than those normally used in underwater digs. A screen on the bottom of the tube prevented objects from being sucked up before the diver could rescue them. An even finer screen on the barge served as the receptacle for the sediment and debris coming up the tube and allowed the four men on the barge to retrieve very small items such as pins or beads.

Plotting artifacts' position and stratigraphic depth was difficult in such dirty water; however, by trial and error we found a functional method. At the beginning of each day's excavation, we placed four buoys in a square around the area in which we were diving. As each major artifact was brought up, the skiff attendant recorded the position of the top of the airlift tube in relation to the four buoys. At the end of the day the exact position where each artifact was recovered was plotted on a grid chart. To determine stratigraphic depth, the skiff attendant had only to record the length of airlift tube protruding above the surface. We could establish the stratigraphic depth of each major artifact when we knew the depth of water we were working in, the state of the tide, and the depth that the airlift tube was beneath the surface. Occasionally, however, when the sides of a hole we were excavating collapsed and artifacts fell down deeper into it, mixing with the sediment, it was impossible to determine their original position and depth.

On May 1, 1966, at 7:00 a.m., the dig began in a spot about 100 feet (30 m) from the shore. After removing little more than 1 foot (30 cm) of sediment, we turned up one artifact after another, and by the end of the first hour we had filled three baskets with clay smoking pipes, ceramic shards, some unbroken onion bottles (so named because of their shape) and various coral-encrusted iron objects. We were off to a good start despite the fact that visibility was less than 1 foot (30 cm) in the turbid water, and we had to rely primarily on our sense of touch.

Our first major discovery was a fallen wall. As I excavated along one side of the wall, objects began dropping into the hole I was making—a pewter spoon, then a pewter meat platter with four pewter plates stacked neatly on top of it. I realized that the wall was tilting over the hole, and I shut off the airlift, debating whether or not to disassemble the wall before proceeding further. Signaling to the team to keep hands off the wall until it was level again, I began pumping away sediment from the opposite side. At once I came upon a cluster of four pewter spoons. I was excited and recklessly began pumping deeper. Suddenly, the wall slid over on top of me, pinning my head and torso to the bottom.

It smashed the airlift tube but fortunately didn't break my air hose. The men on the barge realized something was wrong and Kelly came looking for me. It took him a while to find me but as soon as he did, he disconnected the air hose from the broken tube and used it as an air jet to blow away the sediment under my body. It was a risky maneuver; there was every chance that the wall would slide further, trapping him too, but it worked. After that, the rule was take a wall apart before it could take you apart.

In the vicinity of the first wall we found six others of similar construction, along with seven roof beams. I felt we were working on the site of a single house. Whose house? We had a clue in the initials RC marked on two pewter plates and two pewter spoons found under the first wall. Consulting a map of old Port Royal at the Institute

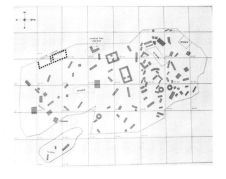

Plot chart showing the areas excavated during the first year of the Port Royal project.

of Jamaica, I discovered that at the time of the earthquake a Richard Collins had owned property near where we found the pewterware bearing his initials, so it is a fair assumption that the house belonged to him.

Aside from the fact that he owned property, nothing is known about the man, but I think he either kept a tavern or rented part of his land to someone who did because in the area around the house we found quantities of onion bottles, ceramic beer mugs, broken wine glasses and more than 500 clay smoking pipes. The drinking paraphernalia could have belonged to a tippler with a lot of friends, but no man would have owned so many clay pipes. Many of them had been smoked so they weren't stock from a shop that sold pipes. The most plausible explanation was a tavern since in those days a man owned several clay pipes and customarily left one at each of his favorite taverns.

Pewter and silver ware and ceramic objects found in a kitchen of one of the standing buildings.

Fairly soon after I exercised my powers of deduction on the tavern site, I had a new mystery on my hands. For about two weeks we excavated an area roughly 50 feet (16 m) square in which we came upon few clay pipes or household relics. Instead, we found thousands of artifacts from a ship including iron nails, caulking tools, brass ship fittings, copper wire, copper hull patches and lead draught markers. The evidence pointed to a shipwreck, but where was it? As a rule, no matter how much sediment covers a wreck, the pile of the ship's ballast protrudes above the seafloor. But we didn't find any ballast and whoever heard of a ship without it? I was baffled. The English "broad arrow" was marked on the brass and copper artifacts, proof that they were Crown property. This told me they could not have come from a ship chandlery, for no shop would have been allowed to possess Crown property. The Roman numerals VII, IX and XI on the draught markers indicated the wreck was a large one, because a small sloop would never draw that much water

A week later, we found the keel and ribs of a ship of 250 to 300 tons. The size of the cannon nearby, along with the absence of barrel staves or other artifacts normally carried by merchant vessels, indicated that she was a warship. The brick walls found above and below a part of the keel showed that she had sunk during the earthquake. What ship was she? A period of detective work began, involving a search through contemporary documents and extensive correspondence with the British Admiralty. The only English warship reported lost during the earthquake was the HMS *Swan*. She measured 80 feet (25 m) in length and with a normal load her depth in the water would have been about 20 feet (6 m) and her weight 305 tons—statistics perfectly in keeping with our wreck. The most interesting information to come to light about the *Swan* was that she was being careened at the time of the earthquake. Careening necessitates the removal of ballast, the explanation of why we found none. Without ballast (at least 100 tons of it for a ship her size), the *Swan* would have been light in the water, light enough for the tidal wave to fling her from her original position into the middle of town where we found her.

A major discovery like the *Swan* invariably gave us a big lift. The average working day, however, consisted of grueling hours underwater that yielded modest discoveries. On some days the bucket came up with nothing but clay pipes and ceramic shards. We recorded the stratigraphic and horizontal position of everything we excavated. At the end of each day we had to photograph, draw, measure and catalogue the day's finds and start the appropriate preservation treatment for each type of artifact. There were constant hazards. We had to expect the unexpected because the water was usually so black that we could see our reflections in our face masks. Sea urchins and slivers of glass caught in the airlift screen frequently lacerated our hands. Sometimes objects fell from the collapsing sides of the hole onto us. Although we made a tour of inspection every morning, groping around the hole for anything large, a few times we overlooked large coral heads. Two of them seemed to have eyes; one aimed for Kelly's knees, and the other's target was my back.

Sewage spewing into Kingston Harbor from a pipe near the site not only contributed to the divers' frequent infections but also attracted uninvited visitors. More often than not, they were upon us before we saw them. One day Kelly felt himself nudged as he was surfacing out of the gloom. An instant later, a manta ray, some 12 feet (3.5) wide, embraced him with its wings. Manta rays are playful by nature, but now and then their romps in the water have carried them onto a ship's deck, where they have crushed people to death with their weight—a fact of which Kelly was well aware. He remained perfectly still until the manta ray, probably deciding that Kelly was not much fun as a playmate, unfolded its wings and swam away.

Another time, I was working on the bottom when I was shoved from behind. Intent on my task, I reached out a hand to push the intruder away and touched something that had the texture of sandpaper. I whirled to find myself facing a hammerhead shark only inches away. Possibly my sudden movement scared it, or perhaps my rubber suit and glass face mask did not make me a very appetizing morsel. In any case, it disappeared.

Pharmaceutical jars, bronze mortar and pestles, and scale weights found in the apothecary shop.

Despite the dangers and the delays that now and then forced work to a standstill, we made discovery after discovery. An apothecary's pestle and a wooden chest containing twenty-one small glass medicine bottles and two ceramic medicine vases told us we were on the site of an apothecary's shop. Awls, pieces of leather, heels, soles and completed shoes were evidence of a cobbler's shop. A carpenter's shop was indicated by hammers, saws, adzes, chisels, files, scrapers, nails, tacks and a wooden table and chair. Ships' rigging and fittings (not marked with the broad arrow this time) were the signs of a ship chandlery. We came upon an area in which one-third contained fish bones and the rest the bones of cows, horses, pigs, goats and wild boars. We had found the fish and meat markets.

The shops and the markets were what I expected to find in this area of the sunken city on which bones were piled as much as a yard (1 m) high. One find that did surprise us was the uncovering of two turtle crawls side by side. We knew that turtles, which provided the meat staple for Port Royal's inhabitants, had been kept in fenced areas before slaughter, but we thought that a tidal wave powerful enough to lift the *Swan* would have swept away the wooden fences. Instead, most of the posts were still standing, and we found thousands of turtle bones inside them.

Why the turtles did not swim to safety when the area sank under water is a mystery. Their legs may have been bound together (a common practice of the age) or perhaps they were buried under an avalanche of mud before they could escape. Whatever the reason for the existence of the relics, I was delighted with them, as I was with other relics that had miraculously lasted through almost three centuries: a handful of human hair, a complete tobacco leaf in a remarkable state of preservation, and a petrified chunk of butter.

A high point of the dig was the discovery of two standing buildings. We excavated around the exterior and a portion of the interior of the first building before having to quit for the day. The next morning we were disappointed to see that the walls had collapsed during the night. Soon afterward we came upon the second standing building, and I decided to excavate differently, removing no more than 1 foot (30 cm) of sediment outside the walls before doing the same inside, thus attempting to keep external and internal pressure equal. I hoped to brace the wall after the excavation, so that the building would remain standing.

It was a full day's work merely to clear the topmost 6 feet (2 m) of the building, which was 35 feet (11 m) long, 20 feet (5.5 m) wide and had walls 2 feet (60 cm) thick. The next morning we were elated to find that the building was still standing. It was the only happy event of the day. The first sour note was the breakdown of the Aquanaut. We descended with scuba gear and had been down only a few minutes when Kelly gashed his hand on a piece of glass. I sent him to the doctor and continued the excavation with Wayne's help. When the building was almost totally excavated, Wayne complained of a sinus headache, so I sent him to the surface.

Before stopping work myself (as a rule we didn't dive alone for reasons of safety), I decided to complete my sketch of the building, since I knew that there was every chance it might collapse during the night. I went to examine the wall with the entrance; the next thing I knew I woke up to find myself pinned under the wall, my mask gone and my eyes smarting from the salt and dirt of the water. Fortunately, I had fallen face downward and the wall's weight had pressed my face against the purge button of my mouthpiece regulator so that I had received air while unconscious. As soon as I realized where I was, I tried to push the wall off my back, but it was impossible to move—the section that had fallen on me was a solid mass. I knew I could not count on being rescued, so the only thing to do was to dig straight ahead with my hands. After what seemed years, my fingertips touched the end of the wall. I crawled through the handmade tunnel until my arms and head were free. I could see a glimmer of sunlight filtering down through the murky water as I crawled out a little farther, then suddenly my regulator got caught between two bricks in the wall.

I wasted precious minutes of my dwindling air supply in a futile attempt to free the regulator. With most of my body still pinned to the bottom, I was unable to maneuver well enough to remove the entire tank. It became harder to draw air with each breath. There was only one chance. I jerked my body forward with every ounce of strength I could muster. The regulator snapped, and I found my torso clear of the wall. Another jerk, and I shot toward the surface.

For several days after that narrow escape, walls were the enemy. The reconciliation occurred when I excavated a fallen wall and came upon the single most valuable artifact recovered during the entire dig. It was a round object so thickly encrusted with coral that I hadn't a clue to its identity. An X-ray outlined a man's pocket watch; removal of the coral and cleaning showed its remarkable state of preservation. The cover of the silver watch shone like a mirror; on it the name of the maker, Gibbs, and place of origin, London, were as legible as they had been the day the watch left the workshop.

Almost immediately after the recovery of the watch, the supply of artifacts petered out. Most days we surfaced empty-handed. We expected a quick end to the run of bad luck, but it continued for more than a month. It was bewildering. All along we had been recovering artifacts steadily. The pewter we had already excavated constituted the most extensive collection of pewterware of that period ever found. Now we found no pewter and few other artifacts. We were working in an area that contained no fallen walls; even onion bottles, clay pipes and pottery shards—things we usually found strewn over the seafloor—were becoming rarities.

We eventually moved to an area about 100 feet (30 m) to the north of the hole where Kelly found four silver Spanish pieces of eight, so well preserved that all the markings were clearly visible. I hadn't been able to believe my eyes. Ordinarily coins found underwater are so badly sulfated that even after cleaning, their impressions are barely discernible. Making out the date on one coin in a hundred is cause for rejoicing among numismatists. We found hundreds more, all in the same miraculous state of preservation thanks to the remains of a wooden chest that had protected the coins over the centuries.

Spanish silver pieces of eight, the brass keyhole plate and part of a brass key found on a wooden treasure chest.

The discovery of this unexpected treasure proved to be a nuisance. Our project had received very little publicity on the island, but word of the coins spread quickly. The value was wildly exaggerated and work was hindered for several weeks while the police tried to keep crowds of curious Jamaicans at bay. Documents in the Archives of the Indies in Seville, Spain, revealed why a treasure chest with a keyhole plate bearing the coat-of-arms of the King of Spain was found in Port Royal. In 1690, two years before the earthquake, three Spanish galleons wrecked near Jamaica, and Port Royal divers and fishermen had salvaged a great part of the treasure they carried.

In March 1967 we discovered another shipwreck. It lay relatively close to the surface of the seafloor and was broken into two sections. From artifacts recovered from it and from documents in the Jamaican archives we learned that this was a French warship that sunk during a hurricane in 1722. The ship's principal cargo consisted of thousands of 150-pound (68 kg) iron mortar balls. We brought up a few dozen of these balls and then spent several weeks moving the rest to an area we had already excavated so that we could dig deeper in the sediment under the wreck, where we discovered many fallen walls and a large number of artifacts. Between the two sections of the shipwreck we encountered a virtual forest of tree branches and trunks, which also had to be removed by hand. This area proved to be a warehouse containing tons of dyewoods, no doubt awaiting shipment to England.

April started off well when we discovered a cookhouse containing hundreds of culinary items such as dinnerware, silverware, bottles, pots and pans. Two items of special interest were a large intact barrel full of lime with the shipper's mark still clearly visible on it and a large wooden mortar containing cornmeal. We found our first gold artifact by accident. By April we had over fifty large tanks full of coral-encrusted iron artifacts, the majority of which were unidentifiable unless X-rayed or broken open; the first option was impossible because of lack of funds and the second was out of the question since we didn't have adequate means to preserve the iron. All we could do was immerse the conglomerates in fresh water and hope for funding to take them apart and preserve the artifacts within. One day, to test my underwater metal detector I placed a random piece of coral-encrusted iron in front of the detector head. Much to my surprise, it gave a nonferrous reading, and out of curiosity I carefully broke the encrustation apart and discovered a gold ring among some badly oxidized nails. I wondered what else might lie hidden in the thousands of artifacts in those storage tanks.

Throughout the course of the excavation we found the majority of artifacts dating from the 1692 earthquake 3 to 9 feet (1 to 3 m) deep in the sediment, although we generally excavated as deep as 15 feet (5 m). On several occasions we discovered a few artifacts of the indigenous Arawaks, who disappeared from the West Indies after the advent of the colonial era. The artifacts were found below the stratigraphic level of artifacts from the time of the earthquake and included pottery shards and a stone metate (used to grind grain). In the spring of 1967 we found seven intact Arawak pots, hundreds of pottery shards, fishing sinkers, axe heads, one projectile point and a limestone mold of unknown use. The volume of these artifacts indicates that Port Royal must have once been an Arawak settlement and not merely a fishing outpost.

May and June were the only two months throughout the excavation that were free of accidents or loss of diving hours due to colds, cuts or other mishaps. However, the work became even more tedious because about 80 percent of the sediment consisted of fragments of house bricks and small pieces of dead coral that had to be excavated by hand and sent up in buckets because they were too large to move through the airlift tube. From beneath all of the fallen brick we recovered thousands of fascinating artifacts including plates, bowls, tankards, spoons, porringers and other items in pewter and silver; many intact ceramic cups, mugs, bowls and plates; candlesticks, pots, skimmers, ladles, buckles, buttons and an apothecary's mortar and pestle in brass and copper; as well as many other artifacts of iron, lead, glass, wood, bone and leather.

We had previously recovered about 6 tons of bones, most of which were turtle bones from the crawls and fish, fowl and domestic animal bones from the site of the fish and meat markets; but none were human. During May and June we found several hundred human bones, most under fallen walls, where people had been trapped during the disaster. During the first two weeks of July we excavated the area of another tavern and another cookhouse. One of the most remarkable finds was a large brass oil lamp of Mediterranean origin, which we believe we recovered from the site of the synagogue that served Port Royal's Jewish community.

Then unfortunately, or fortunately, depending on one's perspective, we discovered another treasure, several thousand Spanish silver coins, in a remarkable state of preservation like the first find. In addition, we excavated a great amount of silverware, gold rings and cuff links, and fragments of a large clock. The most spectacular artifact was a beautiful Chinese porcelain statue, 13 inches (35 cm) high, of a woman holding a child in her lap. Research proved that it was the goddess of fertility and childbirth, dating from the Kuan-Yin period of the Ching dynasty and made in Tu-Hu, China. All evidence pointed to this being the site of a pewterer's or silversmith's shop.

Word of the find spread like wildfire throughout the island. Once again the police were needed not only to keep people from interrupting work but also to protect us, because the local criminal element threatened our lives if we would not hand over a portion of the treasure. Politics entered the picture when Jamaica's opposition party claimed that the find was much larger than reported and accused the party in power of stealing the treasure and using part of it in various illegal ways. When the subject came up for debate in Jamaica's Parliament, the government was almost forced to call a halt to the whole project; however, the matter was finally resolved and we were able to continue working.

Preserving the thousands of artifacts we had brought up was a monumental job. The project had such a bare-bones budget that we could do little more than store them in water-filled tanks, and many began to show signs of disintegration. The Jamaican government approached the United Nations for assistance, and UNESCO assigned two preservation experts to help us.

Our excavation continued until the end of May 1968, when I called a halt to the project for several reasons. For one thing, the site was no longer threatened since the proposed dredging operation was cancelled. For another, by devoting most of my efforts to excavating, I had little time to write archaeological reports. I wanted to devote my time to recording the results of the excavation while so many facts were still vivid in my mind and in the hundreds of pages of daily notes I had kept. After three years of intensive work at Port Royal (two and a half spent excavating), we had barely made a dent on the site. Less than 5 percent of the overall area of the sunken city had been uncovered, but the massive amount of archaeological data produced persuaded many archaeologists and historians that Port Royal is the most important marine archaeological site in the western hemisphere.

Aerial view of the site showing the barge with the airlift depositing sediment on it.

Five years after I left Port Royal a team of archaeologists and graduate students from the Institute of Nautical Archaeology of Texas A&M University, led by Dr. Donny Hamilton, began working on the site. They excavated the site of several submerged buildings and recovered a nice array of artifacts. After six summer seasons the Jamaican government terminated their contract without saying why.

In 1999 Jenifer, my wife, whom I had met at Port Royal in 1966, and I returned to Port Royal to participate in an Arts & Entertainment television documentary entitled "Sin City, Jamaica." We were heartbroken to find that more than 90 percent of the artifacts and treasure brought up during my excavation of the site in the sixties had disappeared. Government officials had no explanation for this, but local inhabitants of Port Royal told us that the finds had been sold to tourists visiting the site by the very people who were in charge of running my old preservation laboratory. Fortunately I had kept precise archaeological records of the entire excavation, and I wrote some fifty archaeological reports, so the important information gleaned from the excavation will always be available for scholars to study.

Many land archaeologists, while admitting that examination of such sites contributes to a better understanding of the past, feel that their excavation is not merited since there are so many similar sites waiting to be excavated on land where it is less difficult and less expensive to work. However, there are many submerged settlements well worth excavating around the globe. Some, located in harbors and bays, have already been destroyed by dredging or filling and others are likely to be obliterated soon.

During the spring of 1974, dredging and construction of a large deep-water pier began at the Caribbean island of St. Eustatius. In the course of work a large portion of the sunken city of Orangestaad, drowned in an earthquake in 1687, was destroyed. Similar sites are fast disappearing throughout the world, and it is imperative that they be catalogued and that as many as possible be excavated.

In the Mediterranean at least 280 such submerged sites merit attention. Those that sank as a result of catastrophes such as earthquakes and volcanic action are of the time-capsule variety, similar to Pompeii or a ship sunk in deep water. Few land sites can compare with them; although a number of sites were submerged because of isostatic movements of the earth's crust and are more similar to land sites. In these cases, the water level didn't rise, but, rather, the land sank slowly over a long period. A smaller number of sites of very ancient human habitation were inundated by a gradual rise in sea level of several inches per century. Usually where sites were slowly covered by water, most of the buildings were destroyed, the material reduced to indecipherable rubble. This is especially true in areas where the sites were exposed to the open sea and heavy wave action.

Except for the work at Port Royal, no submerged cities or ports have been excavated. A few test holes have been dug on a number of sites in the Mediterranean, but none approaches the scope of an excavation. Most of the work on those sites has been restricted to surveying and mapping the remains protruding through the seafloor from under tons of sediment. Enthusiasm for work on underwater settlements appears to be limited, primarily because of the expense and time required. Many of these sites encompass vast areas and are covered by centuries of sedimentation. This is especially true of those located near river mouths. Whereas a shipwreck may only take a season or two to excavate, one of these sites could take many years. In addition, few people are qualified to undertake such projects and there is reluctance on the part of land-bound archaeologists to work with divers. There is hope for the future, however, if archaeologists develop programs that utilize the voluntary assistance of amateur underwater archaeologists and if governments and international cultural organizations contribute to such cultural projects.

Humans have explored the seas for at least 6,500 years. We have gone from free-diving in the clear, familiar shallows for sunken dugouts to plumbing the abyss for centuries-old shipwrecks. The technology that can take us up to the moon and beyond is now at our disposal to voyage to the deepest frontier of our watery planet, where so much of our heritage lies. With each passing year new technological advances will enable us to bring more of the past to light through excavation and study of ancient shipwrecks.

Since the future of underwater exploration lies largely, although not entirely, in the profoundly deep waters that for so long defied our efforts to plumb their depths, it is reasonable to anticipate that increasingly sophisticated electronic devices and developments in chemistry will make it possible to recover and preserve entire shipwrecks and their cargoes to an unprecedented degree.

The future also holds the promise of exciting discoveries in shallow waters where wreck sites are likely to have been ravaged and scattered by the elements or scavenged by generations of salvors. Technology and archival sleuthing will account for some of the finds, but others, perhaps the most thrilling of all, will be serendipitous discoveries made by skin-divers or other amateurs who spot a pile of ballast stones or make out a coral-encrusted cannon camouflaged on a tropical reef.

Even in today's jaded world, who can resist the lure of sunken treasure? Finding a shipwreck and unraveling its secrets is an unparalleled thrill. Whether a shipwreck is discovered after an intensive hunt by a high-tech team of searchers and scientists armed with archival research, or chanced upon by a couple of vacationing recreational divers, pulses quicken and hearts pound. There is nothing like the first sight of ocean treasure, whether seen through a face mask in shallow sun-dappled water or viewed on the small screen of a shipboard monitor connected to an ROV a mile (1660 m) below.

APPENDIX
METHODS USED IN UNDERWATER ARCHAEOLOGY

Visual Search If a shipwreck target has been narrowed down through historical research to an area where the water is relatively clear and less than 50 feet (15 m) deep (more than 95 percent of all shipwrecks lost are in shallow water), the first search method employed to cover a large area is a visual search using small airplanes, helicopters or hot-air balloons.

Divers use underwater scooters to search visually for traces of a shipwreck. In the top photograph on this page, the scooter is equipped with a metal detector mounted on the bow. The detector indicates the presence of any metallic material that may be buried under the bottom sediment or in coral. Sometimes a diver holds onto a line and is towed behind a small boat that follows a predetermined search pattern; the diver visually combs the seafloor for shipwreck traces.

Diver flying a Pegasus in search of a shipwreck. Note lights and motion picture camera mounted on the unit.

Proton Magnetometer The magnetometer is the most common tool used in locating shipwrecks that are buried and not visible. One or more sensor heads connected to a surface monitor by cable are towed behind a small boat. The instrument can also be moved along on the bottom by a diver who holds the sensor heads. A magnetometer detects only ferrous metal (iron or steel). It can detect a 1-ton mass of ferrous material, such as cannons or anchors, as much as 150 yards (165 m) from the sensor head. A large steel ship can be detected up to one-quarter mile (400 m) away.

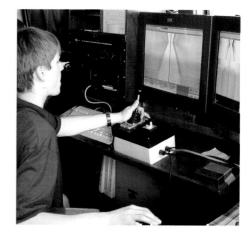

Side-Scan Sonar This method is used to locate shipwrecks lying deeper than 50 feet (15 m). It indicates only objects protruding above the seafloor, which is sufficient for detecting most shipwrecks in deeper water.

A sonar operator is monitoring the sonar recorder for possible targets.

Subbottom Profiling Sonar This type of sonar can be employed to search for the remains of shipwrecks that are completely buried. However, it has its limitations. It will penetrate more than 100 feet (30 m) deep in mud or silt, but less than 10 feet (3 m) in sand, and not at all in coral. It is especially useful for locating ships lost in muddy harbors.

Pre-disturbance Plot Chart After a shipwreck has been located, a chart is made in order to define the limits of the overall site and aid in planning the excavation phase. Accurate measurements of the positions of all visible objects are obtained by using a plane table, which is similar to a surveyor's transit. As an excavation progresses, the major finds are plotted on a similar chart.

Underwater Metal Detector This instrument is used to detect all types of metal, both ferrous and nonferrous. It detects metal buried in coral as well as under sediment. A detector is used during the survey of the site and subsequently during the

An underwater archaeologist at work measuring the ship's timbers on a Dutch East Indiamen wreck off South Africa.

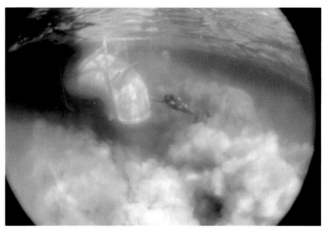

Diver using an airlift to uncover a Portuguese sixteenth-century anchor in the Bahamas.

A prop-wash being used to blow away the sand covering a shipwreck off Haiti.

Diver using an underwater metal detector to find small metallic objects hidden under the sand.

excavation to locate metals that may be hidden in small cracks after the sediment has been removed. It can locate a coin or a musket ball about a foot (30 cm) away from the sensor head, or a 1-ton mass of metal at a distance of 10 feet (3 m).

Airlift The airlift is the most common tool used in excavating a shipwreck buried in sand or mud. It works in much the same way as a vacuum-cleaner. A hose carries a steady stream of compressed air from a surface air compressor to the bottom of a plastic or metal pipe, which is positioned over the area to be excavated. As the air rises in the pipe, it creates suction and removes the bottom sediment.

Airlifts cannot be used on sites buried in coral. These are the most difficult to excavate, since each object has to be extracted by hand, using hammer and chisel or pneumatic hammers. Dynamite or other explosives cannot be used, because they would destroy artifacts.

Prop-wash This tool is employed to remove large amounts of bottom sediment covering shipwreck sites. The prop-wash is placed over the propeller of a salvage vessel and secured after the vessel has been anchored both fore and aft to prevent any movement. Then the boat's engine is run. The prop-wash diverts the "wash" or wake of the propeller downward, causing a whirlpool action that blows away the bottom sediment. The prop-wash is effective only in shallow water; beyond 50 feet (15 m) its power diminishes significantly. Some wreck sites in the Bahamas are covered by more than 30 feet (9 m) of sand and would be impossible to excavate without a prop-wash.

The self-contained one-atmosphere robotics diving suit WASP is capable of reaching depths of 3,000 feet (914 m).

SELECTED BIBLIOGRAPHY

Ballard, Robert D. *The Discovery of the Bismarck*. New York: Warner/Madison Press, 1990.

——. *The Discovery of the Titanic*. New York: Viking, 1987.

Bass, George F. *Ships and Shipwrecks of the Americas*. London: Thames & Hudson, 1988.

——. *History of Seafaring*. London: Thames & Hudson, 1972.

——. *Archaeology under Water*. New York: St. Martin's Press, 1966.

Blackman, D.J. *Marine Archaeology*. London: Butterworth, 1973.

Blair, Clay, Jr. *Diving for Pleasure and Treasure*. Cleveland: Crown, 1960.

Burgess, Robert F. *Sunken Treasure: Six Who Found Fortunes*. New York: Dodd, Mead & Co., 1988.

——. *They Found Treasure*. New York: Dodd, Mead, 1977.

Burgess, Robert F. and C.J. Clausen. *Gold, Galleons & Archaeology*. New York: Dodd Mead & Co, 1990.

Bush Romero, Pablo. *Under the Waters of Mexico*. Mexico City: CEDAM, 1964.

Boudriot, Jean. *La Belle*. Paris: Editions A.N.C.R.E., 2000.

Bound, Mensun. *Lost Ships*. New York: Simon & Schuster, 1998

Bowers, O. David. *The Treasure Ship* Brother Jonathan. Los Angeles: Wolfeboro, 1998.

Casson, Lionel. *The Ancient Mariners*. New York: Macmillan, 1959.

Clifford, Barry. *Expedition* Whyda. New York: Cliff Street Books, 1998.

Dash, Mike. *Batavia's Graveyard*. New York: Crown Publishing Co., 2002.

Davis, Robert H. *Deep Diving and Submarine Operations*. London: Seibe Gorman Co., 1951.

Delgado, James P., ed. *Encyclopedia of Underwater and Maritime Archaeology*. New Haven: Yale University Press, 1997.

Duffy, James. *Shipwrecks and Empire*. Cambridge: Harvard University Press, 1955.

Dugan, James. *Man under the Sea*. New York: Collier Books, 1956.

Dumas, Frederic. *Deep-Water Archaeology*. London: Routledge & Kegan, 1962.

Edwards, Hugh. *Treasures of the Deep*. Sydney: HarperCollins Publishing Co., 2000.

Esquemeling, John. *The Buccaneers of America*. London: Peter Balaguer & Son, 1684.

Franzén, Anders. *The Warship Vasa*. New York: Doubleday, 1960.

Furneaux, Rupert. *The Great Treasure Hunts*. New York: Taplinger Publishing Co., 1969.

Gores, Joseph N. *Marine Salvage*. New York: Doubleday, 1971.

Grissim, John. *The Lost Treasure of Concepción*. New York: William Morrow & Co., 1980.

Guilmartin, John F,. Jr., *Galleons and Galleys*. London: Cassel & Co., 2002.

Henderson, Graeme. *Unfinished Voyages: Western Australian Shipwrecks*. Perth: University of Western Australia Press, 1988.

Jefferis, Roger & Kendall McDonald. *The Wreck Hunters*. London: Harrap, 1966

Konstam, Angus. *The History of Shipwrecks*. New York. The Lyon Press: 1999.

Latil, Pierre & Jean Rivoire. *Sunken Treasure*. New York: Hill & Wang, 1962.

Lyon, Eugene. *The Search for the Atocha*. New York: Harper & Row, 1979.

Martin, Colin. *Full Fathom Five: Wrecks of the Spanish Armada*. London: Chatto & Windus, 1975.

Marx, Jenifer G. *Pirates and Privateers of the Caribbean*. Malabar, Fla.: R.E. Krieger Publishing Co., 1991.

——. *The Magic of Gold*. New York: Doubleday, 1978.

Marx, Robert F. *The History of Underwater Explorations*. New York: Dover, 1990.

——. *Sunken Treasure: How to Find It*. Dallas: Rain Publishing Co., 1990.

——. *Into the Deep*. New York: Mason Charter, 1978.

——. *The Capture of the Spanish Treasure Fleet, 1628*. New York: David McKay, 1976.

——. *The Lure of Sunken Treasure*. New York: David McKay, 1973.

——. *Sea Fever: Famous Underwater Explorers*. New York: Doubleday, 1972.

——. *Treasure Fleets of the Spanish Main*. New York: World Publishing Co., 1968.

——. *The Battle of the Spanish Armada, 1588*. New York: World Publishing Co., 1965.

Marx, Robert F. and Jenifer G. *In the Wake of Galleons*. Flagstaff: Best Publishing Co., 2000.

——. *Deep, Deeper, Deepest*. Flagstaff: Best Publishing Co., 1998.

——. *The Underwater Dig*. New York: H.Z. Walck, 1975.

Masters, David. *Epics of Salvage*. Boston: Little, Brown & Co., 1952.

McKee, Alexander. *History under the Sea*. London: Hutchinson, 1968.

Muckleroy, Keith, ed. *Archaeology under Water*. New York: Cambridge University Press, 1980.

National Geographic Society. *Undersea Treasures*. Washington, D.C.: National Geographic Society, 1974.

Peterson, Mendel. *The Funnel of Gold*. Boston: Little, Brown & Co., 1975.

——. *History under the Sea*. Washington, D.C.: Smithsonian Institution Press, 1965.

Potter, John S., Jr. *The Treasure Diver's Guide*. New York: Doubleday, 1960.

Rackl, Hanns-Wolf. *Diving into the Past: Archaeology under Water*. New York: Charles Scribners Sons, 1968.

Rule, Margaret. *The Mary Rose: The Excavation and Raising of Henry VIII's Flagship*. London: Conway Maritime Press, 1982.

Schurz, William L. *The Manila Galleon*. New York: E.P. Dutton, 1939.

Stenuit, Robert. *L'Or à La Tonne*. Paris: Glenat, 1990.

——. *Treasures of the Armada*. Newton Abbot: David & Charles, 1972.

Throckmorton, Peter. *Shipwrecks and Archaeology*. Boston: Little, Brown & Co., 1969.

Tucker, Teddy. *Treasure Diving with Teddy Tucker*. Hamilton: Bermuda Tourist Board, 1966.

Turner, Malcolm. *Shipwrecks and Salvage in South Africa*. Cape Town: C. Struik Co., 1988.

Wagner, Kip and Taylor, LB., Jr. *Pieces of Eight*. New York: E.P. Dutton, 1966.

Wignall, Sydney. *In Search of Spanish Treasure*. London: David & Charles, 1982.

PHOTO CREDITS

INDEX